Y convexity of a bond

ΔP estimated change in bond price

ΔP_D change in bond price due to duration

ΔP_Y change in bond price due to convexity

Option Pricing

X_c exercise price of a call option

X_p exercise price of a put option

V_c value of a call option or cap option

V_p value of a put option or floor option

V_t value of a cap or floor option maturing at time t

S price of an asset underlying an option

x_c exercise price of a cap option

x_p exercise price of a floor option

Δ_c delta of a call option

Δ_p delta of a put option

ΔS change in the value of the underlying asset

τ time to expiration of an individual cap or floor option

T time to expiration of a cap or floor option

σ standard deviation of an asset price

σ^2 variance of an asset price

Mathematical Operators

ln natural logarithm

e 2.7182, the base for the natural logarithm and the continuous compounding discount factor

$N(\cdot)$ cumulative normal probability function, the probability that a normally distributed random variable will be less than or equal to the value in parenthesis

MAX the maximum number of a series, for example $MAX[1,2,3] = 3$

MIN the minimum number of a series, for example $MIN[1,2,3] = 1$

$\sum$ summation operator, for example
$$\sum_{x=1}^{5} x = 1 + 2 + 3 + 4 + 5 = 15$$

$\prod$ product operator, for example
$$\prod_{x=1}^{5} = 1 \times 2 \times 3 \times 4 \times 5 = 120$$

MUNICIPAL DERIVATIVE SECURITIES
USES AND VALUATION

MUNICIPAL
DERIVATIVE
SECURITIES
USES AND VALUATION

Gary Gray, Ph.D.
Patrick Cusatis, Ph.D.

IRWIN
Professional Publishing

Burr Ridge, Illinois
New York, New York

This publication is designed to provide accurate and
authoritative information in regard to the subject matter
covered. It is sold with the understanding that neither the
author or the publisher is engaged in rendering legal, accounting,
or other professional service. If legal advice or other expert
assistance is required, the services of a competent professional
person should be sought.

From a Declaration of Principles jointly adopted by a Committee
of the American Bar Association and a Committee of Publishers.

Project editor:	Lynne Basler
Production manager:	Pat Frederickson
Designer:	Larry J. Cope
Art coordinator:	Heather Burbridge
Compositor:	Graphic Sciences Corporation
Typeface:	11/13 Palatino
Printer:	R. R. Donnelley & Sons Company

Library of Congress Cataloging-in-Publication Data

Gray, Gary
  Municipal derivative securities : uses and valuation / by Gary
Gray, Patrick Cusatis.
    p. cm.
  Includes index.
  ISBN 0-7863-0251-8
  1. Municipal bonds. 2. Municipal bonds—United States.
  3. Derivative securities—Prices—United States—Mathematical
  models. I. Cusatis, Patrick. II. Title.
  HG4726.G73   1995
  332.63′233′0973—dc20   94–17987

Printed in the United States of America
1 2 3 4 5 6 7 8 9 0 DO 1 0 9 8 7 6 5 4

To my wife, Katie O'Toole, whose support, understanding, and encouragement are much appreciated, and to my six wonderful children: Ali, David, Momo, John, Claire and Tom.

G.J.G.

To my wife, Deborah, who is always a source of motivation and support.

P.J.C.

PREFACE

To many market participants, the term *derivative securities* conjures up nightmares! The values and rates necessary to calculate swap rates, to derive option values, and to estimate a derivative security's cash flows appear to have popped out of a *black box*. The internal workings of the black box seem to be understood only by a select few financial alchemists—the so-called "rocket scientists of Wall Street." In an effort to make derivative securities more understandable, this book attempts to pry open the black box and shed some light by explaining rationally the *pricing and valuation mechanisms* of derivative securities.

In this book, we develop and present a framework to help participants in the financial markets to understand and value the complex new securities that are rapidly being introduced into the municipal marketplace. Although the focus is on *municipal* derivative securities, the approach developed works equally well for corporate or government derivative debt securities. We sincerely hope that participants in the capital market agree with us and that corporate and government debt professionals find this book helpful.

To illustrate our valuation framework, we use a security pricing model that we call the *Derivative Asset Pricing Model* to value five specific complex securities: Residual Interest Bonds RIBS, inverse floating rate bonds, cap bonds, BEAR Floaters, and BULL Forward Bond Payment Obligations. The model has the flexibility to value derivative securities introduced into the market in the future.

It is unfortunate for Wall Street's investment banks that it is either impossible or impractical to properly patent, protect and/or copyright new financial securities. Once a security is introduced by an investment bank, it can easily be copied by a competitor, without the copier incurring the very significant development cost of the inventors. There is a saying among financial engineers: "Good products are imitated and quickly copied, and poor products writhe and die a lonely death." RIBS, inverse floaters, BEAR Floaters, cap bonds, and Bond Payment Obligations have all been widely copied and renamed under various acronyms.

Derivative securities, by their nature, are often confusing. Many textbooks fail to explain derivative securities adequately and often leave the reader bewildered. In an attempt to appeal to readers with varying levels of technical expertise, we have developed a basic, result-oriented approach. But, try as we may to simplify the telling, the derivative story is still complex. As Mark Twain once said: "Everyone wants to go to Heaven, but no one wants to die to get there." Dying is not a prerequisite to understanding derivative securities, but the painful investment of a lot of time to expand one's skill set is necessary.

This book is organized as follows. Chapter 1 is the introduction and overview of the book. Chapter 2 provides an overview of the municipal bond market. Chapter 3 reviews valuation and risk concepts, including yield-to-maturity, price volatility, duration, and convexity, that are associated with investments in fixed-income securities. Chapter 4 addresses what we call *expectational analysis*—how today's yield curve works to quantify market participants estimates of future unknown interest rate levels. In it we show how to calculate *implied forward rates*, which are an essential ingredient in understanding derivative securities.

In Chapter 5, we begin the process by explaining the basic valuation procedures underlying derivative securities. We closely examine the *building blocks* for municipal derivative products starting with debt components. Chapter 6 looks at hedging component building blocks, which include forwards, futures, and swaps. We describe how interest rate swap rates are set on both a current and forward basis, how swaps are valued in the secondary market, and how forwards and futures contracts are valued. Chapter 7 focuses on option component building blocks, which include interest rate cap and floor options, and we show how these options are valued using simple, easy-to-understand examples. Chapter 8 employs the Derivative Asset Pricing Model to value the above-mentioned complex municipal derivative securities.

As investment bankers specializing in new-product development in the tax-exempt market, we are acutely aware of the current confusion among market participants regarding municipal derivative securities. Most market participants are not familiar with the assumptions underlying *expectational analysis*, and many market participants probably wish that inverse floaters, embedded swaps and caps, and all the various acronyms would just go away. Others, however, are determined to take the time and invest the energy to understand derivative securities. It is for the brave participants—those who are willing to learn new skills—that we have written this book.

Gary Gray
Patrick Cusatis

ACKNOWLEDGMENTS

We would very much like to acknowledge the assistance, support, and encouragement of a number of individuals in the development of this book. Particularly important were four of our closest associates: J. Nicholas Rozsman, who has been a principal architect of a number of the products discussed herein; Manny Puello, who can trade and value municipal derivatives better than anyone we have yet encountered; and John Wilson, who possesses a unique ability to express in simplified terms the benefits of complex municipal derivative securities to institutional accounts. Also of considerable assistance and importance was David Seltzer, a close friend and business associate over the last 17 years, who gave the manuscript a thorough critique and was incredibly helpful with his suggestions.

Sir Isaac Newton once said, "If I have seen farther, it is by standing on the shoulders of giants." In the broadest sense, the new products described in this book are derivative from earlier innovations by key participants in the tax-exempt market. Therefore, we would like to acknowledge and thank the *innovators in the field of municipal finance*—the investment bankers and lawyers who helped to design many of the financing structures that are described here and are now well accepted in the marketplace. We would like to mention several of the best whom we've had the privilege to work with and learn from over the years—Jim Lopp, Bob Kutak (in memoriam), Fred Weisner, Willis Ritter, Ron Gallatin, Dale Collinson, Dick Sammis, Dan Horowitz, Steve Huff, and Jere Thompson.

We'd also like to thank the members of the Aspen Ski Institute, who in lift lines and apres ski have provided significant input for the book and furnished the necessary spiritual support in the development of various municipal derivative products. This illustrious group includes: Alec Arader, Tom Carroll, David Eckhart, Jerry Fallon, John H. Foote IV, Bob Jones, Rusty Lewis, Patrick Mooney, Scott Perper and J. Randall Woolridge. Additionally, the comments of Marcia Stigum, James Kurish, and Jim Angel were much appreciated, as was a clever title suggestion by our friend Bill McLucas that was rejected by our editor. We would also like to thank Ralph Reeves, our publisher, and Lynne Basler, our project editor.

Finally, a very big thank you to Chris Spero, who had to decipher horrendous handwriting and correct abysmal grammatical mistakes in the typing of this manuscript and to Jeff Gertz, Arjuna Costa, and Sridhar Ganeshan, who provided valuable technical assistance.

CONTENTS

CHAPTER 1

OVERVIEW OF MUNICIPAL DERIVATIVE SECURITIES

INTRODUCTION

Derivative securities have been a focal point of the financial markets in the 1990s and have created quite a stir among capital market participants and market regulators. To many participants in the municipal bond market, the term "derivative securities" is a mystifying phrase that sends a reader glassy-eyed to the coffee shop seeking a double espresso. This book attempts to explain derivative securities in a simple manner so that they may be understood and used by people who are not rocket scientists.

Definition of Derivative Securities

Derivative securities are financial instruments the value of which is derived from, or based upon, either the value of another security or the level of an interest rate, or interest rate index, or stock market index. For example, a call option on a stock is an *equity-based* derivative security; its value is dependent upon, among other things, the value of an underlying share of common stock.

The J. J. Kenny Index is a municipal interest rate index that tracks short-term (30-day) interest rates in the municipal bond market. In the tax-exempt marketplace, a Kenny-based interest rate cap is a *debt-based* derivative security that is an interest rate call option. The value of such a security is principally dependent upon the present and expected future levels of the Kenny Index relative to a contractual fixed interest rate. Call options, interest rate caps, and interest rate options are explained in Chapter 7.

In the municipal bond market, the term "derivative securities" also refers to *debt-based* financial instruments that have complex variable-rate interest payment structures with option-like or swaplike features. These instruments have payment structures that resemble the payment structures of interest rate swaps, interest rate caps and floors, and interest rate forwards and futures contracts. We will later explain all these interest payment structures.

Why should an issuer of municipal bonds consider using municipal derivative securities? Why not maintain the status quo and issue only traditional fixed-rate debt? The reason is that, if municipal derivative securities are properly structured, they may create unique payment streams that are more highly valued by investors than the payment streams of other instruments. This may allow an issuer of these securities to:

1. Lower its financing costs, as compared to the costs of traditional fixed-rate issues.
2. Broaden its universe of investors by accessing buyers who will purchase the derivative structure but would not purchase the issuer's fixed-rate debt.
3. Create a market segmentation effect for a bond issue that reduces the amount of fixed-rate bonds, thereby reducing price pressures on the fixed-rate bonds and enabling a reduction of the conventional fixed-rate offering yield.

Debt-based derivative securities generally are designed in a way that makes their cash flows and market values more dependent upon changes in short- and/or long-term interest rates, or yield levels, as compared to fixed-rate debt instruments. A *bullish* derivative debt-based product is structured such that a *decrease* in interest rates *increases* the cash flows associated with the derivative product. A decrease in interest rates is bullish for investors in fixed income securities because the *market price* of the security generally *increases*. Bull derivative securities exhibit a greater change in the ratio of market price to change in yield than do fixed-rate bonds with comparable maturities. This ratio, known as *price volatility*, is estimated using a calculation that measures *duration*. Duration and price volatility are discussed in Chapter 3.

A *bearish* derivative debt-based security is structured such that an *increase* in interest rates *increases* the cash flows associated with the derivative security. An increase in interest rates is bearish for investors in fixed-income securities because the *market price* of the security generally *decreases*. Bear derivative securities have a lower price volatility measure than do fixed-rate bonds with comparable maturities.

The price volatility and duration characteristics of municipal derivative securities are valuable to certain investors. With increased price volatility and longer duration, there are higher expected returns. Hence, bullish municipal derivative securities have a higher expected return, all else equal, than do comparable fixed-rate bonds. Conversely, bearish municipal derivative securities due to their decreased price volatility, have a lower expected return than do comparable fixed-rate bonds.

Derivative securities are used by portfolio managers either to increase a portfolio's duration and price volatility or to decrease a portfolio's duration and price volatility. Price volatility is not necessarily a bad characteristic. If a derivative security is well structured and properly priced, and if investors are fairly compensated for increasing volatility, derivatives give the best risk–reward payoffs available in the market. Understanding municipal derivative securities, their payment characteristics, and their price volatility, and valuing them properly is what this book is about.

Understanding Derivative Securities

Why are derivative securities so misunderstood? Why are they so difficult to value? Why do the various acronyms and abbreviations (and their full names as well)—such as RIBS® (Residual Interest Bonds℠), SAVRS® (Select Auction Variable Rate Securities℠), BPOs℠ (Bond Payment Obligations℠), FLOATs℠ (Floating Auction Tax-exempts℠), RITES℠ (Residual Interest Tax-exempt Securities℠), PARS℠ (Periodic Auction Reset Securities℠), and INFLOS℠ (Inverse Floating Rate Securities℠)—send municipal market professionals to the medicine cabinet in search of Excedrin?[1] The principal reason for this confusion is that the future cash flows on these securities are *unknown*. The cash flows associated with many derivative securities and, therefore, their values are dependent to some extent upon future uncertain levels of interest rates.

Three basic concepts can help in quantifying these unknown interest rates and the expected cash flows of derivative securities for valuation purposes. These concepts are essential to an understanding and valuation of any debt-based derivative security—municipal, corporate, or government. The three concepts are:

1. *The yield curve and expectational analysis.* Expectational analysis is a way of studying the process by which today's yield curve works to quantify current expectations regarding future unknown interest rates.
2. *The components or building blocks of derivative securities.* In the building-blocks approach, a derivative security is divided into:
   a. Debt components (bond instruments).
   b. Hedging components (futures, forwards, and swaps).
   c. Option components (interest rate caps and floors).
3. *The derivative asset pricing (DAP) model.* The DAP model values the underlying components and adjusts for positive or negative inherent attributes, or *structure value,* of the instrument.

The valuations of the derivative securities that are examined in this book are dependent upon *expectational analysis*. Using this procedure, the cash flow and valuation of an asset are not found by simply discounting a known cash flow on a bond calculator. Rather, they are dependent upon expectations of future levels of interest rates and the volatility of those rates. To value these deriv-

---

[1]SAVRS® and RIBS® are registered trademarks of Lehman Brothers, Inc. Select Auction Variable Rate Securities℠, Residual Interest Bonds℠, Bond Payment Obligations℠, and BPOs℠ are service marks of Lehman Brothers, Inc. FLOATS℠, Floating Auction Tax-Exempts℠, RITEs℠ and Residual Interest Tax-Exempt Securities℠ are service marks of Merrill Lynch & Company Inc. Periodic Auction Reset Securities℠, PARS℠, Inverse Floating Rate Securities℠ and INFLOS℠ are service marks of Goldman Sachs & Company. Excedrin is a trademark of Bristol-Myers Company.

ative municipal bonds, it is important to understand the mechanism by which a bond's interest rate is set, as well as how the expectations of future interest rates are incorporated into the valuation process. To that end, we examine how the yield curve quantifies, to some degree, expectations of future uncertain interest rates. In Chapter 4, the reader is guided through the mathematics underlying expectational analysis, including the full-coupon yield curve, the implied zero-coupon yield curve, implied forward rates, and, finally, implied tax-exempt forward rates.

In Chapters 5 through 8, our approach is to focus on a complex security, such as an inverse floater, a cap bond, a RIB, a BEAR Floater, or a BULL Forward BPO[2] and to analytically divide it into simpler securities, or building blocks. Then we value and sum the underlying components, using a derivative asset pricing (DAP) model.[3] The DAP model is easily applied in dealing with derivative securities. It is possible for financial engineers to build, model, and value complex derivative securities with optionlike features by analyzing them as combinations of the simpler underlying financial building blocks (e.g., fixed-rate bonds, zero-coupon bonds, swaps and forward contracts, and option contracts).[4] While this approach is commonly used in corporate finance, it is relatively new to municipal finance.

Structure Value of Derivatives

The process of financial innovation and security design in the corporate finance market is examined by John Finnerty, who cites three ways in which securities innovation can add value for investors and issuers.[5] The three ways are:

---

[2]BEAR Floater[SM] and BULL Forward BPO[SM] are service marks of Lehman Brothers, Inc.

[3]This is the approach taken by G Gray and P Cusatis, "Understanding and Valuing Municipal Derivative Securities," *Municipal Finance Journal*, vol. 14, no. 2 (summer 1993), pp. 1–41.

[4]This is the approach taken by C Smithson, "A LEGO Approach to Financial Engineering: An Introduction to Forwards, Futures, SWAPS and Options," *Midland Corporate Finance Journal*, vol. 4, no. 4, 1987, pp. 16–28.

[5]See J Finnerty, "Financial Engineering in Corporate Finance: An Overview," *Financial Management*, vol. 1, no. 4, 1989, pp. 49–58

1. Introducing *structural features* into a security. These features reduce risk to an investor or reallocate risk to another entity.
2. Developing *financing structures* that have lower issuance expenses and underwriting discounts.
3. Developing *financing structures* that enhance the tax characteristics of the cash flows, thereby increasing the value of a derivative security.

In successful and innovative derivative products, such as Collateralized Mortgage Obligations (CMOs) in the mortgage market, Certificates of Accrual on Treasury Securities^{SM} (CATS^{SM})[6] and Treasury Investment Growth Receipts^{SM} (TIGRS^{SM})[7] in the US Treasury market, and RIBS in the municipal market, combinations of unique cash-flow streams are created that are more highly valued by certain investors than is a simple aggregate sum of the underlying streams. In other words, successful derivative products have a *positive structure value*. The value of the whole or the output is greater than the sum of the value of the parts or the inputs. At least temporarily, until arbitrage activity takes away the structure value, investors may be willing to discount these unique streams at a lower rate, and to pay a higher price for a derivative security. Unique structural aspects of a transaction may also enhance the tax characteristics of the cash flows, thereby increasing the value of a derivative security.

BASIC CONCEPTS UNDERLYING DERIVATIVES

There are three basic concepts underlying derivative securities. First, expectational analysis forms the basis for valuation of derivatives. Expectational analysis uses today's yield curve to estimate future levels of interest rates. Second, each derivative security can be evaluated as a collection of simpler securities or building

---

[6]Certificates of Accrual on Treasury Securities^{SM} and CATS^{SM} are service marks of Salomon Brothers.

[7]Treasury Investment Growth Receipts^{SM} and TIGRS^{SM} are service marks of Merrill Lynch & Company, Inc.

blocks. Finally, the Derivative Asset Pricing Model is the method of combining the values of each of the building blocks into one valuation for a derivative security.

Expectational Analysis and Implied Forward Rates

The corporate derivatives market is quite familiar with the valuation of securities with cash flows that depend on unknown future interest rates. Since the introduction of interest rate swaps in the early 1980s, corporate inverse floating-rate notes in 1985, and the trading of interest rate cap and floor options based on interest rate indexes in the early 1980's, market participants have developed valuation models that attempt to project levels of future interest rates. As a basis for projections, the models generally incorporate the *term structure of interest rates.* This concept is examined more closely in Chapter 4.

There are numerous models of the term structure. Expectational analysis uses the *pure expectations model* of the term structure of interest rates to estimate *expected future* or *implied forward interest rates.* In this model, investors expect that future long-term rates will adjust in such a way that all investors will receive equivalent returns over any given holding period. For example, an investor would expect to receive an equivalent return for any 10-year investment, whether it consisted of a series of 10 consecutive issues with maturities of one year, or of two consecutive issues with maturities of five years, or of a single security with a 10-year maturity. The traditional form of this hypothesis posits that the expected average annual return on a long-term bond is the geometric mean of expected short-term rates. According to this theory, investors are assumed to be risk-neutral, and a flat yield curve is implied when investors expect that short-term rates will remain constant. The pure expectations model is discussed in Chapter 4.

If we know the taxable, full-coupon yield curve [Treasury or London Interbank Offered Rate (LIBOR)], which is published daily in *The Wall Street Journal,* and given the assumptions inherent in the pure expectations model of the yield curve, two relatively simple equations allow us to derive implied zero-coupon rates and implied forward rates. *The valuations of derivative securities are crucially dependent upon implied forward rates and implied zero rates.* A method for calculating implied forward rates is shown in detail in Chapter 4.

It is important to understand that, in calculating the value of a derivative security, *the set of implied forward rates is used to determine the expected future cash flows.* In addition, the *implied zero rates* have much the same valuation function as *yield* has in discounting the cash flows associated with a fixed-rate security. Once these relationships are understood, valuing derivative securities becomes much easier.

The Building Blocks of Derivative Securities

Any complex derivative security can be analyzed as a package of simpler, more basic securities. The value of a derivative security depends on the value of the underlying simple securities, or *building blocks,* with an adjustment (*positive* or *negative*) for structure value. For the purpose of valuing municipal derivative securities, these building blocks can be grouped into three broad categories: *debt components* (bond instruments), *hedging components* (forward-like, futurelike, and swaplike instruments), and *option components* (interest rate cap and floor instruments).

Debt Components

Debt components are the cash-flow obligations of the derivative securities; they may be thought of as the repayment of the principal portion of the security plus the *normal* payment or accretion of a fixed rate of interest on the security. The three types of debt components that will be considered in depth in Chapter 5 are: (1) a fixed-rate bond component with semiannual interest payments, (2) a zero-coupon bond component with a semiannually accreting interest payment plus a principal repayment at maturity, and (3) a level-amortizing bond component which pays both interest and principal semiannually.

The value of the debt component of a derivative security is familiar to all market participants: its present value increases as the discount rate, or yield, decreases, and vice versa. The value of the debt component of a derivative security at issuance typically ranges between 90 and 100 percent of the price of the security.

Hedging Components
This is where things begin to get interesting! The hedging components consist of *contingent* interest payments, the amount and valuation of which are dependent upon future levels of interest rates or upon an interest rate index. These building blocks are called *hedging* components because contracts of this type are often used by market participants to *hedge* or offset interest rate risk caused by other financial assets or liabilities held in a portfolio. The nature of a hedge is that its value reacts to a change in interest rates in a manner *opposite* to the change in value of the asset or liability that is being hedged. This is where the interest rates determined by expectational analysis come into play in valuation.

Two types of hedging components are considered in Chapter 6: (1) instruments that offer forwardlike and futurelike payments and (2) instruments that have interest rate swaplike payment streams. As with any financial contract, the present value of a forward contract, a futures contract, or an interest rate swap equals the *discounted value of its anticipated future cash flows.* Depending on the current yield curve and the implied forward rates, these hedging components may have *positive, zero,* or *negative* present values. At issuance, the hedging component of a new municipal derivative security generally is structured to have a zero present value. Exhibit 6–14 (see Chapter 6) shows how to calculate and set the *swap rate* in a municipal derivative security so that the embedded interest rate swap will have a zero present value at issuance. As interest rates move and the yield curve shifts, the values of the hedging components change. Typically, the value of a hedging component is between +10 percent and –10 percent of the total value of the municipal derivative security.

Option Components
The level of complexity increases a notch with options contracts. The option components of municipal derivative securities consist of contingent interest obligations with payment characteristics that depend upon future levels of interest rates or upon an interest rate index. The value of the option component depends not only upon *expectations* of future interest rates, but also upon the *volatility* of interest rates.

Two types of option components are considered in Chapter 7:

interest rate caps and interest rate floors. An *interest rate cap* is a call option on interest rates that is designed to trigger periodic payments only when interest rates *rise* above a specified level or *cap rate*. If interest rates do not rise above the specified cap rate level, no payment is made under the contract. The contract expires after a preset period of time (e.g., five years). It can be thought of as a contract between two parties—the *cap writer* and the *cap owner*. The cap writer, in consideration of an up-front payment, agrees to make periodic payments to the cap owner only in the event that an interest rate index exceeds the cap rate (e.g., 3.5 percent) for a period of time.

An *interest rate floor* is a put option on interest rates. The opposite of an interest rate cap, it is designed to trigger periodic payments when interest rates *fall* below a specified level or *floor rate*. Each interest rate floor contract involves an agreement between a floor writer and a floor owner.

The valuation of interest rate options such as caps and floors involves estimating both uncertain future cash flows (based on expectational analysis) and the *probabilities* that the interest rate index will exceed the specified cap and floor rates. The inputs to a typical option valuation model (which are discussed in detail in Chapter 7) are (1) the current yield curve, (2) the time to maturity of the option, (3) the specified levels of the cap and floor rates, (4) the volatility of interest rates, and (5) the risk-free rates of interest used to discount expected future cash flows. The option components of municipal derivative securities usually lie between +10 percent and –10 percent of the total value.

Derivative Asset Pricing Model

Financial engineers have shown that complex derivative securities can be broken down into simple, more basic securities, which may be easily valued.[8] However, the cash flows associated with derivative securities may have unique features. For example, the cash-flow characteristics of municipal inverse floating-rate bonds

---

[8]See D Smith, "The Arithmetic of Financial Engineering," *The Journal of Applied Corporate Finance*, winter 1989, pp. 49–58.

(IFRBs) can be created synthetically (as discussed in Chapter 8) by owning a fixed-rate, tax-exempt bond and being the floating-rate payer in an interest rate swap. In this example, the cash flows are the same, but the treatment for federal income tax purposes is quite different for the inverse floater and its synthetic replication. All the interest associated with inverse floaters is treated as *tax-exempt* income, while the interest associated with an interest rate swap that is not embedded in a tax-exempt bond generally is treated as *taxable* income. This difference is significant for a municipal bond fund that has the goal of maximizing *tax-free* income for fund holders.

To address the unique structural aspects of a derivative security, a *structure value* is incorporated into the valuation process. The DAP model[9] is a valuation approach in which the building blocks are modeled and valued and a *subjective* structure value is assigned. A positive structure value (a lower discount rate or yield) results if there are beneficial tax aspects, lower intermediation costs, or efficiencies of structure (we explain structure value in detail in Chapter 8). A negative value (a higher discount rate or yield) results if there are negative tax aspects, higher intermediation costs, and lower liquidity of the instrument. Successful derivative products will have positive structure values—generally due to advantageous tax treatment, in excess of negative structure values—because of the reduced liquidity of the security. *The value of a successful derivative security will be greater than the sum of the simpler underlying cash flows.*

THE VALUATION PROCESS

The focus of this book is practical rather than theoretical. Application is in the foreground, with financial theory supporting its implementation.

To say that there is currently a degree of uncertainty (i.e., wide price dispersion) among traders, underwriters, and investors in

---

[9] See G Gray and K Engebretson, "Residual Interest Bonds (RIBS)," *Municipal Finance Journal*, vol. 13, no. 1 (spring 1992), pp. 1–29. They refer to their pricing model as a *synthetic-asset pricing model*.

the valuation of complex municipal derivative securities would be an understatement. To help overcome this confusion, five specific municipal derivative securities that are currently being offered for sale in the marketplace are valued: RIBS, an inverse floater, a cap bond, a BEAR Floater, and a BULL Forward BPO. For each of the theoretical valuations, a valuation date of January 3, 1994, is assumed, and the Treasury yield curve at the close of business is used as the basis for valuing contingent interest payments. Expectational analysis is used to project implied forward rates. Each derivative security is broken down into its building block components, and the DAP model is used to calculate its value. Descriptions and graphs of the interest payment profiles of each of the five securities are given below.

Residual Interest Bonds
An AA-rated revenue bond of the sort known as *Residual Interest Bonds* (RIBS) that matures on August 1, 2014, is callable on August 1, 2003, at a price of 104 percent. The *linked bond* pays interest every 35 days at a linked coupon rate of 6.173 percent, which has a bond equivalent yield (BEY) of 6.25 percent. The RIBS rate is calculated at a BEY rate of 2 times 6.25 percent *minus* an interest rate (the current 35-day Dutch auction rate plus expenses), on a variable-rate security, SAVRS. As an option, the RIBS can be *linked* with an equal amount of 35-day auction securities to form a 6.25 percent (BEY) fixed-rate bond. RIBS and the linking procedures are explained more fully in Chapter 8, and SAVRS are described in Chapter 2. (See Exhibit 1–1.)

Inverse Floater
An AA-rated hospital revenue bond that matures on August 15, 2012, is callable on August 15, 2002, at a price of 102 percent. It pays interest on August 15 and February 15, at the annual rate of 6.15 percent *plus* a variable rate equal to 4.70 percent minus the Kenny Index, prior to August 15, 1999. Thereafter, interest is paid at a fixed rate of 6.15 percent until maturity. (See Exhibit 1–2.)

Cap Bond
A Baa-1-rated general obligation bond that matures on October 1, 2016, is callable on October 1, 2002, at a price of 101.5 percent. It pays interest on October 1 and April 1, at the annual rate of 6.60

EXHIBIT 1-1
RIBS Interest Rate Profile

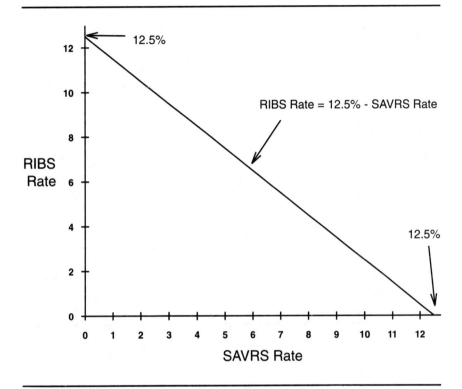

percent *plus* a variable rate equal to the *greater* of 0 percent or the PSA Index minus 3.5 percent, prior to October 1, 1997. Thereafter, interest is paid at a fixed interest rate of 6.60 percent until maturity. (See Exhibit 1-3.)

BEAR Floater

An AAA-rated insured hospital revenue bond that matures on August 15, 2022, is callable on August 15, 2002, at a price of 102 percent. It pays interest on August 15 and February 15, at the annual rate of 6.10 percent *plus* a variable rate equal to 2 times the Kenny Index minus 5 percent, subject to a minimum interest rate of 4 percent and a maximum interest rate of 8.2 percent prior to August 15, 2002. Thereafter, interest is paid at a fixed rate of 6.10 percent until maturity. (See Exhibit 1-4.)

EXHIBIT 1–2
Inverse Floater Interest Rate Profile

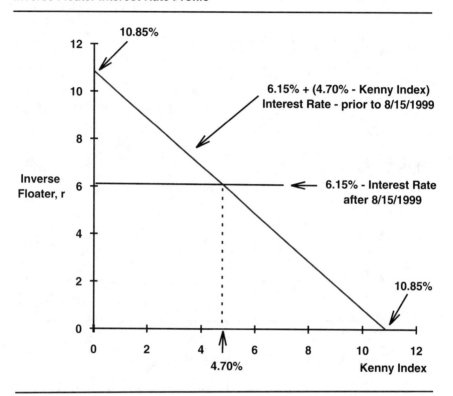

BULL Forward BPO

An AAA-rated insured water-system revenue bond that matures on June 15, 2005, is noncallable. It pays interest on June 15, 1994, at the rate of 5.20 percent. Thereafter, it pays interest on each June 15 and December 15 until maturity, at a rate equal to 5.20 percent *plus* a fixed rate equal to 3 times the interest rate adjustment. The interest rate adjustment may be positive or negative. The interest rate adjustment is designed to create a change in the present value of the BULL Forward on June 15, 1994 (the interest adjustment date), that would be similar to the present value of the payoff from a tax-exempt interest rate futures contract, which is discussed in Chapter 8 (see Exhibit 1–5).

EXHIBIT 1–3
Cap Bond Interest Rate Profile

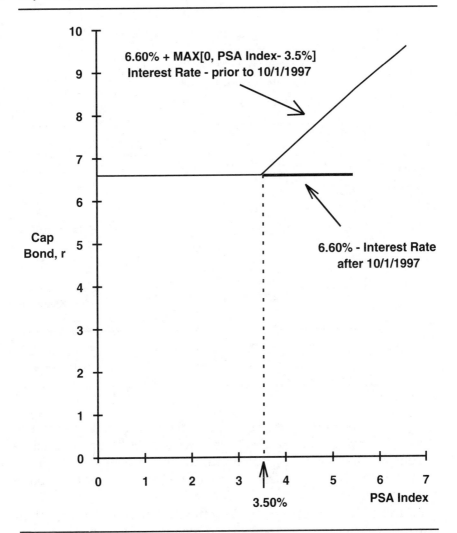

SUMMARY

In this chapter we presented an introduction and an overview of the book. Derivative securities are financial instruments the value of which is derived from or based upon the value of another security or

EXHIBIT 1–4
BEAR Floater Interest Rate Profile

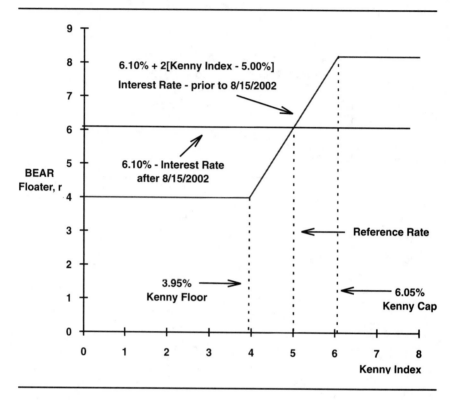

on the level of an interest rate index. In the municipal bond market, the term "derivative securities" also refers to debt-based financial instruments that have complex interest payment structures with optionlike or swaplike features that are embedded in a fixed-rate bond instrument.

Derivative securities are designed in such a way that their cash flows and market values are dependent upon changes in interest rates. Bullish derivative securities have greater price volatility and a longer duration than do fixed-rate bonds of comparable maturity. Conversely, bearish derivative securities have less price volatility and a shorter duration than fixed-rate bonds of comparable maturity. These unique price volatility and duration characteristics are valued by certain investors.

We also introduced the three basic concepts that are essential

EXHIBIT 1–5
BULL Forward BPO Interest Rate Profile

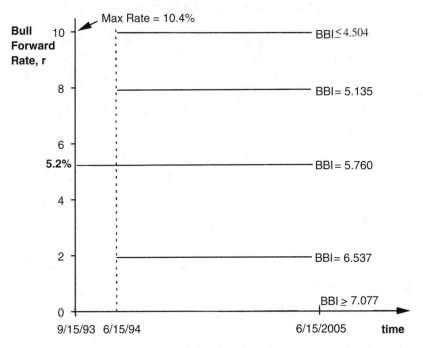

BULL Forward Rate = 5.20% prior to 6/15/1994
Initial Yield-to-Maturity on Bond Buyer 40 Bond Index = 5.76%
BULL Forward Rate after 6/15/1994 depends on Yield to
Maturity of Bond Buyer 40 Bond Index on 6/15/1994

to the understanding and valuation of any debt-based derivative security—municipal, corporate or government. These concepts are:

1. The yield curve and expectational analysis.
2. The components or building blocks of derivative securities.
3. The DAP model.

We then described five different municipal derivative securities, which will be further examined in the chapters that follow. The valuation procedures of the above securities may seem a little confusing at this point. The common denominator of the securities, and the principal source of confusion for most market participants, is that their interest rates, at least prior to their respective conversion dates, are unknown. The interest rate profile diagrams for the five securities that we will value are designed to show how the payment of interest on each of these securities is dependent upon another variable or input. How to better understand and value these types of securities and how to address uncertainty will be discussed herein.

Once expectational analysis is understood, expected interest rates on the municipal derivative securities can be estimated. Once the building-block approach is understood, the complex securities can be broken down and modeled. Once the DAP model is understood, the securities can be valued. All this lies ahead in the next seven chapters.

CHAPTER 2

THE MUNICIPAL BOND MARKET

OVERVIEW

Municipal bonds are debt instruments issued by states, cities, municipal authorities, and other entities. Although municipal entities occasionally issue *taxable* bonds, in this book, we address only *tax-exempt* bonds. The overwhelming attraction of municipal bonds for investors is the exemption of interest income on the bonds from federal and certain state and local income taxation. Because of this interest income exemption, an investor's decision to invest in tax-exempt bonds is based upon an *after-tax* interest income comparison with other fixed-income securities, taking into account the investor's marginal tax bracket.

Municipal entities generally issue debt for two purposes. The first purpose is to temporarily fund short-term operating expenses, which typically are paid on a current basis from operating revenue of the entity. The second purpose is to permanently fund longer-term capital expenditures, which typically are *amortized* over a long period of time. Because of seasonal disparities which may arise in the timing between the receipt of revenue and the payment of operating expenses within a fiscal period, municipalities fund temporary working capital deficits by issuing short-term tax anticipation notes (TANS) and/or revenue anticipation notes (RANS). The combined form—tax and revenue anticipation notes (TRANS)—most often has fixed interest rates and maturities of less than one year. To finance capital expenditures, municipal entities generally issue long-term debt. This book focuses on long-term municipal bonds, or bonds with maturities longer than one year.

The municipal bond market is a huge, diverse, and extremely complicated marketplace. There are estimated to be 37,000 municipal issuers,[1] and the outstanding aggregate face value of bonds on the market was $1.24 trillion as of September 30, 1993. The volume of newly issued long-term municipal bonds sold during calendar year 1993 was a record $289 billion. The securities underlying municipal bond issues range in complexity from a general obligation unlimited taxing power pledge to revenues from garbage facility tipping fees. This variety of security structures makes credit analysis difficult. In addition, unusual redemption features associated with municipal bonds often make the timing of expected cash flows uncertain and further complicate valuation.

Credit risk analysis of municipal security structures has been adequately addressed in other sources.[2] We will closely examine *interest rate risk* in later chapters. In this chapter, we examine the municipal bond marketplace, the municipal bond instrument itself, and the structures—fixed-rate and variable-rate—of the issues themselves.

THE MUNICIPAL BOND MARKET—GENERAL

Types and Volume of Issues

General Obligation Bonds
General obligation bonds are issued by cities, states, and political subdivisions and are secured by the issuer's full faith, credit, and taxing powers. The amount of taxing power may be limited or unlimited. Sources of revenue, depending on the powers of the issuer, may include real estate taxes, personal property taxes, occupational taxes, personal and corporate income taxes, and other miscellaneous taxes. Proceeds of general obligation bonds usually are used to construct projects for the general good of the community: roads, street lighting, school buildings, municipal buildings, etc. Such projects are associated with no specific or substantial revenue source.

---

[1]See S Feldstein and F Fabozzi, "Municipal Bonds," in *The Handbook of Fixed Income Securities*, 3d ed., Dow Jones–Irwin, Homewood, IL, 1991, Chapter 21.

[2]See S Feldstein and F Fabozzi, *The Dow Jones–Irwin Guide to Municipal Bonds*, Dow Jones–Irwin, Homewood, IL, 1987.

Revenue Bonds

Municipal revenue bonds are issued by cities, states, political sub-divisions, and municipal authorities. They are payable principally from revenues generated by the facility or system constructed with the proceeds of the bonds. Examples of projects financed with municipal revenue bonds include: sewer and water, gas, and hydroelectric utilities; bridges, tunnels, and turnpikes; airports; parking facilities, hospitals, and dormitories; rapid transit; pollution control; municipal power stations; student loan programs; agriculture; multifamily and single family housing; and municipal stadiums.

Volume of Issues

Over the last 20 years, the total issuance of municipal bonds has increased dramatically (see Exhibit 2–1) as a result of various factors, including increased demand for public services, reduced federal funding, and fiscal limitations on pay-as-you-go funding of capital outlays. Another contributing factor has been the development of creative new uses for tax-exempt bonds by public officials, bond lawyers, and investment bankers.

Purchasers of Municipal Bonds

Prior to the enactment of the *Tax Reform Act of 1986* (which is also called the *1986 Tax Act*) the principal purchasers of municipal bonds were individuals, commercial banks, and property and casualty insurance companies. Certain aspects of the Tax Reform Act made municipal bonds less desirable for property and casualty insurance companies and, with the exception of certain governmental bonds, undesirable on an after-tax basis for commercial banks.

Currently, the largest categories of purchasers of municipal bonds are individual investors in high and moderate marginal tax brackets and their institutional proxies—mutual funds, trust departments, and investment advisers. With the recent enactment of the Omnibus Budget Reconciliation Act of 1993, investors in the highest marginal tax bracket are subject to effective federal taxes of 39.6 percent. Therefore, a 5.5 percent municipal bond would be the equivalent of a 9.106 percent [5.5% / (1 – 39.6%)] yield on a corporate bond. Certain municipal bonds are exempt from state and local income taxation. If state income taxes (the New York State tax rate is

EXHIBIT 2-1
Volume by Type of Issue ($ in billions)

Year	Number of Issues	General Obligation	Revenue	Total	Total Outstanding
1993	13,916	$92.42	$197.44	$289.86	$1239.50*
1992	12,709	81.74	153.28	235.03	1197.30
1991	11,087	58.02	115.23	173.25	1131.60
1990	8,843	40.37	87.66	128.03	1062.10
1989	9,359	38.42	86.47	124.89	1004.70
1988	8,309	31.15	86.65	117.81	939.40
1987	7,079	30.53	74.63	105.16	873.10
1986	7,717	45.16	105.66	150.82	789.60
1985	10,062	40.42	166.57	206.99	743.00
1984	6,392	27.51	74.37	101.88	564.40
1983	6,290	22.58	60.76	83.35	505.70
1982	6,079	23.28	53.90	77.18	451.30
1981	4,242	13.99	32.15	46.13	398.30
1980	5,550	16.35	30.79	47.13	365.40
1979	5,116	12.61	29.65	42.26	341.50
1978	5,061	17.89	28.32	46.21	313.50
1977	5,130	17.91	27.17	45.08	273.60
1976	4,768	16.91	16.93	33.84	243.90
1975	4,724	15.01	14.32	29.33	223.00
1974	4,287	13.03	9.79	22.82	208.00
1973	4,741	12.82	10.13	22.95	188.49

*Preliminary and unadjusted figures from third quarter.

Source: *The Bond Buyer Yearbook,* 1993. *The Bond Buyer,* Feb. 25, 1992, and Jan. 12, 1994. Taken from the Federal Reserve Board, Flow of Funds Accounts, and Financial Assets and Liabilities.

7.875 percent, and the California tax rate is 11.00 percent) and city income taxes (the New York City tax rate is 4.46 percent, and the Philadelphia tax rate is 4.96 percent) are factored into the after-tax investment return analysis, the allure of tax-exempt municipal bond income to individuals in high tax brackets is quite evident.

Individual investors participate in the purchase of municipal bonds in several ways: through individual purchases directly from municipal bond dealers; through purchases through bank trust departments or money managers; through the purchase of unit trusts or managed bond funds. In recent years, unit trusts and bond funds have represented an increasing share of the new-issue municipal bond market, as reflected in total outstanding holdings of municipal bonds (see Exhibit 2–2).

Tax Exemption

Tax laws inevitably change. Because of the need to amortize an ever-increasing federal deficit, the tax rules relating to municipal bonds seem to be changing with increasing frequency. We have written this section with the recognition that the tax laws that affect the *supply* of municipal bonds may change. Tax law changes may affect allowable uses, as well as the *demand* for municipal bonds, higher marginal tax brackets, and the extent to which municipal bonds are exempt from taxes. Keep in mind also that tax laws are complex and that the descriptions that follow are simplified and general.

EXHIBIT 2–2
Holders of Outstanding Municipal Bonds ($ in billions)

Year	House-holds	Long-Term Mutual Funds	Money Market Mutual Funds	Comm. Banks	Property & Casualty Insurers	Other	Total
1992	$508.9	$173.4	$94.8	$97.5	$134.3	$188.50	$1197.40
1991	503.8	137.1	89.9	103.2	126.8	170.80	1131.60
1990	468.9	109.1	83.6	117.4	136.9	146.10	1062.00
1989	442.2	93.6	69.4	133.8	134.8	130.90	1004.70
1988	391.8	78.7	65.7	151.6	134.1	117.60	939.50
1987	332.8	70.7	61.4	174.3	124.8	109.30	873.30
1986	242.9	65.3	63.8	203.4	101.9	112.50	789.80
1985	255.2	33.5	36.3	231.7	88.2	97.90	742.80
1984	186.3	19.1	23.8	174.6	84.7	75.90	564.40
1983	159.4	13.4	16.8	162.1	86.7	67.40	505.80

Source: *The Bond Buyer*, Jan. 12, 1994. Taken from the Federal Reserve Board, Flow of Funds Accounts, and Financial Assets and Liabilities.

The interest income on the obligations of a state, a territory, or a possession of the United States, any political subdivision of any of the foregoing, or the District of Columbia has been excluded from gross income since the Federal Income Tax Law was adopted in 1913.

The Tax Reform Act of 1986 introduced significant changes for the municipal bond market.[3] The 1986 Tax Act lowered marginal tax rates, thereby reducing demand; restricted the supply of municipal bonds by curtailing certain uses; introduced the alternative minimum tax (AMT), which subjected certain municipal bonds to partial federal taxation; and altered the tax treatment of interest on municipal bonds for property and casualty insurance companies and for commercial banks.

---

[3]Ibid., "Appendix A: The 1986 Tax Reform Law."

The 1986 Tax Act reduced the highest marginal tax rate for individuals from a rate of 50 percent to an effective rate of 33 percent, which included surcharges. This lowering of marginal tax rates negatively affects the demand for municipal bonds and, all else equal, should increase yields on municipal bonds relative to Treasury bonds. The 1986 Tax Act also eliminated many tax shelters, leaving municipal bonds as one of the few remaining tax-advantaged investments. This change increased the demand for municipal bonds.

The 1986 Tax Act reduced the supply of municipal bonds by defining two categories of municipal bonds—governmental use and private activity bonds—and by severely restricting the ability to issue private activity bonds. *Governmental use* bonds finance "traditional" government capital expenditures such as schools and municipal buildings and government-owned and operated utility systems. *Private activity* bonds are issued to finance projects, if more than 10 percent of the bond proceeds are used in a private trade or business, or if more than 5 percent are loaned to a private entity. Classified as private activity bonds are certain bonds issued for airports, mass commuting facilities, student loans, single and multifamily mortgages, hydroelectric, and solid waste, among other purposes. The 1986 Tax Act enacted state-specific limitations on the aggregate volume of certain private activity bonds that can be issued in a calendar year. The respective annual state caps are the greater of $50 per capita or $150 million. The 1986 Tax Act also restricted the ability of an issuer to advance-refund its outstanding debt and introduced a *rebate* procedure. Under the rebate provisions, an issuer must return to the US Treasury any investment profits earned on the investment of certain funds, in excess of the yield on its bonds.

As mentioned above, the 1986 Tax Act introduced the AMT calculation. This calculation requires that individuals and corporations compute their tax liabilities both on a conventional basis and under AMT procedures. The calculation is a complicated process that includes interest earnings on private activity municipal bonds, but not on governmental use bonds. Because interest income on private activity bonds is taxable to certain investors, the market for AMT municipal bonds is not as broad as the market for governmental use bonds, and yields on AMT bonds are higher than yields on comparable non-AMT issues.

Also affected by the 1986 Tax Act is the tax-exempt characterization of interest income on tax-exempt bonds held by commercial banks and by property and casualty insurance companies. The 1986 Tax Act requires property and casualty insurance companies to decrease

Regulation of the Municipal Bond Market[4]

Municipal bonds are exempt from registration under the *Securities Act of 1933* as amended (also called the *1933 act*) and from the reporting requirements of the *Securities Exchange Act of 1934* (also called the 1934 act). They do, however, come under certain antifraud provisions of the 1933 act and the 1934 act.

During the early 1970s the Securities and Exchange Commission (SEC) brought legal action against a number of municipal market participants regarding their selling techniques and marketing procedures. In reaction to perceived abuses in and growth of the municipal bond market, the US Congress included a regulatory program for municipal bonds at the federal level in the *Securities Act Amendments of 1975* (also called the 1975 amendments). The 1975 amendments resulted in the establishment of the Municipal Securities Rulemaking Board (MSRB), and gave the SEC certain rule-making and enforcement authority over brokers and dealers in the municipal bond market.

The MSRB was established as a self-regulatory organization for dealers and brokers in the municipal market. Its 15-member board includes representatives of noncommercial bank broker-

---

their deductions for losses incurred but not paid by an amount equal to 15 percent of their tax-exempt interest income. This effectively reduces the after-tax interest income on municipal bonds for property and casualty insurance companies. Prior to the 1986 Tax Act, banks were allowed to deduct 80 percent of the interest expense incurred on borrowed funds used to purchase tax-exempt bonds. The 1986 Tax Act repealed this deduction, with the exception of certain *bank-qualified* obligations of issuers that do not expect to issue more than $10 million per year. Because of the appeal of bank-qualified bonds to banks, which broadens the demand for these bonds, yields on bank-qualified bonds are lower than yields on comparable non-bank-qualified bonds.

The state and local tax treatment of interest income on municipal bonds varies state by state and city by city. Many states and cities have individual income taxes. Interest income on bonds issued by in-state entities is exempt from state income taxation in the majority of states. Interest income on bonds issued by local entities (e.g., New York City and its authorities, the City of Philadelphia and its authorities) generally is exempt from local, in-city income taxation. Interest income on tax-exempt bonds issued by territories (e.g., Puerto Rico, Guam, and the Virgin Islands, and their respective entities) is exempt from all state and local income taxation, and these triple-tax-exempt bonds are desired by investors in high-tax states such as California and New York.

[4]See "Staff Report on the Municipal Securities Market," *The Division of Market Regulation, US Securities and Exchange Commission*, September 1993.

dealers, bank broker-dealers, and members of the public, including a representative from a municipal bond issuer. The MSRB has no inspection or enforcement powers; rather, it is a rule-making body under the supervision of the SEC.

Responsibility for enforcement of the MSRB rules resides with the National Association of Securities Dealers (NASD) for nonbank firms and with bank regulatory agencies for bank municipal bond dealers. The SEC has the overall disciplinary authority over and responsibility for the market participants—the brokers, the dealers, and their associated personnel.

The 1975 amendments expressly limited both the SEC's and the MSRB's authority to promulgate or require specific issuer disclosure language in its offering statements. The MSRB is prohibited from requiring issuers to provide documents, reports, or other information that are not generally available from a source other than the issuer itself. The sections of the 1975 amendments that limit the SEC's and the MSRB's powers to require issuers to provide certain information are collectively known as the *Tower Amendment*. During 1993 the Tower Amendment came under significant political scrutiny, and changes were proposed in a September 1993 SEC staff report.

The Primary and Secondary Markets

The *primary market* is the marketing process involved in the *initial offering* of a bond to the investing public. It represents the direct issuance of the debt by the issuer, through underwriters, to the end investors. The bond, its security, and its terms are described in an official statement that accompanies the offering. Primary offerings are marketed either on a negotiated basis, through the negotiation of terms between a predetermined underwriting syndicate of investment banks, or on a competitive basis, in which a number of underwriting syndicates bid on a bond issue at a predetermined time and date. In calendar year 1993, a $231.9 billion principal amount of bonds was marketed on a negotiated basis and $55.6 billion was marketed on a competitive basis. The *secondary market* is the over-the-counter (OTC) dealer marketplace, in which bonds are traded after initial issuance. Billions of dollars worth of municipal bonds are traded in the secondary market by approximately 2600 municipal bond dealers. Most outstanding municipal bonds are plain-vanilla bonds with a fixed interest rate, a specified maturity date, and the possibility of an early redemption after a predetermined optional redemption date.

As with other fixed-rate debt instruments, the market value or price of a municipal bond increases as interest rates fall, adjusting the bond's yield to reflect prevailing market conditions. Conversely, municipal bond prices fall as interest rates on comparable securities rise. If market interest rates are above the coupon or current interest payment on a municipal bond, dealers assume that this *discount* bond will be outstanding until maturity, and the market value is calculated with the cash flows *discounted to maturity.* If market interest rates are below the coupon payment, dealers assume that this *premium* bond will be called by the issuer at the first optional redemption date, and the market value is calculated with the cash flows discounted to the *first call date.*

The *secondary market* is also the process by which a municipal bond dealer overlays an outstanding municipal bond with certain credit, liquidity, or structural features that make the bond a *derivative security.* As a derivative security, it may become more highly desirable to certain investors. When a dealer does such a structural overlay, it is important to address any effects that the enhancement may have on the municipal bond's basic exemption from the 1933 act, the 1934 act, and the *Investment Company Act of 1940* (also called the *1940 act*).

Many of the debt-service structures discussed in this book can be implemented by the issuer in the primary market or by dealers in the secondary market. Because of securities law concerns, issuer-initiated primary market transactions have a distinct advantage over dealer-manufactured secondary market structures. However, innovative dealers have introduced secondary market derivative structures that have been quite successful.

THE MUNICIPAL BOND INSTRUMENT

Municipal bonds are debt instruments that have a specified *maturity date,* specified *redemption features,* and either fixed-rate or variable-rate *interest payments.* Many long-term municipal bonds (i.e., bonds with maturities longer than 10 years) have early redemption features which dictate when and at what price an issuer may call the bonds. Maturity date, interest payment, redemption price, and redemption date are the four key inputs in valuing any municipal bond. These are the features that determine the *amount* and *timing* of the bond's expected cash flows.

The *security and credit* aspects of a municipal bond reflect an issuer's *pledged* sources of payments and its *ability* to make its promised payments. A greater ability to pay means a more secure investment, which should translate into a higher-rated bond and lower interest rates. The description of a municipal bond, including all relevant security features, is summarized in the official statement by the issuer that accompanies the initial offering to the public.

When an issuer comes to market with a bond issue, generally a number of bonds are offered under the same official statement. Each bond that is offered has a specific maturity date and an interest payment and redemption feature. In the typical upward-sloping municipal yield curve, bonds with shorter maturities will have lower interest rates, assuming that they are not sold at a discount, than bonds with longer maturities. The Committee on Uniform Security Identification Procedures (CUSIP) has established a systematic method for identifying bond maturities. A CUSIP number is a nine-digit identification number, consisting of numerals and letters, that distinguishes each maturity.

In this section, we focus on new issues of municipal bonds—that is, on the primary market.

Security

Municipal bonds can be secured in many ways. This section explains the security and credit aspects and the pledged sources of payments for municipal bonds.

Primary Security

The primary security associated with a municipal bond is the issuer's revenue sources that are pledged for payment of interest and principal on the bonds. General obligation bonds are secured by the issuer's taxing powers, which may be limited or unlimited, and other revenues of the issuer. Revenue bonds are payable principally from revenues generated by the facility or system constructed with the proceeds of the bonds. Examples of revenue bonds and their primary security sources[5] are:

1. *Sewer and water revenue bonds.* User charges and tapping and connection fees.
2. *Gas and electric revenue bonds.* Utility user charges.
3. *Bridges, tunnel, and turnpike revenue bonds.* Toll collections, gas taxes, and driving-related fees.
4. *Airport revenue bonds.* Landing fees, terminal rentals, and concession fees.
5. *Mortgage revenue bonds.* Mortgages and mortgage-loan repayments.
6. *Hospital revenue bonds.* Patient payments, third-party commercial payers, and federal and state reimbursement programs.
7. *Student loan revenue bonds.* Student loan repayments (usually insured *or reinsured* by the federal government).
8. *Resource recovery bonds.* Garbage tipping fees; revenues from sale of scrap, electricity, or steam.
9. *Special tax bonds.* Generally limited pledges of a specific tax source (e.g., sales tax) dedicated to repayment of certain bonds. These bonds are analyzed as revenue bonds rather than as tax-backed bonds.

Secondary Security

Secondary security structures are credit overlays that enhance or support the primary security of an issue. The two principal sources of secondary security structures are insurance companies, through bond insurance, and commercial banks, through letters of credit (LOCs) and liquidity facilities.

Municipal Bond Insurance.   Municipal bond insurance is issued in the form of a financial guaranty contract written by an insurance company. It pays scheduled interest and principal on a bond issue in the event that payments are not made by the issuer. The insurance policy effectively superimposes an insurance

---

[5]See Feldstein and Fabozzi, op. cit., Chapter 1.

company's credit on top of the issuer's pledged repayment sources. The insurer charges an insurance premium for issuing the insurance policy, which runs for the term of the bonds. Most bond insurance policies are purchased by the issuer of the bonds at the time of initial issuance, and the bonds are offered to the public as insured bonds. However, secondary market insurance programs have also been developed. In the secondary market, a dealer or investor can purchase insurance on bonds of an outstanding bond issue, obtain a new CUSIP number, and establish a custodial receipt representing ownership interest in the insured bonds.

Municipal bond insurance was first introduced by the American Municipal Bond Assurance Corporation (AMBAC) in 1971. Since then, several monoline and multiline insurance companies have entered the bond insurance field. Major participants at this time include AMBAC, the Municipal Bond Insurance Association (MBIA), the Financial Guaranty Insurance Company (FGIC), the Financial Security Association (FSA), and the Capital Guaranty Insurance Company (Cap Guaranty), among others. In calendar year 1993, a $107.45 billion principal amount of municipal bonds, representing 37 percent of the total principal amount of bonds issued, was insured.

Municipal bond insurance represents a very strong credit enhancement. Most of the insurance policies have been structured to provide timely payment of interest and principal. Bonds that have been insured by AMBAC, MBIA, FGIC, or Capital Guaranty are rated AAA by Standard and Poor's Corporation (S&P) and/or Aaa by Moody's Investors Service, Inc. (Moody's) and/or AAA by Fitch Investors Service, Inc. (Fitch).

The increased security created by bond insurance results in higher ratings for issuers, reduced borrowing costs for certain issuers, and reduced risks for investors. Generally, the reduction in interest rate for most issuers whose bonds would otherwise be rated below AA more than offsets the cost of the insurance premium. However, insured Aaa/AAA bonds have rates that are generally higher than otherwise comparable noninsured Aaa/AAA bonds (see Exhibit 2–3 on page 33)[6].

---

[6]See J Angel, "The Municipal Bond Insurance Riddle," *Financier*, Volume 1 (1) 48–63, 1994

Commercial Banks. Commercial banks have been active in providing credit and liquidity facilities for municipal bond issues. In a *letter of credit,* a commercial bank guarantees the payment of scheduled debt service on the municipal bonds to an investor. However, in contrast to bond insurance policies, LOCs typically extend out only five to seven years (until the LOC expiration date). If the LOC is not renewed or replaced on its expiration date, the issuer effectively has to buy back the bond from the investor. The legal structure of an LOC is complicated by bankruptcy law and related rating agency concerns, but the LOC provides a strong secondary security structure for a municipal bond issue. A properly structured LOC-backed municipal bond will attain rating levels from Moody's, S&P, and Fitch equivalent to the rating of the commercial bank that issued the LOC. In calendar year 1993, $11.56 billion in municipal bonds secured by LOCs was marketed.

Liquidity facilities are issued by commercial banks to reduce the *effective maturity* of a municipal bond from its stated maturity (e.g., 30 years) to a shorter period (the *put period,* e.g., seven days). This shortening of maturity is extremely important to money market municipal bond funds that can invest only in instruments with an effective maturity of less than 397 days. Liquidity facilities are usually linked with municipal bonds that have a floating, or variable, rate of interest. They do not guarantee payment of debt service, and, typically, they are automatically terminated in the event of a payment default of the municipal bond issue, a bankruptcy of the municipal bond issuer, or a credit downgrade of the bonds by the rating agencies below a certain rating level, usually Baa/BBB. In an upward-sloping yield curve, the existence of a liquidity facility, which reduces the effective maturity of a bond, allows a lower interest rate to be set and paid by the issuer. However, because the interest rate on the bonds floats, the issuer bears the risks associated with increasing interest rates.

Commercial banks charge a fee for issuing LOCs and liquidity facilities, which can be purchased by issuers in the primary markets and by dealers who set up a liquidity facility-backed municipal derivative bond structure in the secondary market. LOC-supported municipal bond issues were very popular in the 1980s, when LOCs were treated as *off-balance sheet liabilities* of banks and LOCs had zero or minimal bank capital allocation considerations. Changes in banking laws in 1990 that led to stricter bank capital requirements have made LOCs more expensive and less available than in the 1980s.

The Effect of Increased Security on Municipal Bond Interest Rates
Reoffering yields associated with municipal bonds decrease as security and credit ratings increase. Exhibit 2–3, which shows general obligation AAA, AAA (insured), AA, and A par reoffering interest rate levels associated with 1- to 30-year maturities, illustrates this relationship. It is interesting to note that AAA (insured) bonds trade at slightly higher yields than lesser-rated AA bonds, as shown in Exhibit 2–3, reflecting the fact that investors in insured bonds, to a certain extent, look past the insurance to the issuer's underlying source of repayment.

Interest Rates

The mechanism by which interest rates are set is the cause of most investors' confusion about municipal derivative products. In this section, we describe a number of interest rate payment structures for municipal bonds.

The interest rate on a municipal bond is the annual interest, expressed on a percentage basis, that accrues or is paid to the holder of the bond. The interest rate may be fixed or variable. While the upward-sloping nature of the municipal yield curve (see Chapter 4 for a description of yield curves) consists of comparatively lower short-term rates rather than long-term rates, most issuers of municipal bonds are *risk-averse* and are concerned about the potential for higher interest rates with variable-rate debt. Interest rate risk also causes concern at rating agencies when credit ratings for a municipal bond issue are being assessed. To overcome this risk, investment bankers have devised two approaches to the creation of fixed-rate obligations for issues of variable-rate debt. Those approaches are called the *mirrored-security fixed-rate structure* and the *synthetic-asset fixed-rate structure*. The following section describes the various fixed-rate and variable-rate structures that have been introduced into the municipal bond market over the last decade. An understanding of these interest rate structures will

EXHIBIT 2–3

Municipal Market Data
General Obligation Yields

Figures are for 2:30 p.m. EST, Jan. 3, 1994. These data are provided by Municipal Market Data, (617) 345-2900, and are considered proprietary. Although they have been obtained from sources considered reliable, there is no guarantee of completeness or accuracy.

Year	AAA	AAA (ins)	AA	A
1995	2.30	2.40	2.40	2.60
1996	3.10	3.25	3.20	3.40
1997	3.45	3.65	3.55	3.75
1998	3.70	3.85	3.80	4.00
1999	3.85	4.05	3.95	4.05
2000	4.00	4.20	4.10	4.30
2001	4.15	4.35	4.25	4.44
2002	4.25	4.45	4.35	4.55
2003	4.35	4.55	4.45	4.65
2004	4.45	4.65	4.55	4.75
2005	4.55	4.75	4.65	4.85
2006	4.65	4.85	4.75	4.95
2007	4.75	4.95	4.85	5.05
2008	4.85	5.05	4.95	5.15
2009	4.95	5.15	5.05	5.25
2010	5.00	5.20	5.10	5.30
2011	5.05	5.25	5.15	5.35
2012	5.10	5.30	5.20	5.40
2013	5.10	5.30	5.20	5.40
2014	5.15	5.35	5.25	5.45
2015	5.15	5.35	5.25	5.45
2016	5.20	5.40	5.30	5.50
2017	5.20	5.40	5.30	5.50
2018	5.20	5.40	5.30	5.50
2019	5.20	5.40	5.30	5.50
2020	5.25	5.45	5.35	5.55
2021	5.25	5.45	5.35	5.55
2022	5.25	5.45	5.35	5.55
2023	5.25	5.45	5.35	5.55
2024	5.25	5.45	5.35	5.55

Source: *The Bond Buyer,* Jan. 4, 1994, page 25.

help in analysis of the municipal derivatives products that we will examine in later chapters.

Fixed-Rate Bonds

Fixed-rate bonds are the most common type of bonds in the municipal market. The coupon payments are fixed over the life of the bond and the issuer is certain of the payments. The different types of fixed-rate bonds are described in this section.

Fixed-Rate Par Bonds.   The fixed-rate par bond is by far the most popular and often-used form in which bonds are issued in the primary market. The issuer, along with its underwriter and/or financial adviser, determines the *interest rate* (e.g., 5 percent) assigned to a particular maturity (e.g., 20 years) that results in a market value of par, or 100 percent, at the time of bond pricing. In this example, the offering yield will be equal to the 5 percent coupon. The bonds are then offered to the investing public at par by the underwriters, and the issuer receives par, less the underwriter's discount. The issuer then pays the annual coupon of 5 percent (2.5 percent every six months), on predetermined semiannual interest payment dates, until the redemption of the bond, when it pays the redemption price, which is par at maturity and usually 102 percent at the first optional redemption date of 10 years. This is the *plain-vanilla* fixed-rate bond, which serves as a basis or reference point for the evaluation of all alternative structures.

Fixed-Rate Discount Bonds.   The fixed-rate discount bond is another popular bond in the primary market. It is important that an issuer understand the advantages and disadvantages of issuing a bond with an original issue discount (OID). In a discount offering, the issuer will market a bond through its underwriters to the investing public, with an interest rate (e.g., 4 percent) assigned to a particular maturity (e.g., 20 years) that creates a market value less than 100 percent at the time of pricing, and an offering yield (e.g., 5 percent) that is higher than the coupon. Based on the above example (a 4 percent coupon, 20-year-maturity, 5 percent offering yield), the offering price of this discount bond would be 87.449 percent. The issuer pays the annual coupon of 4 percent (2 percent every six months), until the maturity of the bond or until an earlier redemption date and pays the redemption price, which is par at maturity or par plus any call premium if the bonds are redeemed earlier.

What are the advantages and disadvantages of OID bonds? The advantage for the issuer, assuming an upward-sloping municipal yield curve, is that the coupon associated with a discount bond is *lower* than the coupon of a par bond. The lower coupon means lower current interest payments for the discount bond, which frees up a portion of debt-service cash flows that can be used to pack in additional debt of the issuer in shorter-term, lower-yielding bonds maturing prior to the OID bond. In more analytical terms, the weighted average cash flows, or *duration* (see Chapter 3), of an OID bond are *longer* than the duration of an otherwise comparable par bond offered at the same yield. The benefit of increasing the duration of a discount bond and allowing the packing-in of additional lower-cost, shorter-term debt can be estimated by the issuer's investment banker and/or its financial adviser.

The disadvantage of a discount bond is that, due to the lower current coupon payment, there is a reduced probability that the issuer's early redemption option, the call option, will be exercised. The call option has a quantifiable value to the issuer. The reduction in value of the call option can be estimated by the issuer's investment banker and/or financial adviser. The issuer can then make a rational decision about the benefits and costs of discount bonds as compared to a par bond. Typically, bonds issued at a coupon rate that results in a small discount to the market (e.g., a 90 percent issue price or higher) can be offered at a slightly lower yield than a par bond, reflecting the greater call protection for the investors. An additional concern to some issuers is that discount bonds require a larger face amount of principal than that required by par bonds to generate the same net proceeds. This is of particular concern to issuers that face statutory debt capacity limitations.

1. *Zero-coupon bonds and capital appreciation bonds.* Two extreme examples of discount bonds are zero-coupon bonds (zeroes) and capital appreciation bonds (CABs). These deeply discounted bonds are offered with *no* current interest associated; their current coupon is 0 percent. For example, a zero that matures in 20 years and is offered at a yield of 5 percent has an offering price of 37.243 percent. The first zero-coupon bonds were sold in 1982 at a deep discount from their face value of par paid at maturity. However, certain issuers have prescribed debt limits and political concerns that prevent them from issuing pure zero-coupon bonds. To overcome this concern, CABs were developed. CABs are issued at an offering price and a face value which *accrete* along an *accreted value schedule* to par value at maturity.

The advantage, from an issuer's perspective, is that there is no current interest payment on a zero or a CAB. This allows the issuer to pack in the maximum amount possible of additional lower-cost, shorter-term debt. The duration of a zero is equal to its maturity—much longer than the duration of a comparable par bond.

In 1982, in connection with zeroes and CABs sold by Tampa Water and Sewer Authority and Bellefonte Area School District, E.F. Hutton & Co. introduced the concept of early redemption based on the compound accreted value of the zero or the CAB. Based on mathematical compounding formulas, the compound accreted value call generally has no negative impact on or hidden cost associated with an issuer's ability to call a CAB or a zero, as compared to a normal par bond call provision.

What disadvantages does the issuer face, in offering zeroes and CABs? From the investor's perspective, the internal compounding or accreting nature of a zero or a CAB eliminates any reinvestment risk associated with reinvestment of coupon interest payments. However, the increased duration of a zero's cash flow means that its price or market value will be more volatile than that of a par bond with a comparable maturity. To compensate for this increased volatility and as a natural consequence of longer duration in an upward-sloping yield curve, investors often require zeroes and CABs to have a *higher offering yield than a comparable par bond*. Again, the benefit of packing in lower-yield, short-term debt versus the cost of a higher yield on the zero or CAB can be quantified and examined by the issuer.

2. *Deferred-interest bonds.* In 1983, Goldman Sachs introduced Growth and Income Securities[SM] (GAINS[SM]) into the municipal bond market.[7] GAINS are deferred-interest bonds (DIBs), with no current interest payments for a period of time (e.g., 10 years)

---

[7]GAINS[SM] and Growth and Income Securities[SM] is a service mark of Goldman Sachs & Company.

and with current interest payable at a specified coupon rate (e.g., 5 percent) for the remaining life of the bond (e.g., 20 years). DIBs are priced at issuance to accrete along an accreted value schedule to par and, thereafter, to pay current interest. For example, a DIB that matures in 20 years accretes interest for the first 10 years; has a 5 percent coupon for years 11 through 20; and, if offered at a yield of 5 percent, has an offering price of 61.027 percent. The compound accreted value of the DIB is 100 percent in year 10.

From the issuer's perspective, since there is no current coupon payment on the DIB for 10 years, lower-cost, shorter-term debt can be packed in for the 10-year accretion period. The duration of a DIB is longer than that of a par bond but shorter than that of a zero or a CAB. Because of increased duration and increased price volatility, DIBS are often required to have a *higher offering yield than a comparable par bond.* There is generally no disadvantage or loss of value in the redemption features of DIBs, as compared to par bonds. Again, the cost of the higher yield on DIBs versus par bonds may be easily compared to the benefit of lower-cost, shorter-maturity debt instruments.

Fixed-Rate Premium Bonds. The fixed-rate premium bond is frequently used in competitive bidding on bonds that are not subject to early redemption. In a premium offering, the issuer will market a bond through its underwriters, with an interest rate (e.g., 6 percent) assigned to a particular maturity (e.g., 20 years) that creates a market value greater than 100 percent at the time of pricing, and an offering yield (e.g., 5 percent) lower than the coupon. A premium bond with a 6 percent coupon, 20-year maturity, and a 5 percent offering yield has an offering price of 112.551 percent. The issuer will pay the annual coupon of 6 percent (3 percent every six months) until the maturity of the bond or until an earlier redemption date. However, most initial-issue premium bonds are noncallable prior to maturity.

For an issuer, what are the disadvantages and advantages of premium bonds? The first disadvantage is the converse of the packing-in benefit of a discount bond. That is, the coupon associated with a premium bond is *higher* than the coupon of a par bond. The higher coupon requires larger current interest payments for the premium bond. This requirement crowds out a portion of debt-service cash flows that, otherwise, would have been used to amortize lower-cost, shorter-term debt maturing prior to the premium bond. In other words, the duration of a premium bond is *shorter* than the duration of an otherwise comparable par bond offered at the same yield. The second disadvantage of premium bonds is that, generally, they are not callable prior to maturity. This disadvantage is irrelevant for shorter-maturity serial bonds that otherwise would not be callable, but it becomes more important with longer-maturity premium bonds.

What are the advantages of premium bonds, for an issuer? Lower yields! Why? First, investors recognize the value of noncallability in a bond; because of this value, the required yield on noncallable bonds is lower for all noncallable bonds (par, discount, and premium) than for otherwise comparable callable bonds. Second, because of the shorter duration and lower price volatility, investors generally will accept a lower yield on premium bonds than on par bonds. The benefits of lower-yield, noncallable premium bonds versus the cost of crowding out lower-yielding debt-service payments and the loss of the call option can be quantified. The issuer can decide whether or not to use premium bonds. Another advantage is that premium bonds require a smaller face amount of principal than par bonds to generate the same net proceeds. This characteristic is particularly beneficial to issuers that face statutory debt capacity limitations.

Variable-Rate Bonds
The municipal bond market has generally exhibited an upward-sloping yield curve. The benefit of variable-rate bonds is that, historically, the interest rates that investors accept for municipal variable-rate bonds with interest rate mechanisms designed to create *par* instruments are considerably lower (see Chapter 4) than the interest rates associated with comparable-maturity, fixed-rate par bonds. The major risk of variable-rate bonds for an issuer is interest rate increases.

As previously discussed, most traditional municipal entities—states, cities, school districts, etc.—are reluctant to assume the risk of upward-floating interest rates associated with variable-rate bonds. Most treasurers of municipalities rightly feel that they are not compensated to *gamble* on the outcomes of interest rates: if they're right, they are lucky if they receive a handshake, and if they're wrong, their jobs are in jeopardy. This is known as a *non-symmetrical outcome.*

There are many situations, however, in which tax-exempt bonds may be issued by a municipal entity to fund certain facilities on behalf of large corporations that are more familiar with the benefits and risks associated with variable-rate debt, and are also more familiar with techniques for hedging against higher interest rates. Members of these corporate finance staffs are compensated for taking risks and are rewarded for successful outcomes. Hospitals, investor-owned utilities, and other private-use issuers are examples. These types of issuers have often used straight variable-rate bonds to fund their long-term capital needs.

There is a significant demand for variable-rate municipal bonds by a number of bond funds and investment managers that desire interest payment and price performance characteristics associated with variable-rate bonds. This demand typically exceeds the supply provided by the private-use marketplace. To better meet this demand and also to create savings for traditional municipal entities, investment bankers have created variable-rate bonds that result in a fixed rate for the issuer when these bonds are combined with other bonds or financing instruments. Various variable-rate debt structures are examined below.

Floating-Rate Bonds. In 1980, with the commercial bank prime interest rate approaching 21 percent, investment bankers at E.F. Hutton & Co. launched the first publicly offered, long-term, floating-rate municipal bonds. The floating-rate bonds paid semiannual interest rates at levels that were based on a *taxable* interest rate index, subject to a minimum and maximum rate. For example, the interest rate was to be a floating interest rate of not less than X (e.g., 7 percent), nor more than Y (e.g., 12.5 percent). The rate per annum, determined weekly, would be the *higher* of A percent (e.g., 67 percent) of 13-week US Treasury bills, or B percent (e.g., 74 percent) of the interest rates applicable to 30-year constant-maturity Treasury bonds. This interest rate mechanism was intended to adjust in such a manner that the floating-rate bonds would always trade at or near par value.

Twenty-eight of these bond issues, totaling approximately $500 million, were marketed, and many bonds were purchased by retail investors. Unfortunately, the interest rate formula was rigid and did not take into account the possibility of changes in tax laws, marginal tax rates, or the security and credit ratings of the bonds. As a result of declining credit quality of a number of the obligors, the market value and liquidity of floating-rate bonds declined precipitously. Floating-rate bonds waned in popularity when they were replaced with structures that better accommodated tax law changes and credit changes.

In the early 1980s, investment bankers at Prudential-Bache Securities Inc. introduced Tax-Exempt Exchangeable Securities℠ or TEES℠.[8] The interest on TEES was fixed (e.g., 6.75 percent) for a period of time (e.g., three years) called the *fixed-rate period*. On any interest payment date after the fixed-rate period, the TEES, at the option of the holder, could be converted into bonds with a variable interest rate (*variable-rate bonds*); otherwise, they would continue to pay the fixed rate of 6.75 percent. Once converted, the variable-rate bonds could not be converted back to fixed-rate bonds.

The variable-rate bonds paid interest semiannually, at a rate calculated by Kenny Information Systems, a municipal bond valuation service, to be the *higher* of (1) the minimum rate required to produce a par bid for the variable-rate bonds, assuming a maturity of six months; or (2) a rate that was 1.00 percent higher than comparably rated securities, with a maturity of six months. There were also minimum rates (e.g., 5.00 percent) and maximum rates (e.g., 9.50 percent) on the variable-rate bonds.

A number of TEES were marketed by Prudential-Bache, but the program never caught on with other investment banking firms. Possibly because investors sensed a lack of liquidity, a broad institutional investor base was never established.

Variable-Rate Demand Notes.   In September 1981, investment bankers at E.F. Hutton & Co. introduced variable-rate demand notes (VRDNs) for municipal bonds. The first VRDNs were issued on behalf of the Tucson Electric Company. VRDNs have a periodic interest rate resetting mechanism, whereby interest rates are reset within certain parameters by a remarketing agent, based on a short-term tax-exempt market rate, at a level designed to *clear the market*. To ensure that rates are set at an appropriate level,

---

[8]Tax-Exempt Exchangeable Securities℠ and TEES℠ are service marks of Prudential-Bache Securities Inc.

VRDNs have either an LOC or a liquidity facility, usually provided by a commercial bank, which allows a holder to put its VRDN to the trustee or the provider of the liquidity facility at a price of par plus accrued interest. The interest rates may be reset daily, weekly, monthly, quarterly, or yearly. The reset periods coincide with the put period feature of the liquidity facility.

VRDNs have proved to be a popular method of variable-rate financing, and billions of dollars worth of VRDNs were issued during the 1980s and 1990s. Because the interest rate on VRDNs is set by the remarketing agent at a market clearing price, and not by a rigid formula, and because it is based on a tax-exempt rate, VRDNs are very successful variable-rate instruments. Their market values equal par on each interest reset date. The duration of a VRDN is essentially the term of the put period (e.g., one week). Tax-exempt money market funds are the principal purchasers of VRDNs, because the LOC or liquidity facility gives a VRDN an *effective* maturity equal to the put period (less than 397 days). Because of more stringent bank capital requirements that fully took effect at the end of 1992, LOCs have become more costly and less available. For this reason, most VRDN transactions that are currently being completed rely on either the issuer and/or bond insurance for credit enhancement, and on commercial banks solely for liquidity facilities.

Auction-Rate Securities. In 1984, investment bankers at Shearson Lehman Brothers, Inc., introduced an auction-rate security into the preferred stock arena. This security, called *Money Market Preferred Stock*[SM] (*MMP*[SM]), became a popular method of issuing preferred stock.[9]

In 1988, investment bankers at Goldman Sachs & Company used the auction-rate mechanism developed in MMP in the municipal market for a $121,400,000 principal amount of PARS issued by The Industrial Development Authority of the County of Pima (Arizona). PARS were quickly replicated by Shearson Lehman Hutton Inc. in issuing a $50 million principal amount of SAVRS for the Department of Budget and Finance of the State of Hawaii.

---

[9] Money Market Preferred Stock[SM] and MMP[SM] are service marks of Lehman Brothers, Inc.

In auction-rate securities such as PARS and SAVRS, interest rates are set periodically (typically every 28 days, 35 days, six months, or longer) through a Dutch auction process conducted by an auction agent. The auction agent is usually a large money center commercial bank such as Chemical Bank, Bank of New York, or Banker's Trust Company. A Dutch auction is an interest rate setting procedure in which holders or potential buyers or sellers of an auction-rate bond submit buy, hold, or sell orders on the bond based on an interest rate determined in the Dutch auction. Assuming that sufficient clearing bids (buy and hold orders) exist, the interest rate for that period (e.g., the next 35 days) is the minimum interest rate at which sell orders, at that minimum interest rate or lower, are offset by buy and hold orders, at that minimum interest rate or higher.

Ideally, demand by potential investors to participate in an auction is generated by the broker-dealers (e.g., Lehman Brothers, Goldman Sachs, or Merrill Lynch) that normally participate in remarketing auction-rate securities. Interest rates on municipal auction-rate securities tend to move in concert with Treasury bill rates. The interest rates of these securities are closely correlated with the interest rates in the taxable marketplace, as adjusted for the marginal tax rate for corporations. Their correlation with a short-term, tax-exempt index like the 30-day Kenny Index, which changes on a weekly basis, is more volatile. However, a study performed by Lehman Brothers in late 1993, which compares the Kenny Index to the Lehman Brothers SAVRS Rate Index, shows that, on average, the auction rate is approximately 22 BPs higher on the SAVRS Rate Index than on the Kenny Index.[10]

It should be noted that the broker-dealers who solicit investor participation in the Dutch auction help to determine a market clearing interest rate in an auction rate security, in much the same way as a remarketing agent does in a VRDN. However, the issuer of an auction-rate security does not have to bear the liquidity facility costs associated with VRDNs. This cost is currently in excess of the 22 BPs which, as shown in the Lehman Brothers study, repre-

---

[10]See L Chuey, "Tax-Exempt Dutch Auction Securities," *Municipal Market Review*, December 1993. Published by Lehman Brothers, Inc.

sent the average differential between Dutch auction rates and the Kenny Index.

How effective are Dutch auctions? Merrill Lynch performed a study in 1991 in which 472 auction rate securities (municipal bonds, preferred stock, and corporate debt) were surveyed. Only eight failed auction events were found, all of which were related to credit deterioration.

Inverse Floating-Rate Securities.   In March 1990, investment bankers at Shearson Lehman Brothers introduced inverse floating-rate bonds (IFRBs) called *Residual Interest Bonds (RIBS)* into the municipal bond market in two offerings: a $100 million housing bond issue for Nebraska Investment Finance Authority (NIFA) and a $75 million student loan bond issue for Pennsylvania Higher Education Assistance Agency (PHEAA). Since then, the development and introduction of municipal derivative securities have gone into high gear. RIBS are inverse floating-rate securities the interest rate of which *goes down* as the interest rate on a short-duration companion floating-rate security, the SAVRS, *goes up*. As the interest rate on the companion SAVRS *goes down*, the interest rate on RIBS *goes up*.

RIBS are long-term (generally 20- to 40-year) bonds that, when issued with companion SAVRS, combine to give an interest rate formula that results in an *absolutely fixed* interest rate for an issuer. The RIBS interest rate formula on the NIFA transaction is as follows:

NIFA RIBS rate = 15.222% – SAVRS rate

The RIBS interest rate formula on the PHEAA transaction is as follows:

PHEAA RIBS rate = 15.100% – SAVRS rate

The interest rate formula for RIBS-style issues stays in effect for the life of the RIBS.

Interest on RIBS is payable in concert with interest on SAVRS, generally every 35 days or every 6 months. Any comparisons of interest rates between plain-vanilla bonds and RIBS or SAVRS and similar securities should take into effect and adjust for different compounding periods. That is, yield comparisons should be made in terms of BEYs which are based upon a 30/360-day count with semiannual payments, rather than payments every 28 or 35 days.

Other investment banks have introduced similar *linked-rate* structures with acronyms such as PARS, INFLOS, FLOATS, and RITES. Such issues have been extremely well received, with over $8 billion in principal amount issued in more than 100 primary issues through December 31, 1993.

Investment bankers at Morgan Stanley introduced another type of IFRB in November 1991, called a *Structured Yield Curve Note*[SM] *(SYCN*[SM])*,*[11] for the City of Los Angeles. The interest rate formula for this transaction was as follows:

SYCN rate = 6.60% + (4.91% − Kenny Index) until 11/1/1996
SYCN rate = 6.60% after 11/1/1996

IFRBs, like RIBS, are securities on which the rate also *goes down* as the level of an interest rate index *goes up.* The converse relationship between interest rates also holds. IFRB rates are dependent on a short-term interest rate index, such as the Kenny Index or the PSA Index. There is no companion security, similar to a SAVRS, and there is no auction-rate mechanism with an IFRB. It is typical for the interest rate on an IFRB to be variable for a period of time (e.g., 5 to 10 years), and then to convert, on a specified conversion date, to a fixed rate of interest (e.g., 6.60 percent).

It also is not unusual for an inverse floater to be *leveraged* so that it has a multiplier effect of greater than 1 for the inverse variable-rate portion, which is equal to a reference rate (e.g., 5.4 percent) minus the interest rate index (e.g., the Kenny Index). For example, a BULL Floater[SM] was introduced by Lehman Brothers, Inc. for a portion of a $119,999,773 Puerto Rico Housing Finance Corporation Single Family Mortgage Revenue Bond Issue.[12] Series C BULL Floaters in the amount of $7,300,000 were due on August 1, 2014, with an interest formula as shown below.

BULL Floater rate = 6.60% + 2 (5.4% − Kenny Index)
prior to 2/1/2002
BULL Floater rate = 6.60% after 2/1/2002

---

[11]Structured Yield Curve Notes[SM] and SYCN[SM] are service marks of Morgan Stanley & Company Inc.

[12]BULL Floater[SM] is a service mark of Lehman Brothers, Inc.

In many inverse floating-rate transactions, the investor has an option, prior to the IFRB conversion date, to convert the variable-rate interest payment to a fixed-rate payment. The conversion option involves either a positive or a negative interest rate adjustment, depending on the movements in the interest rate index and the hypothetical swap agreement. This type of interest rate adjustment is examined further in Chapter 8. The interest rates on all municipal floating-rate and inverse floating-rate bonds of which the authors are aware can never go below zero, and many have interest rate ceilings which they cannot go above. This limitation of interest rate swings creates embedded interest rate *caps* and *floors* that have value; these are described in Chapter 7.

Cap Bonds and Superfloaters. In 1992, Goldman Sachs & Company introduced cap bonds to the municipal bond market. Cap bonds pay interest semiannually at a *base fixed interest rate* (e.g., 6.60 percent), plus a *variable rate* equal to the maximum (*MAX*) of either 0 percent or the difference between a specified rate of interest (e.g., 3.5 percent) and a short-term municipal bond interest index like the Kenny Index or the PSA Index. For example a Baal-rated cap bond, which we will examine in Chapter 8, was marketed by the City of New York through First Boston in October 1992. This issue matures on October 1, 2016; is callable on October 1, 2002 at a price of 101.5 percent; and pays interest as follows:

$$\text{Cap bond rate} = 6.60\% + MAX\ (0\%, \text{PSA Index} - 3.5\%)$$
$$\text{until } 10/1/1997$$
$$\text{Cap bond rate} = 6.60\% \text{ after } 10/1/1997$$

Cap bonds help to protect investors in a rising interest rate environment by giving them additional tax-exempt interest income above the base fixed interest rate if short-term interest rates rise above a certain threshold, or cap rate. If short-term interest rates stay below the cap rate, the investors receive only the base fixed interest rate.

Superfloaters are simply leveraged versions of floating-rate securities that are designed to give investors additional tax-exempt interest income if short-term interest rates rise. They also provide less interest income if short-term rates fall. For example, the *mirrored* companion security to the BULL Floater on the previously-mentioned Puerto Rico Housing Finance Corporation transaction is a BEAR Floater. The BEAR Floater has a leveraged factor of 2; a maturity date of August 1, 2014; an optional redemption feature of August 1, 2002, at 102 percent; and an interest rate formula as follows:

BEAR Floater rate = 6.60% + 2 (Kenny Index–5.4%)
prior to 2/1/2002
BEAR Floater rate = 6.60% after 2/1/2002

Whereas typical adjustable-rate bonds such as VRDNs and auction-rate securities are designed by investment bankers with interest rate mechanisms that make them par securities with little or no price volatility, superfloaters, which are leveraged instruments, exhibit price volatility. For example, as short-term interest rates increase, the interest rates on BEAR Floaters increase twice as much. How this type of leverage affects valuation is addressed in Chapter 8.

Stepped-Coupon Bonds, and BULL and BEAR Forward BPOs. In 1982, the Florida-based investment banking firm of Arch W. Roberts & Co. introduced the industry's first *stepped-coupon* interest rate mechanism for a $16,400,000 Lee County, Florida, issue. The issue consisted solely of stepped-coupon bonds with serial maturities from 1982 to 2005. The interest rate on the stepped-coupon bonds began at 8.00 percent in 1982 and increased periodically until it reached 18.00 percent in the years 1999 to 2005. All the stepped-coupon bonds, regardless of their maturity dates, would bear the same rate of interest in each year. The stepped-coupon bonds resulted in an overall yield on the Lee County bonds that was significantly lower than the yield of a comparable-term, fixed-rate bond issue.

The municipal bond market at that time was unprepared to value this type of security. The interest rate setting mechanism and redemption features of these bonds were extremely sophisticated, and large institutional buyers may have been concerned about secondary market liquidity. Also, many institutional buyers did not want to sacrifice current yield in the early years of the stepped-coupon bond for the higher interest rates in the later years. This type of structure may be revived as the quantitative skills of municipal market participants improve and they become better able to understand and value this type of security.

On August 26, 1993, the City of Philadelphia issued a $1,157,585,000 principal amount of Water and Wastewater Revenue Bonds, Series 1993, through underwriters led by Smith Barney Shearson Inc. This huge transaction had discount and premium fixed-rate bonds and several municipal derivative securities, including Smith Barney's version of floating-rate—inverse floating-rate bonds, *called AIRS*[SM],[13] and Lehman Brothers' Bond Payment Obligations (BPOs). Certain of the BPOs, called *2005 BEAR Forward BPOs* and *2005 BULL Forward BPOs*[14] have a stepped-coupon interest rate that is dependent on the future level of a yield on a long-term municipal bond index. The municipal index used was the yield to maturity on the Bond Buyer 40 Municipal Bond Index (BBI-40 rate), a general municipal market yield indicator published daily in *The Bond Buyer*.

Initially, interest payments on the Philadelphia BULL Forward and BEAR Forward holders were equal, 5.2 percent, until June 15, 1994—(the interest adjustment date, IAD). On the IAD the market index agent, Lehman Brothers, was to determine the interest rate adjustment. The present value of the interest rate adjustment, which may be a positive or a negative number, was designed to equal the change in value of a *futures contract* on a 20-year, non-callable municipal bond, with a coupon rate equal to the BBI-40 rate at the time of the initial pricing, which was 5.76 percent. The interest rate formulas for BULL Forward BPOs and BEAR Forward BPOs after the IAD were as follows:

BULL Forward BPO rate = 5.20% + 3 (interest rate adjustment)

BEAR Forward BPO rate = 5.20% − 3 (interest rate adjustment)

If the BBI-40 rate on the IAD increases above 5.76 percent, the interest rate adjustment is negative. The BEAR Forward BPO holder receives an increased interest rate until its maturity, and the BULL Forward BPO holder receives a decreased interest rate. The converse relationship also holds: a decrease in the BBI-40 rate increases the interest rate to the BULL Forward holder and decreases the interest rate to the BEAR Forward holder. Consequently, purchasers of both BULL and BEAR Forward BPOs have a stepped-coupon instrument

---

[13] AIRS[SM] is a service mark of Smith Barney Shearson Inc.

[14] BEAR Forward BPOs[SM] is a service mark of Lehman Brothers, Inc.

with a 5.2 percent initial rate for approximately 1 year and an un-known fixed-rate for the next 11 years. The Philadelphia BULL For-ward BPOs are examined in detail in Chapter 8.

Mirrored-Security Fixed-Rate Structures

As previously stated, most traditional issuers of municipal govern-mental use bonds are less than enthusiastic about accepting the risk of adverse consequences associated with variable-rate debt. However, there is significant demand from certain investors for variable-rate municipal bonds with interest rate setting mecha-nisms that would better meet their investment needs.

An approach developed by investment bankers to meet both the desires of issuers and the demands of investors is called the *mirrored-security fixed-rate structure*. These issues are also known as *linked-rate* or *paired* obligations. Under a mirrored-security struc-ture, *combinations of securities* are marketed at original issuance. The proportions are such that the debt service associated with those combinations of securities, along with the required retire-ment of the securities, results in an *absolutely fixed rate* to the issuer in all interest rate scenarios.

The first mirrored-security structure was the RIBS–SAVRS. From an issuer's perspective, this floater–inverse floater program raises long-term funds with an aggregate fixed interest rate. The program segments the issuer's fixed payment stream into two com-ponents, each of which is sold to investors as a separate security. The components are issued in equal principal amounts, as follows:

- *Floaters,* which are variable-rate securities with their interest rate reset periodically (e.g., every 35 days) through a Dutch auction.
- *Inverse floaters,* which have an interest rate equal to the dif-ference between the issuer's fixed-interest payment stream and the interest and expenses paid on the floaters.

Many investment banks have introduced floater–inverse floater structures, under various acronyms. Some of these struc-tures have been further leveraged. For example, in September 1993, Kidder Peabody & Company Inc. marketed for Puerto Rico Housing Finance Corporation a premium coupon structure (a 7.50 percent linked bond in a 5.30 percent market) with a ratio of three floating-rate bonds to one inverse floating-rate bond. The IFRBs had an offering price of 182 percent, and the floating-rate bonds had an offering price of 100 percent. All the programs require that there be a proportional percentage of floaters and inverse floaters retired such that the issuer always pays a known, fixed rate of interest.

BULL Floaters and BEAR Floaters are mirrored securities that have an interest rate setting mechanism and a requirement of proportional debt retirement that also results in a fixed interest rate to an issuer. The BPO structures (see Chapter 8) that were first marketed in 1993 do the same thing.

Synthetic-Asset Fixed-Rate Structures

Another approach developed by investment bankers pairs variable-rate debt with a private contract entered into between the issuer of debt and a financial institution to synthetically set the combined obligations of the issuer at a fixed rate of interest.

In the mid-1980s, Merrill Lynch was very successful in designing financings in which a municipal issuer would market VRDNs and would simultaneously enter into an interest rate swap with a subsidiary of Merrill Lynch. The issuer would receive from the Merrill Lynch subsidiary a variable swap rate based on the Kenny Index; the swap rate was intended to match the variable-rate debt-service exposure. The issuer would pay a fixed swap rate to the Merrill Lynch subsidiary, thereby creating a *synthetic* fixed cost of funding.

This same approach is generally taken on the other types of floating-rate obligations. Typically, a municipal issuer hedges IFRBs by entering into an interest rate swap with a financial institution. The IFRB issuer will receive an inverse floating swap rate from the swap partner and will pay a fixed rate, synthetically creating a fixed rate for the issuer. Issuers of cap bonds and superfloaters usually hedge their obligations effectively by entering into private contracts with financial institutions that synthetically create a fixed rate for the issuer, which is lower than the plain-vanilla comparable bond rate.

This method of synthetically fixing a variable-rate obligation is not without risks. The risks include: counterparty risk, basis risk, and credit facility rollover risk. In addition, some structures may make it impossible to take full advantage of refunding opportunities.

Maturity, Redemption and Mandatory Tenders

Every municipal bond that is issued has a stated maturity date on which the issuer is obligated to retire the bond at a predetermined price, usually its face value. Period!

The redemption or call features of a municipal bond are not nearly as easy to understand as its maturity. The complexity of the early redemption feature and the uncertainty of the bond's cash flows, associated with the possibility of early redemption, make valuation of municipal bonds difficult. This section illustrates how confusing municipal redemption features can be.

The classifications of redemption features associated with different types of municipal bonds are optional redemption, mandatory sinking fund redemption, extraordinary redemption, and mandatory tender. These redemption features are discussed below.

Optional Redemption

In most municipal bond issues, the issuer reserves the option (the *Call Option*) to redeem the bonds prior to their stated maturity at a predetermined price, usually 102 percent, which declines over time to 100 percent. The call option can be exercised on or after a predetermined date, usually 10 years. The call option has a quantifiable and discernible cost to the issuer, which is paid in the form of a slightly higher borrowing rate. That is, investors require a higher yield on callable bonds than on otherwise comparable noncallable bonds.

The optimal time for the issuer to exercise the call option is when it becomes financially desirable to do so, that is when and if interest rates drop and the issuer can refund or advance-refund its outstanding bonds. Therefore, the investor that owns a callable bond is subject to considerable uncertainty about cash flows on its callable municipal bonds; this uncertainty exacts a price that is measured by higher required yields. The effect of the call option on the pricing of municipal bonds is discussed in Chapter 3.

Mandatory Sinking Fund Redemption

Many long-term municipal bond issues are marketed with a number of shorter-term (1- to 15-year) serial bonds, which are bonds with a certain maturity date coming due every year, and with one or more *term* bonds, which are longer-term bonds that have a specified final maturity date and are subject to an annual or semiannual call in accordance with a prespecified schedule. This redemption schedule is referred to as a *sinking fund redemption.* Even otherwise noncallable bonds may be subject to sinking fund redemptions. This early redemption requirement introduces further holding period uncertainty for the investor.

Extraordinary Redemption

Different types of municipal bonds have provisions that, in the event of certain unusual occurrences, present the possibility of an unexpected mandatory redemption and a truncation of cash flows. The most complex redemption provisions are usually associated with pooled-asset revenue bonds such as mortgage revenue bonds or student loan bonds.

Mortgage revenue bonds typically include the following extraordinary mandatory redemption events: unexpended proceeds redemption, mortgage prepayment redemption, excess revenue redemption, transfer from other revenue funds redemption, condemnation redemption, mortgage default and foreclosure redemption, and hazard and/or title insurance proceed redemption.

Student loan revenue bonds typically include unexpended proceeds redemption, lack of recycling redemption, and "unreasonable burden or excessive liabilities from making certain amounts of further Education Loans" redemption.

Pooled-asset revenue bonds, a popular financing structure of the mid-1980s, have many of the redemption features associated with mortgage revenue bonds plus redemption features associated with expiration and/or replacement of investment agreements supporting the bonds.

Many revenue bonds that are partially secured by buildings and structures (such as hospitals and power plants) have extraordinary mandatory redemption features in the event of damage to, destruction of, or condemnation of facilities, to the extent of the proceeds of insurance or condemnation awards.

Mandatory Tenders

During the early 1980s, the concept of mandatory tender was introduced to the municipal marketplace. A mandatory tender allows an issuer of municipal bonds to require current bondholders to put back or tender bonds to the bond trustee, on or after a specific date, and allows the bonds to be remarketed to other investors. This is in contrast to a call for redemption, which involves extinguishing the debt. This procedure was used in situations in which the security on a bond issue was about to change or the interest rate was to be reset. For example, when an LOC from a commercial bank expired and was replaced by another LOC or by a different security source, it was very important, from the rating agencies' perspective, to require a mandatory tender of the bonds.

Most mandatory tenders are structured such that, if the bondholders do not respond to the tender notice, they are deemed to have tendered their bonds. The bonds are then purchased by the issuer at par value. In many cases, a bondholder can elect to retain the bond through an affirmative notice to the trustee for the bond issue and can, effectively, become an owner of the remarketed security, with its new security and terms in place. Some mandatory tenders do not allow an investor to retain the bond in any event.

A popular feature analogous to mandatory tenders, introduced by PaineWebber in 1992, is called *detachable call options* or *call rights*. Under this type of program, an issuer may elect to sell separate call options which give an owner the right, on or after a certain date, to require a mandatory tender of a specified bond for purchase at a predetermined price (e.g., 102 percent of par after 10 years, declining to par after 12 years). From the issuer's perspective, the Omnibus Budget Reconciliation Act of 1993 has called into question certain tax aspects associated with call rights.

From the perspective of an investor in a bond which is subject to mandatory tender, if the investor has no right to retain the bond, the mandatory tender feature of the bond should be viewed similarly to a comparable optional redemption feature. Therefore, a mandatory tender at a premium price (e.g., 102 percent) may create a capital gain or loss with associated tax considerations.

Legal Opinions[15]

All municipal bonds are issued with legal opinions written by an independent law firm that acts as *bond counsel* on a transaction. The opinion written by bond counsel states that the issuer has the power to issue the bonds, that the requisite security structure is in place, and that the bonds are validly issued and are binding obligations of the issuer. Bond counsel or special tax counsel also opines that the interest on the bonds is exempt from federal income taxation, and from state and some local taxation, if applicable.

It is extremely important to have recognized, high-caliber law firms as bond counsel or co-bond counsel on a transaction. Investment bankers and institutional investors know the importance of a legal opinion written by recognized experts in the field. In fact, transactions in which less recognized firms take an aggressive tax or securities law position often will have significantly higher interest rates than comparable transactions with the same legal opinion from a more recognized firm. The additional interest expense to the issuer often is many times greater than the cost of the legal opinion.

Ratings

Most municipal bonds that are offered to the investing public have a *rating* from Moody's, S&P, and/or Fitch. The rating is generally purchased by the issuer, who provides the various rating agencies with the information necessary for assignment of a credit rating.

The rating is designed to be a proxy measuring the strength of security of a bond. The highest-quality rating categories are Aaa, AAA, and AAA from Moody's, S&P, and Fitch, respectively. The lowest-quality rating categories are C, D, and D, which represent bonds that are in default, with interest and/or principal in arrears. Many investors restrict their purchases to securities that are *investment grade*, that is, securities with ratings of Baa, BBB, BBB, or higher. Some high-yield funds invest in higher-yield bonds with lower credit ratings—lower than investment-grade ratings.

A rating acts only as a proxy for credit quality. In infrequent but highly visible situations, such as Washington Public Power

---

[13]See S Conlon and V Aquilino, *Tax-Exempt Derivatives*, American Bar Association, 1994, for an excellent description of legal issues associated with tax-exempt derivative securities.

Supply System Projects 4 and 5, revenue bonds with investment grade ratings have defaulted. Ultimately, investors are making a credit assessment decision when they purchase a security.

SUMMARY

In this chapter, we have described the municipal bond market and its various nuances. The overwhelming attraction of municipal bonds for investors is the exemption of interest income on the bonds from federal and certain state and local income taxation. Individual investors in moderate and high marginal tax brackets, and their institutional proxies—mutual funds, trust departments, and investment advisers—are the largest category of purchasers of municipal bonds.

The municipal bond market is a huge, diverse, and extremely complicated market. There are numerous issuers of bonds, and the security structures of municipal bonds range from a full-faith, credit, and taxing power general obligation pledge to pledged revenues from toll collections and gas taxes. In 1993 alone, there were 13,916 different issues totaling $289.86 billion; 32 percent of these were general obligation bonds, and 68 percent were supported by revenue pledges.

The four key features that determine the *amount* and *timing* of a municipal bond's cash flows are the interest payment, the maturity date, the redemption price, and the redemption date. The security or credit aspects of a municipal bond reflect an issuer's sources of payments and its *ability* to make its promised payments. In this chapter, we looked at security, maturity, and redemption features, but we expended most of our effort on the *interest payment characteristics* of a number of different types of municipal bonds.

It is the interest payment characteristic that differentiates the types of municipal bonds. This characteristic is also the key structural aspect in the design, understanding, and valuation of municipal derivative securities. The interest payment feature will be our focus in the chapters that follow.

CHAPTER 3

THE MATHEMATICS OF MUNICIPAL BONDS

In this chapter we explain the basics of bond pricing and the measures of bond price volatility. The basis for all bond valuation, like most asset valuation, is present value. In this chapter, we develop the steps involved in pricing municipal bonds, because an understanding of the pricing concepts involved with debt instruments helps an investor to fully understand the risks involved in investing in the municipal market. In addition, we describe the risk and return measures of duration and convexity. These concepts are important for investors in municipal as well as corporate and government bonds.

INTRODUCTION

The risks involved in municipal bonds are the same as the risks of investing in other fixed-rate debt instruments. The four basic categories of risk are as follows:

1. *Default risk* is the risk that the issuer of a bond will not make its scheduled debt service payments.
2. *Reinvestment risk* arises from the periodic interest payment of coupon bonds. Since payments are received over the life of a coupon-bearing bond, an investor faces the risk of reinvesting coupon payments at uncertain future interest rates that may be lower than the yield on the bond.
3. *Prepayment risk* arises from the ability of an issuer to call bonds prior to their stated maturity. A municipal issuer

may exercise its option to call bonds on or after a specified call date. Mortgage-backed securities also allow loan pre-payments to be used to retire bonds. In either case, the pre-payments tend to increase in periods of lower interest rates and therefore also contribute to reinvestment risk.

4. *Interest rate risk* is the risk that changes in market levels of interest rates will adversely effect the value of an investment.

Our focus in this chapter is on developing the tools necessary for pricing debt-based securities, and on describing and analyzing *interest rate risk*. Debt-based derivative securities generally are designed in a way that makes their cash flows and market values more dependent upon changes in interest rates. *Bullish* derivative securities are designed to increase interest rate risk, and *bearish* derivative securities are designed to decrease interest rate risk relative to fixed-rate bonds.

In this chapter and the chapters that follow, we value municipal bonds and the components that make up municipal derivatives securities, using financial theories and valuation techniques developed by academicians and financial practitioners. Most of these valuation techniques are based upon assumptions regarding the capital markets. The assumptions that allow the precise valuation of a security are based upon a conceptual valuation framework known as *perfect capital markets*. The principal characteristics of a perfect capital market include:

1. No transaction costs or external government restrictions.
2. A neutral tax policy which implies either no taxes or equal taxes on interest, dividends, and capital gains.
3. Unlimited borrowing and lending (or investing) at the same rate.
4. Free information for all market participants and equal access to all information.
5. No bankruptcy costs and unrestricted salability of tax losses.

Perfect capital markets are an idealization of the real world. Market imperfections exist and are very significant for certain participants, such as individual investors, and much less significant for large, efficient institutional participants, such as commercial and investment banks. The existence of market imperfections allows market values of securities to drift away, sometimes very greatly, from their theoretical values.

How do investors generally handle the risks mentioned above? Default risk can be reduced by purchasing bond insurance or letters of credit. Reinvestment risk can be eliminated by buying zero-coupon bonds. Prepayment risk can be eliminated by buying noncallable securities. The risk that is most difficult to assess and address is interest rate risk!

Derivative securities are a vehicle for directly addressing interest rate risk and price volatility! The proxy that attempts to measure interest rate risk—a security's change in price/change in interest rate ratio—is called duration. Duration measures the time weighted average maturity of a bond's cash flows. Greater duration means greater price volatility. With greater price volatility, there is an expectation of higher returns.

$$D = \frac{\partial P}{\Delta i}$$

PRESENT VALUE, BOND PRICING, AND COMPUTATION OF YIELD

In order to understand interest-bearing securities, you must first understand concepts of discounting and compounding. The sum of $1 invested today is worth more than $1 in the future. *How much more depends on the rate of interest, the method of compounding, and the length of time between today and the future payment date.*

Present Value

Consider an investment that requires a principal investment today and pays principal and interest in one year.

Let:

F = principal invested today or present value of the investment

c = one year interest rate in percentage

C = interest cash flow or coupon rate in dollars

The interest received at the end of one year is as follows:

$$cF = C$$

In total, the investor will receive, at the end of the one-year period:

$$C + F = F(1 + c)$$

The initial investment, F, is the present value, PV, of the investment, and the principal and interest at the end of the time period, $C + F$, is the expected cash flow in one year. If we rearrange the terms from the above expression, we can arrive at the present value of this investment, as follows:

$$PV = \frac{C}{1 + c} + \frac{F}{1 + c}$$

The denominator in the expression above, $1 + c$, represents the discount factor and c represents the yield on the investment. The yield will change with changes in market interest rates and will change the present value of the investment. To avoid confusion, we replace the c with y to represent a market yield that changes over time, as shown below.

$$PV = \frac{C}{1 + y} + \frac{F}{1 + y}$$

If interest is received over more than one period, then we sum each of the cash flows over the time period and adjust the discount factors to reflect the time period when they are received. For example, a two-period investment would have the following present value:

$$PV = \frac{C}{1 + y} + \frac{C}{(1 + y)^2} + \frac{F}{(1 + y)^2}$$

In general, when many cash flows are expected, we can express the summing of cash flows with the summation operator $\sum$.
Let:

PV = present value of investment

C = interest payment or coupon payment in dollars

F = face value or principal at maturity

y = annual yield on the investment

t = time

p = number of times interest is compounded per year

n = number of years

$\sum$ = summation operator; for example, $\sum_{t=1}^{3} t = 1 + 2 + 3 = 6$

Then:

$$PV = \sum_{t=1}^{n} \frac{C}{(1 + y)^t} + \frac{F}{(1 + y)^n}$$

If interest is compounded on a different frequency, such as semiannually, monthly, or daily, the interest rate, the coupon payment, and the number of compounding periods must be adjusted to reflect the frequency of the compounding.

Let:

p = frequency of compounding (2 for semiannually, 4 for quarterly, etc.)

Then:

$$PV = \sum_{t=1}^{np} \frac{C/p}{(1 + y/p)^t} + \frac{F}{(1 + y/p)^{np}}$$

Bond Pricing: Coupon Bearing Bonds

The coupon on a fixed-rate municipal bond is typically paid semiannually on a 30/360-day basis. That is, every year is assumed to have 360 *bond days*, with each month having exactly 30 bond days. The semiannual coupon is expressed in terms of an annual rate of interest or a *bond equivalent yield*. Interest accrues beginning on the *dated date*, and thereafter interest is paid semiannually until maturity. For example, if a *plain-vanilla* bond is dated and delivered January 1, 1994, and has a maturity date of January 1, 2024, the bond will make its first interest payment on July 1, 1994, for the initial period of 180 bond days and will continue to make semiannual payments each January 1 and July 1, thereafter. Exhibit 3–1 shows the cash flows for a 30-year, 6.00 percent full-coupon bond.

The current market price, P, of a bond is equal to the present value of the cash flows received over the life of the bond. The cash flow on a full-coupon bond consists of $2n$ semiannual coupons over n years paid until maturity and the principal or face value, F, at maturity. The cash flows are discounted at the prevailing semiannual market yield for a bond of similar maturity and credit quality.

EXHIBIT 3–1
Interest and Principal Payment on a 30-Year, 6.00 Percent, Full-Coupon Bond

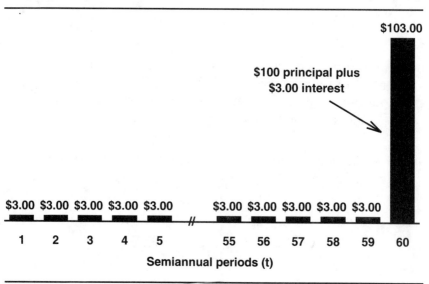

Let:

P = price of the bond

C = annual coupon payment = cF

F = principal at maturity

y = market yield

t = time

n = total number of years

Then:

$$P = \sum_{t=1}^{2n} \frac{C/2}{(1 + y/2)^t} + \frac{F}{(1 + y/2)^{2n}}$$

Example. At issuance, a $100 face-value, noncallable, 30-year bond which pays interest at a rate of 6.00 percent when the market discount rate is 5.00 percent, will be priced as shown below.

Let:

$C = \$6.00$

$F = \$100$

$y = 5.00\%$

$t = 1, 2, 3, \ldots, 60$

$n = 30$

Then:

$$P = \sum_{t=1}^{60} \frac{3.00}{(1.025)^t} + \frac{100}{1.025^{60}}$$

$$P = \$115.45$$

This pricing is appropriate when all the interest payment periods are equal and the first interest period is a full period. When bonds are sold between interest payment periods, the original owner of the bonds is entitled to the interest from the beginning of the interest payment period to the day prior to the settlement date of the sale. The interest over this time period, referred to as *accrued interest*, is calculated by multiplying the interest rate by the number of bond days in the partial interest period and dividing by the total number of bond days in the semiannual period, or 180.

Example. Consider a 30-year municipal bond that makes semiannual interest payments at an annual rate of 6.00 percent on January 1 and July 1 of each year. If the bond is sold with a settlement date of March 15, 1994, the accrued interest, *AI*, is calculated for 74 bond days between January 1, 1994, and March 14, 1994, inclusive, as shown below.

$$AI = \left(\frac{74}{180} \right) \$3.00 = \$1.233$$

The accrued interest for this time period is $1.233 per $100 of bond principal. In calculating the price of a bond, if the first interest period is not a complete period, then the price of the bond must be adjusted to reflect the partial interest period. The compounding periods must be adjusted, and the accrued interest must be subtracted from the price. The bond price can be calculated as follows:

Let:

> P = price of the bond
> C = coupon rate in dollars
> F = face value or principal at maturity
> AI = accrued interest
> y = market yield or discount rate
> t = time
> n = total number of years
> q = the portion of a period the first period represents (for example, if the first interest period is 106 days, q equals $106/180 = 0.589$).

Then:

$$P = \sum_{t=1}^{2n} \frac{C/2}{(1 + y/2)^{t-1+q}} + \frac{F}{(1 + y/2)^{2n-1+q}} - AI$$

Example.   Consider a bond that pays interest semiannually on each January 1 and July 1 at an annual rate of 6.00 percent, has a maturity of January 1, 2024, pays $100 at maturity and is purchased at a yield of 6.00 percent. The bond was purchased with a settlement date of March 15, 1994. The price would be calculated as shown below.

Let:

> $C = \$6.00$
> $F = \$100$
> $AI = 1.233$
> $y = 6.00\%$
> $t = 1, 2, 3, \ldots, 60$
> $n = 30$
> $q = 106/180 = 0.589$

Then:

$$P = \sum_{t=1}^{60} \frac{3.00}{1.03^{t-1+0.589}} + \frac{100}{1.03^{59.589}} - 1.233$$

$$P = \$99.989$$

Bond Pricing: Zero-Coupon Bonds

Zero-coupon bonds do not make semiannual interest payments; instead, they sell at a discount from their face value and increase in value or *accrete* to the par value at maturity. There is only one cash flow associated with a zero-coupon bond, and, therefore, the value is relatively easy to calculate (see Exhibit 3–2).

To calculate the price of a zero-coupon bond, proceed as follows.

Let:

P = price of the bond
F = face value or principal of the bond at maturity
y = market yield
p = frequency of compounding
n = total number of years

EXHIBIT 3–2
Interest and Principal Payment on a 30-Year,
6.00 Percent, Zero-Coupon Bond

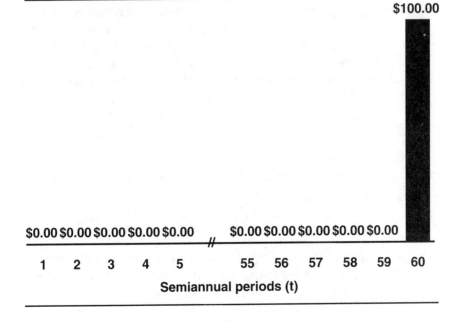

Then:

$$P = \frac{F}{(1 + y/p)^{np}}$$

Example. A noncallable, $100 face-amount, zero-coupon bond that matures in 30 years and is priced at a yield, y, of 6.00 percent would sell for a price calculated in the manner shown below.
Let:

$F = \$100$
$y = 6.00\%$
$n = 30$
$p = 2$

Then:

$$P = \frac{100}{1.03^{60}}$$

$$P = \$16.97$$

This pricing is appropriate when all the interest accretion periods are equal and the first period is a full period. If the first interest period is not a complete period, we must make an adjustment to the calculation. Since zero-coupon bonds do not pay interest, there is no interest accrual between interest payments; therefore, only the compounding periods need to be adjusted. The adjustment to compounding periods is similar to the adjustment for a full-coupon bond.
Let:

P = price of the bond
F = face value or principal amount at maturity
y = market yield
p = frequency of compounding
n = number of years
q = the portion of a period the first period represents (for example, for a semiannual bond, if the first interest period is 106 days, q equals $106/180 = 0.589$).

Then:

$$P = \frac{F}{(1 + y/p)^{np-1+q}}$$

Example.   A zero-coupon bond has a maturity date of January 1, 2024, and interest accretes semiannually based on January 1 and July 1. The bond pays $100 principal at maturity, and the market yield is 6.00 percent. If the bond were purchased for settlement on March 15, 1994, the price of the bond to maturity would be calculated as shown below.

Let:

F = $100
y = 6.00%
p = 2
n = 30
q = 106/180 = 0.589

Then:

$$P = \frac{F}{1.03^{59.589}}$$

$$P = 17.180$$

Computation of Yield

The semiannual coupon payment on a bond represents the current cash flow to an investor. Since the coupon on a long-term bond remains fixed as market rates fluctuate, the value of the bond changes to reflect the changes in rates. *Yield* is a measure of the expected return on a bond based upon its maturity or expected redemption date. The price of a bond, its maturity or redemption date, and the coupon rate jointly determine the yield on a bond. As such, yield to maturity is the interest rate which equates a flow of semiannual coupon payments until maturity to a bond price. *Yield to maturity* is the rate of return earned on a bond at a given price from some date to maturity. *Yield to call* is the rate of return earned on a bond at a given price from some date to the first optional call date.

Example.   A $100 face-value bond, which pays interest semi-annually at 6.00 percent and matures on January 1, 2024, is callable on January 1, 2004, at 102, and sells for $115.45, on January 1, 1994. The bond's yield to maturity is shown below.

Let:

$C = \$6.00$

$F = \$100$

$y_m =$ yield to maturity

$t = 1, 2, 3, \ldots, 60$

$n = 30$

Then:

$$\$115.45 = \sum_{t=1}^{60} \frac{3.00}{(1 + y_m/2)^t} + \frac{100}{(1 + y_m/2)^{60}}$$

Solving for y_m results in a yield to maturity on this bond of 5.00 percent. This means that an investor who buys the bond at a price of 115.45 and holds it until maturity will realize an annualized yield of 5.00 percent over the life of the bond, neglecting reinvestment risk.

Example.   The yield to call, y_c, on the same bond is calculated by solving the equation given below.

Let:

$C = \$6.00$

$F = \$102$

$y_c =$ yield to call

$t = 1, 2, 3, \ldots, 20$

$n = 20$

Then:

$$\$115.45 = \sum_{t=1}^{20} \frac{3.00}{(1 + y_c/2)^t} + \frac{102}{(1 + y_c/2)^{20}}$$

In this example, the yield to call, y_c, is equal to 4.25 percent. An investor who buys this bond at $115.45 and holds it until the first call date (at which time the bonds are redeemed for $102.00) will receive an annualized yield of 4.25 percent over the 10-year period.

An important concept in bond valuation is the relationship among coupon, yield, and price. When a bond is issued, if it is sold at its face value, or *par*, the yield on the bond will exactly equal its coupon. A $100 bond that pays 6.00 percent is *priced at par to yield* 6.00 percent. If the bond is priced below par, the discount from par acts to increase the yield above the coupon. A 30-year bond that sells for $87.53 is priced to yield 7.00 percent. Conversely, if a bond is priced above par, the premium over par acts to decrease the yield below the coupon. A 30-year bond that is priced at $115.45 is priced to yield 5.00 percent. The price of a bond is inversely related to its yield. In Exhibit 3–3, we show the relationship among coupon, yield to maturity, and price for a $100, 6.00 percent bond with 30 years to maturity. We will further examine this relationship when we discuss duration and convexity, later in this chapter.

PRICE VOLATILITY

We now address the quantitative measurements regarding changes in the price/yield relationship of derivative securities. The three measurements that we will examine are: price volatility, duration, and convexity.

EXHIBIT 3–3
Prices and Corresponding Yields of a 6.00 Percent Bond with 30 Years to Maturity

Coupon c	Price P	Yield y
6.00%	$62.14	10.00%
6.00%	$69.04	9.00%
6.00%	$77.37	8.00%
6.00%	$87.53	7.00%
6.00%	$100.00	6.00%
6.00%	$115.45	5.00%
6.00%	$134.76	4.00%
6.00%	$159.07	3.00%
6.00%	$189.91	2.00%

We focus specifically on the duration of derivative securities and show that the classical measurements of duration must be altered to incorporate the interest rate risk peculiar to derivative securities.

Overview of Bond Price Volatility

The *price volatility* of a bond is the extent to which its price changes with fluctuations in market levels of interest rates. We have shown that prices and yields move in opposite directions, other things being equal. However, the magnitude of price movements will differ based on specific bond characteristics. For example, the price volatility of a bond is directly related to its maturity: a *longer-maturity* bond will experience a sharper price adjustment for a given change in market level of interest rates than an otherwise identical *shorter-maturity* bond.

Exhibit 3–4 demonstrates the price sensitivity of three non-callable bonds with maturities of 10, 20, and 30 years to fluctuation in market interest rates. The three bonds have an identical coupon rate of 6.00 percent. The chart reports price changes that correspond to a 1.00 percent decrease and a 1.00 percent increase in yield. For a given change in yield, the price of the 30-year bond changes the most, followed by the 20-year bond price. The 10-year bond exhibits the least price volatility. The longer maturity of the 30-year bond acts to increase the volatility in the bond price.

Price volatility for the variable-rate derivative securities that

EXHIBIT 3–4
Relationship between Maturity and Price of a Bond

Maturity n	Coupon c	Yield y	Price P	Yield y	Price P
10 years	6.00%	5.00%	$107.79	7.00	$92.89
20 years	6.00%	5.00%	$112.55	7.00	$89.32
30 years	6.00%	5.00%	$115.45	7.00	$87.53

we will examine in Chapter 8 is not as simple as the relationship shown in Exhibit 3–4. Because cash flows associated with derivative securities may change with changes in interest rates, price volatility must take into account changes in both cash flows and market interest rates. This complication is addressed below when we discuss the price duration of derivative securities.

The Price–Yield Relationship

As discussed in the previous section, an important relationship exists between bond prices and yield. Recall from Exhibit 3–3 that bond prices increase as bond yields decrease. Conversely, as yields increase, bond prices decrease. Exhibit 3–5 shows this relationship for three noncallable 30-year bonds: a zero-coupon bond, a 6.00 percent full-coupon bond, and a 15.00 percent full-coupon bond.

At a yield of 0.00 percent, the bond prices for all three bonds are equal to the sum of the cash flows to maturity. The zero-coupon bond has a price of $100.00, the 6.00 percent bond has a price of $280.00 = (0.03)(100)(60) + 100, and the 15.00 percent bond has a price of $550.00 = (0.075)(100)(60) + 100. As the yield on the bond increases, the price of the bond decreases, because each of the cash flows is discounted by the new yield to arrive at a price.

An important aspect of this relationship is the speed at which the price decreases for an incremental increase in yield. This determines the *slope* of the price–yield curve (also known as price duration). Initially, the price decreases significantly for a 1.00 percent increase in yield. When yields are increased from 0.00 percent to 1.00 percent, the price drops from $100.00 to $74.14 for the zero-coupon bond, from $280.00 to $229.31 for the 6.00 percent bond, and from $550.00 to $462.08 for the 15.00 percent bond. However, this price change diminishes quickly as yield is increased. For example, when yields are increased from 10.00 percent to 11.00 percent, the price drops from $5.35 to $4.03 for the zero-coupon bond, from $62.14 to $56.36 for the 6.00 percent bond, and from $147.32 to $134.90 for the 15.00 percent bond.

Graphically, this relationship, is represented by a price–yield curve which is convex to the origin (see Exhibit 3–6).

EXHIBIT 3–5
Relationship between Price and Yield

Yield y	Zero-Coupon Bond Price P	6.00% Full-Coupon Bond Price P	15.00% Full-Coupon Bond Price P
0.00%	$100.00	$280.00	$550.00
1.00	74.14	229.31	462.08
2.00	55.04	189.91	392.21
3.00	40.93	159.07	336.28
4.00	30.48	134.76	291.18
5.00	22.74	115.45	254.54
6.00	16.97	100.00	224.54
7.00	12.69	87.53	199.78
8.00	9.51	77.37	179.18
9.00	7.13	69.04	161.91
10.00	5.35	62.14	147.32
11.00	4.03	56.36	134.90
12.00	3.03	51.52	124.24
13.00	2.29	47.38	115.03
14.00	1.73	43.84	107.02
15.00	1.30	40.78	100.00
16.00	0.99	38.12	93.81
17.00	0.75	35.78	88.32
18.00	0.57	33.71	83.43
19.00	0.43	31.87	79.04
20.00	0.33	30.23	75.08

DURATION

The classical measure of duration is the weighted average maturity of a bond's cash flows. The duration of a bond is measured in units of time (e.g., 7.3 years). In the simplest case, the duration of a zero-

EXHIBIT 3–6
Relationship between Prices and Yield

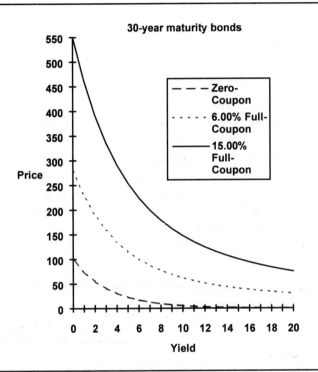

30-year maturity bonds

Legend:
- – – – Zero-Coupon
- · · · · · 6.00% Full-Coupon
- ——— 15.00% Full-Coupon

coupon bond is equal to its current maturity. That is, an investor in zero-coupon bonds must hold the bonds until maturity in order to receive the payment of principal. A coupon-bearing investment has a duration somewhat less than that of a zero-coupon bond of the same maturity, since interest payments are received throughout the life of the bond.

Duration also has come to be defined as a percent change in the price of an asset, divided by a change in interest rates. As such, it is the slope of the line that is tangent to the price/yield curve for a particular security at a specific price. Duration can be represented by the following equation:

Let:

D = Duration
P = dollar price of the bond

ΔP = change in dollar price of the bond

y = market yield

Δy = change in market yield

Then,

$$D = - \frac{\Delta P / P}{\Delta y}.$$

For fixed-rate bonds and for small changes in interest rates, classical measures of duration work well as a proxy for price volatility. However, with derivative securities, adjustments to the computation of duration are needed to incorporate their complex payment structures.

The computation associated with the standard definition of duration, the weighted average maturity of a security's expected cash flows, may be significantly different from the price volatility measure of a derivative security. We find it helpful to compute two duration measures for derivative securities:

(1) Time duration, D_t^*, which is the weighted average expected cash flows of the derivative security; and

(2) Price duration, D_p^*, which measures the change in the theoretical price of a derivative security assuming a small parallel shift in the yield curve.

These two duration measures may give significantly different results. For example, the time duration, D_t^*, of RIBS is 12.76 years, while the price duration, D_p^*, is 23.10 years (see Chapter 8). We examine duration in greater detail, below.

Macaulay's Duration

A standard measure of duration for fixed rate bonds is *Macaulay's duration*, which is the weighted average time to maturity of the cash flows received on a bond. The weights are based on the period in which the payments come due, with later payments being weighted heavier and increasing the duration of the bond.[1]

Let:

---

[1] See Frederick Macaulay, *Some Theoretical Problems Suggested by the Movements of Interest Rates, Bond Yields, and Stock Prices in the United States since 1865*, National Bureau of Economic Research, New York, 1938.

D = Macaulay's duration
P = dollar price of the bond
C = annual coupon payment in dollars
F = face value or redemption value
y = market yield
t = time
n = number of years

Then:

$$D = \sum_{t=1}^{2n} \left\{ \left[\frac{(C/2)/(1 + y/2)^t}{P} \right] \frac{t}{2} \right\} + \left[\frac{F/(1 + y/2)^{2n}}{P} \right] n$$

Each coupon payment is weighted by $t/2$, which corresponds to the payment period of the semiannual coupons. Each cash flow is weighted by the time period when the cash flow is received in years: 0.5, 1.0, 1.5, 2.0, . . ., n. The weighting adjusts the cash flows in each period by the time until the payment is received, thus giving a weighted average maturity of the bond's cash flows.[2]

As stated earlier, the duration of a zero-coupon bond is equal to its maturity. Recall that the price of a zero-coupon bond is found by dividing F by the discount factor, $(1+y/2)^{2n}$. Consider the duration of a zero-coupon bond by substituting the price of a zero-coupon bond and zero for the coupon payment into the duration formula, as follows:

$$D = \sum_{t=1}^{2n} \left\{ \left[\frac{(0/2)/(1 + y/2)^t}{F/(1 + y/2)^{2n}} \right] \frac{t}{p} \right\} + \left[\frac{F/(1 + y/2)^{2n}}{F/(1 + y/2)^{2n}} \right] n$$

$$0 \qquad + \qquad (1)(n) \qquad = n$$

Since duration is a measure of the weighted average maturity of a bond's cash flows, a coupon-bearing bond which makes semian-

---

[2]The duration calculations presented here assume no partial periods. As with the bond valuation equations, an adjustment must be made to calculate duration when the first period is shorter than the others. The adjustments are similar to those of the full-coupon bond equation. The partial period, q, must be used as the first period instead of a whole first period. The adjusted equation is as follows:

$$D = \sum_{t=1}^{2n} \left\{ \left[\frac{(C/2)/(1 + y/2)^{t-1+q}}{P} \right] \left[\frac{t-1+q}{2} \right] \right\} + \left[\frac{F/(1 + y/2)^{2n-1+q}}{P} \right] \left[\frac{2n-1+q}{2} \right]$$

nual payments prior to maturity has a duration that is somewhat less than a zero-coupon bond of the same maturity.

Example. Consider a full-coupon bond that matures in 30 years and is currently trading at par. The bond has a yield of 6.00 percent and pays interest semiannually at an annual rate of 6.00 percent. We can calculate the duration of this bond as shown below.
Let:

$C = \$6.00$
$F = \$100$
$P = \$100$
$t = 1, 2, 3, \ldots, 60$
$n = 30$

Then:

$$D = \sum_{t=1}^{60} \left[\left(\frac{3.00/1.03^t}{100} \right) \frac{t}{2} \right] + \left(\frac{100/1.03^{60}}{100} \right) n = 14.25$$

Exhibit 3–7 shows the duration calculation for this bond. Column 1 represents the time at which each of the cash flows is received, and Column 2 is the time in semiannual periods until the cash flow is received. Since the bond makes payments semiannually at a rate of 3.00 percent and pays the face value at maturity, the cash flows for this bond are as stated in Column 3. Column 4 is the appropriate discount factor for each time period used to calculate the present value of each of the cash flows, as shown in Column 5. After we derive the present value cash flows, we need to weight each cash flow by the period in which the payments are received. This step is accomplished in Column 6. The weighted cash flows from Column 6 are then divided by the bond price of $100. The final step is to sum the results in Column 7 to arrive at a duration. The duration of this bond is 14.253 years.

Effect of Cash Flows on Duration
We can break down the cash flows of a bond into components in order to examine the contribution of specific cash flows to the duration of a bond. For example, as we showed earlier in this chapter, a semiannual full-coupon bond that pays interest at an annual rate of 6.00 percent and matures in 30 years has the following cash flows:

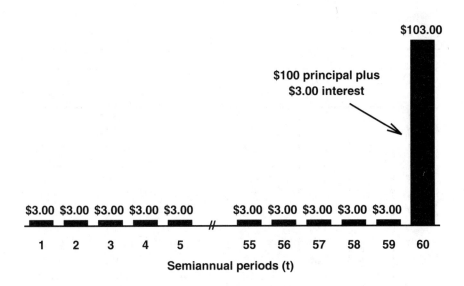

Consider, however, if the bond was broken into a series of separate and distinct cash flows. For example, we can isolate the first 20 semiannual cash flows, the second 40 semiannual cash flows, and the principal into three distinct pieces. The three cash-flow pieces would make payments as shown in Exhibit 3–8.

We can calculate the duration on each of these three pieces by applying the duration formula developed earlier in this chapter. We begin by calculating bond prices for each of the pieces, using a semiannual discount rate of 3.00 percent. The individual prices are:

Piece	P
1	$P_1 = 44.632 = \displaystyle\sum_{t=1}^{20} \frac{3.00}{1.03^t}$
2	$P_2 = 38.395 = \displaystyle\sum_{t=21}^{60} \frac{3.00}{1.03^t}$
3	$P_3 = 16.973 = \dfrac{100}{1.03^{60}}$
Total	$P = 100.00 = \displaystyle\sum_{t=1}^{60} \frac{3.00}{1.03^t} + \frac{100}{1.03^{60}}$

EXHIBIT 3–7
Duration Calculation for a $100, 30-Year, 6.00 Percent Full-Coupon Bond

(1)	(2)	(3)	(4)	(5)	(6)	(7)
t	$t/2$	$C/2$	$1/(1.03)^t$	(3)x(4)	(2)x(5)	(6)/100
1	0.5	3.00	0.9709	2.913	1.456	0.015
2	1.0	3.00	0.9426	2.828	2.828	0.028
3	1.5	3.00	0.9151	2.745	4.118	0.041
4	2.0	3.00	0.8885	2.666	5.331	0.053
5	2.5	3.00	0.8626	2.588	6.470	0.065
6	3.0	3.00	0.8375	2.513	7.538	0.075
7	3.5	3.00	0.8131	2.439	8.538	0.085
8	4.0	3.00	0.7894	2.368	9.473	0.095
9	4.5	3.00	0.7664	2.299	10.346	0.103
10	5.0	3.00	0.7441	2.232	11.162	0.112
11	5.5	3.00	0.7224	2.167	11.920	0.119
12	6.0	3.00	0.7014	2.104	12.625	0.126
13	6.5	3.00	0.6810	2.043	13.280	0.133
14	7.0	3.00	0.6611	1.983	13.883	0.139
15	7.5	3.00	0.6419	1.926	14.443	0.144
16	8.0	3.00	0.6232	1.870	14.957	0.150
17	8.5	3.00	0.6050	1.815	15.428	0.154
18	9.0	3.00	0.5874	1.762	15.860	0.159
19	9.5	3.00	0.5703	1.711	16.254	0.163
20	10.0	3.00	0.5537	1.661	16.611	0.166
21	10.5	3.00	0.5375	1.613	16.931	0.169
22	11.0	3.00	0.5219	1.566	17.223	0.172
23	11.5	3.00	0.5067	1.520	17.481	0.175
24	12.0	3.00	0.4919	1.476	17.708	0.177
25	12.5	3.00	0.4776	1.433	17.910	0.179
26	13.0	3.00	0.4637	1.391	18.084	0.181
27	13.5	3.00	0.4502	1.351	18.233	0.182
28	14.0	3.00	0.4371	1.311	18.358	0.184
29	14.5	3.00	0.4243	1.273	18.457	0.185
30	15.0	3.00	0.4120	1.236	18.540	0.185
31	15.5	3.00	0.4000	1.200	18.600	0.186
32	16.0	3.00	0.3883	1.165	18.638	0.186
33	16.5	3.00	0.3770	1.131	18.662	0.187
34	17.0	3.00	0.3660	1.098	18.666	0.187
35	17.5	3.00	0.3554	1.066	18.659	0.187
36	18.0	3.00	0.3450	1.035	18.630	0.186
37	18.5	3.00	0.3350	1.005	18.593	0.186

EXHIBIT 3-7 *(concluded)*

38	19.0	3.00	0.3252	0.976	18.536	0.185
39	19.5	3.00	0.3158	0.947	18.474	0.185
40	20.0	3.00	0.3066	0.920	18.396	0.184
41	20.5	3.00	0.2976	0.893	18.302	0.183
42	21.0	3.00	0.2890	0.867	18.207	0.182
43	21.5	3.00	0.2805	0.842	18.092	0.181
44	22.0	3.00	0.2724	0.817	17.978	0.180
45	22.5	3.00	0.2644	0.793	17.847	0.178
46	23.0	3.00	0.2567	0.770	17.712	0.177
47	23.5	3.00	0.2493	0.748	17.576	0.176
48	24.0	3.00	0.2420	0.726	17.424	0.174
49	24.5	3.00	0.2350	0.705	17.273	0.173
50	25.0	3.00	0.2281	0.684	17.108	0.171
51	25.5	3.00	0.2215	0.665	16.945	0.169
52	26.0	3.00	0.2150	0.645	16.770	0.168
53	26.5	3.00	0.2088	0.626	16.600	0.166
54	27.0	3.00	0.2027	0.608	16.419	0.164
55	27.5	3.00	0.1968	0.590	16.236	0.162
56	28.0	3.00	0.1910	0.573	16.044	0.160
57	28.5	3.00	0.1855	0.557	15.860	0.159
58	29.0	3.00	0.1801	0.540	15.669	0.157
59	29.5	3.00	0.1748	0.524	15.470	0.155
60	30.0	103.00	0.1697	17.479	524.373	5.245
			Duration			14.253

Using the prices above, the duration for each of these cash flows is calculated as shown below.

Piece 1:

$$\text{Duration} = D_1 = \sum_{t=1}^{20} \left(\frac{3.00/1.03^t}{44.632} \right) \frac{t}{2} + \left(\frac{100/1.03^{20}}{44.632} \right) 10 = 4.762$$

Piece 2:

$$\text{Duration} = D_2 = \sum_{t=21}^{60} \left(\frac{3.00/1.03^t}{38.395} \right) \frac{t}{2} + \left(\frac{100/1.03^{60}}{38.395} \right) 30 = 18.325$$

EXHIBIT 3–8

Cash Flows on a 30-Year, 6.00 Percent Bond Divided into Three Pieces

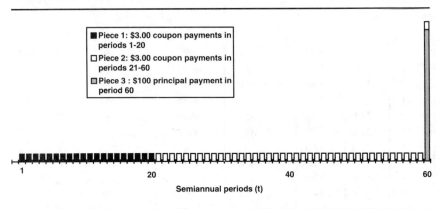

Piece 3:

Duration $= D_3 = 30$

Comparing the durations of the individual pieces, we notice that piece 1 has a much lower duration than pieces 2 and 3. Cash flows up-front act to lower duration, whereas longer maturities and payments at later dates increase duration.

If we weight the individual durations by the appropriate percentage prices, we can derive the duration of the total bond, as follows:

$$D = D_1 \frac{P_1}{100} + D_2 \frac{P_2}{100} + D_3 \frac{P_3}{100}$$

$$D = 4.762 \frac{44.623}{100} + 18.325 \frac{38.395}{100} + 30.0 \frac{16.973}{100} = 14.25$$

From this example, we can see that the duration of this bond is simply the weighted sum of the durations of the individual pieces. This concept is particularly important in evaluation of strippable bonds, such as BPOs, in which certain cash flows can be isolated and removed from the rest of the bond.

Relationship between Duration and Maturity

Certain notable relationships exist between duration and its determinants: maturity, current bond price, coupon, and discount rates. In general, duration increases as time to maturity increases. However, the rate at which it increases is a function of the coupon structure on the bond: the lower the coupon rate, the greater the increase in duration. For coupon-bearing bonds, duration increases at a decreasing rate as maturity increases. Current coupon payments act to decrease duration, and the effects of additional coupon payments are lessened as maturity increases. For a zero-coupon bond, duration always equals maturity, and, therefore, a linear relationship exists between the two (see Exhibit 3–9).

Relationship between Duration and Coupon

Since duration is a measure of the weighted average time of expected cash flows of a bond, increasing the coupon on a bond while keeping the required yield constant increases the price of the

EXHIBIT 3–9
Duration and Maturity

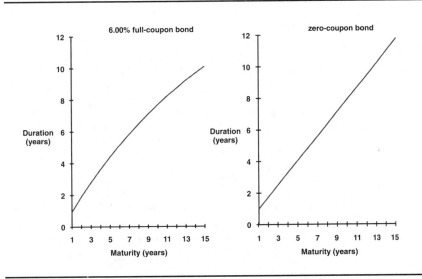

bond and decreases its duration. That is, if two bonds have the same maturity and yield but different coupon rates and different market values, the bond with a higher coupon and higher price, P, will have a shorter duration. Exhibit 3–10 shows the relationship between duration and coupon for a 30-year bond and a 6.00 percent level of market rates. Recall that this bond has a duration of 14.25 if the coupon is 6.00 percent. Notice, however, that as the coupon is increased, the duration decreases significantly and vice versa. Assuming that yield and maturity are unchanged, duration *decreases* as coupon *increases*.

Relationship between Duration and Yield

A similar relationship exists between duration and yield, y, or discount rate. Since duration is highly influenced by the present value of expected cash flows, a change in the yield on a bond signifi-

EXHIBIT 3–10
Duration and Coupon for a 30-Year Maturity, Full-Coupon Bond

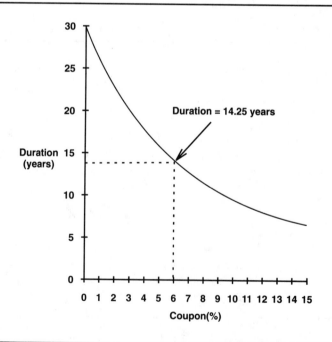

cantly affects the duration. In particular, as the yield on a bond decreases, both the present value of the payments associated with the bond—and the price of the bond itself increase. This causes an increase in duration. The opposite is true for an increase in yield. In higher interest rate settings, the present value of the payments is lower and, therefore, duration is lower. Exhibit 3–11 shows the relationship between duration and market yields for a 30-year, 6.00 percent full-coupon bond. Assuming that coupon and maturity are unchanged, duration *decreases* as yield *increases*.

Modified Duration

An important variation of Macaulay's duration is *modified duration*. Modified duration, a simple transformation of Macaulay's duration, is important for estimating bond prices.

Let:

D_m = modified duration

D = Macaulay's duration

y = market yield

p = frequency of compounding

Then:

$$D_m = \frac{D}{1 + y/p}$$

Example.   A full-coupon bond with 30 years to maturity pays interest semiannually at a rate of 6.00 percent per year, sells for par, and has a duration of 14.25 and a modified duration of 13.83.

Let:

$D = 14.25$

$y = 6.00\%$

$p = 2$

Then:

$$D_m = \frac{14.25}{1 + 0.06/2} = 13.83$$

Modified duration is of particular importance because of its link to the price–yield curve. We can estimate the change in a bond price

EXHIBIT 3–11

Duration and Yield for a 30-Year Maturity, 6.00 Percent Full-Coupon Bond

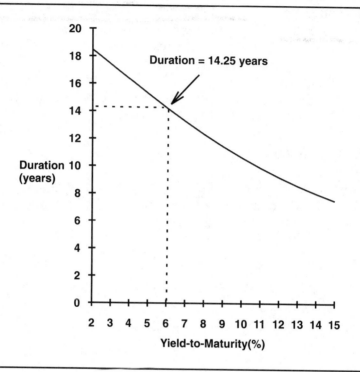

due to duration, ΔP_D, for an incremental change in yield, Δy, by using the modified duration estimate.

Let:

ΔP_D = change in price due to duration

D_m = modified duration

y = market yield

y_n = new yield, $y_n - y = \Delta y$

Then:

$$\Delta P_D = -D_m(y_n - y)(100)$$

The change in price due to duration is the line that is tangent to the price–yield curve shown in Exhibit 3–12. The line touches the price–yield curve where the price is equal to 100. On either side of the tangent point, the line estimates changes in the bond price for corresponding changes in yield.

Example.
Let:

$D_m = 13.83$

$P = \$100$

$y = 6.00\%$

$y_n = 7.00\%$

Then:

$$\Delta P_D = (-13.83)(0.07 - .06)(100)$$
$$\Delta P_D = -\$13.83$$

We can estimate changes in bond yield using modified duration; however, as can be seen from Exhibit 3–12, the tangent line is much different from the plot of actual changes in prices and yields. This is because modified duration is a linear estimate of price changes. However, the price–yield line is generally not linear but convex to the origin (as seen in Exhibit 3–6). As yields move away from the tangent point in either direction, the estimate is less accurate. Modified duration, by itself, provides a cursory estimate of the price–yield relationship. For this reason, we must also estimate the distance between the modified duration tangent line and the price–yield line. The distance between the two lines is commonly referred to as *convexity* and is discussed later in this chapter.

Problems with Classical Measures of Duration for Derivative Securities

Although Macaulay's duration and modified duration work well as a measure of duration for fixed-rate bonds, there are some assumptions that make this model a less accurate predictor of duration for derivative securities. These assumptions include:

1. *The use of a flat yield curve, a constant discount rate, or yield to maturity in the model.* Macaulay's duration, like standard bond-pricing methods, assumes that the yield curve is flat and, as such, that expected future market rates equal today's constant long-term rates. It does not take into account

EXHIBIT 3–12
Price–Yield Curve and Modified Duration Estimate

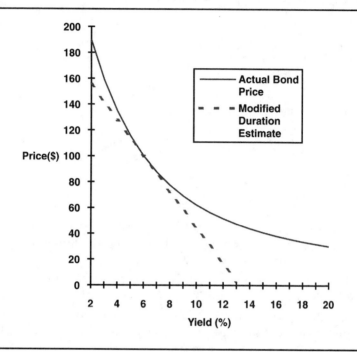

the slope of the yield curve or expectations of future rates implied by the yield curve.

2. *The use of a fixed coupon payment.* Macaulay's duration assumes that all payments on the underlying bond are fixed and uniform. This assumption is inappropriate for many derivative securities with variable payments that are contingent on future levels of interest rates.

3. *An improper weighting of expected cash flows.* Since Macaulay's duration weights the fixed cash flows by their respective times to receipt, it does not properly address expected cash flows of derivative securities. For example, BULL derivatives such as inverse floaters typically have expectations of *higher up-front* and *lower back-end* cash flows, whereas BEAR derivatives may have expectations of *lower up-front* and *higher back-end* cash flows. A duration

measure for derivatives must be adjusted to reflect these disparate expectations.

The payment streams of derivative securities do not fit neatly into a Macaulay's duration framework and require adjustments if the duration is to be properly measured. Just as we must adapt the valuation models to value derivative securities, we must also adapt the standard measures of duration.

Duration Measures of Derivative Securities

As we discussed above, the variable rate cash flows make classical duration measures inappropriate for assessing the price/yield relationship associated with derivative securities. We believe an approach that incorporates two duration measures ; a time duration measure, D_t^*, and a price duration measure, D_p^*, better captures the risks associated with derivative securities.

Time Duration of Derivative Securities

A duration model which incorporates expectations of short-term rates and variable cash flows is known as *Fisher-Weil duration*.[3] This model replaces the constant discount rates and fixed cash-flow assumptions used in Macaulay's duration with a series of expected short-term rates and variable cash flows

In Chapter 4, we develop techniques for using today's yield curve to derive a series of *implied forward rates:* rates expected to prevail in the future. Implied forward rates represent expectations of future levels of short-term rates. These rates are suitable for calculating a derivative security's expected cash flows, and the duration of a security with uncertain future cash flows.

Let's represent the set of semiannual rates expected to prevail from period $t-1$ to period t as $_{t-1}f_t^*$. The present value, PV, of the cash flows on a bond with semiannual payments using these discount factors can be calculated as shown below.

---

[3]See Lawrence Fisher and Romen Weil, "Coping with the Risk of Market Interest Rate Fluctuations: Returns to Bondholders from Naive and Optimal Strategies," *Journal of Business*, 1971, pp. 408–431.

Let:

P^* = price

C = annual coupon payment in dollars

F = principal or redemption amount

$_{t-1}f_t^*$ = tax-exempt forward interest rate from time $t-1$ to t

t = time

n = total number of years

Π = product operator (For example, $\prod_{t=1}^{3} 1.03^t$ = $(1.03)(1.03)^2 (1.03)^3 = 1.194.$)

Then:

$$P^* = \frac{C/2}{1 + {_0}f_1^*} + \frac{C/2}{(1 + {_0}f_1^*)(1 + {_1}f_2^*)} +$$

$$\frac{C/2}{(1 + {_0}f_1^*)(1 + {_1}f_2^*)(1 + {_2}f_3^*)} , \cdots , \frac{F}{\prod_{t=1}^{2n}(1 + {_{t-1}}f_t^*)}$$

Example. Assume that expected short-term rates for six semiannual periods are as shown below.

Semiannual Time Period	Forward Rate
1	$_0f_1^* = 2.50$
2	$_1f_2^* = 2.55$
3	$_2f_3^* = 2.60$
4	$_3f_4^* = 2.65$
5	$_4f_5^* = 2.70$
6	$_5f_6^* = 2.75$

A price measurement that incorporates expectations of changes in semiannual rates can be calculated by discounting each of the cash flows by the appropriate discount factor. To calculate the price of a three-year bond, proceed as follows.

Let:

C = \$6.00

F = \$100

$$_{t-1}f^*_t = {}_0f^*_1 = 2.50, \ {}_1f^*_2 = 2.55, \ {}_2f^*_3 = 2.60, \ {}_3f^*_4 = 2.65, \ {}_4f^*_5 = 2.70,$$
$$_5f^*_6 = 2.75$$
$$t = 1, 2, 3, 4, 5, 6$$
$$n = 3$$

Then:

$$P^* = \frac{3.00}{1.025} + \frac{3.00}{(1.025)(1.0255)} +$$

$$\frac{3.00}{(1.025)(1.0255)(1.026)} \ , \cdots , \ \frac{100}{\prod_{t=1}^{6}(1 + {}_{t-1}f^*_t)}$$

$$P^* = 102.08$$

Using P^* and the expected short-term rates we used to calculate P^*, we can calculate a duration measure that incorporates expected changes in short-term interest rates. The calculation is similar to that of Macaulay's duration, except that we substitute the expected short-term rates for the constant discount factor, as we did in the price calculation.

Let:

D^*_t = duration measure that incorporates movements in short-term rates

C = annual coupon payment in dollars

F = principal or redemption amount

$_{t-1}f^*_t$ = forward interest rate from time $t-1$ to t

t = time

n = total number of years

Then:

$$D^*_t = \sum_{t=1}^{2n} \left\{ \left[\frac{(C/2)/\prod_t(1 + {}_{t-1}f^*_t)}{P^*} \right] \frac{t}{2} \right\} + \frac{F/\prod_t(1 + {}_{t-1}f^*_t)}{P^*} \ n$$

Each expected cash flow is discounted by the appropriate set of short-term discount rates.[4] Using the implied forward rates, we

---

[4] This equation would require the same adjustment for partial periods as did Macaulay's duration, discussed earlier in the chapter (see footnote 2, page 73).

can also adjust the cash flows for interest rate contingent derivative products and, thus, reduce the effects of the problems with standard duration measures. We will further develop and apply this model for the five specific municipal derivative securities in Chapter 8, after we introduce the yield curve and the structural aspects of derivative products.

    Example. We will now calculate the duration of the bond in the example shown above.

    Let:

$$C = \$6.00$$
$$F = \$100$$
$$_{t-1}f_t^* = {}_0f_1^* = 2.50, {}_1f_2^* = 2.55, {}_2f_3^* = 2.60, {}_3f_4^* = 2.65, {}_4f_5^* = 2.70,$$
$$_5f_6^* = 2.75$$
$$t = 1, 2, 3, 4, 5, 6$$
$$n = 3$$

Then:

$$D_t^* = \sum_{t=1}^{6} \left\{ \left[\frac{3.00/\prod_t(1 + {}_{t-1}f_t^*)}{102.08} \right] \frac{t}{2} \right\} + \frac{100/\prod_t(1 + {}_{t-1}f_t^*)}{102.08} \cdot 3$$

$$D_t^* = 2.792$$

Price Duration of Derivative Securities

As we have previously discussed, the $\Delta P/\Delta y$ relationship for derivative securities is not nearly as neat or as constant as for a fixed-rate security. The principal reason for the increased complexity of derivative securities is that their cash flows may change with changes in interest rates or yield levels.

    The capital markets have come to accept the classical measures of duration as a proxy for price volatility. However, with derivative securities that is not the case. Cash flows and prices for derivative securities may react very differently than fixed-rate bonds with changing interest rates. The cash flows and market values of bull derivative securities increase with decreases in interest rates, while the cash flows and market prices of bear derivative securities increase with increasing rates. The complexities associated with derivative securities require that each derivative security be broken down and analyzed as a sum of its various component parts. Once the building blocks of derivative securities are identified, it is possible to examine the value of and duration of each of the components using appropriate valuation techniques.

In the chapters that follow, we show how to use Expectational Analysis (Chapter 4) to quantify the expected cash flows associated with derivative securities. We show (in Chapters 5, 6, and 7) how to divide derivative securities into their appropriate building blocks and calculate the value and duration, whether positive or negative, of each of the components. The total price duration D_p^* of each derivative security is the simple sum of the duration of the underlying components. In Chapter 8, we calculate the duration of each of five municipal derivative securities that we examine.

CONVEXITY

Convexity is a measure that quantifies the difference between the price curve and the modified duration estimate. Mathematically, convexity is the second derivative of the price–yield line divided by price. In this section we develop a model for measuring the convexity of a bond.

Exhibit 3–13 depicts the convexity region for a 6.00 percent full-coupon bond with 30 years to maturity. The convexity region is the area between the modified duration estimate and the price–yield curve.

Let:

Y = convexity in years
P = dollar price of the bond
C = annual coupon payment in dollars
F = face value or redemption value
y = market yield
t = time
n = number of years

Then:

$$Y = \frac{\sum_{t=1}^{2n}\left\{\left[\dfrac{(C/2)/(1 + y/2)^t}{P}\right](t)(t + 1)\right\} + \left\{\left[\dfrac{F/(1 + y/2)^{2n}}{P}\right](2n)(2n + 1)\right\}}{(1 + y/2)^2}$$

Example.
Let:

$P = \$100$
$C = 6.00\%$
$F = \$100$
$y = 6.00\%$
$t = 1, 2, 3, \ldots, 60$
$n = 30$

EXHIBIT 3–13
Convexity Regions for a 6.00 Percent, 30-Year, Noncallable Bond

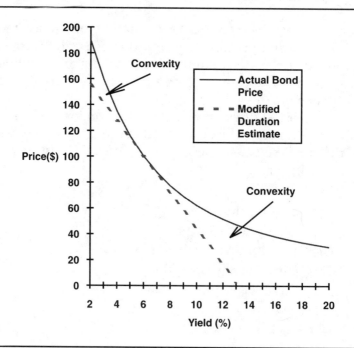

Then:

$$Y = \frac{\sum_{t=1}^{60} \left\{ \left[\dfrac{3.00/(1.03)^t}{100} \right] (t)(t+1) \right\} + \left\{ \left[\dfrac{100/(1.03)^{60}}{100} \right] (60)(61) \right\}}{(1.03)^2} = 269.469$$

Just as we use modified duration to estimate price changes, we use convexity to estimate price changes for a given change in yield, Δy, as shown below.

Let:

ΔP_Y = change in price due to convexity

Y = convexity

y_n = new yield, $y_n - y = \Delta y$

y = market yield

Then:

$$\Delta P_Y = \frac{Y (y_n - y)^2}{2} *100$$

Example.

Let:

Y = 296.469

y_n = 7.00%

y = 6.00%

Then:

$$\Delta P_Y = \frac{269.469(0.01)^2(100)}{2} = 1.347$$

Duration and convexity each provide us with information about price fluctuations. The two together provide an estimate of total price changes, ΔP, for a given change in interest rates, as follows:

$$\Delta P = \Delta P_D + \Delta P_Y$$

Exhibit 3–14 shows the relationship between actual and estimated price changes for a noncallable, 6.00 percent, full-coupon bond with 30 years to maturity.

EXHIBIT 3–14
Convexity Measures for a 6.00 Percent, Noncallable Bond
with 30 Years to Maturity

Δ y	Price P	Actual Price Change	ΔP_D	ΔP_Y	ΔP
-3.00%	$159.07	+$59.07	+$41.49	+13.34	+54.83
-2.00%	134.76	+34.76	+27.66	+5.93	+33.59
-1.00%	115.45	+15.45	+13.83	+1.35	+15.18
0%	100.00	0.00	0.00	0.00	0.00
+1.00%	87.53	-12.47	-13.83	+1.35	-12.48
+2.00%	77.38	-22.62	-27.66	+5.93	-21.73
+3.00%	69.04	-30.96	-41.49	+13.34	-28.15

The estimate of price change, ΔP, is relatively accurate for small incremental changes in the price of bond. In Exhibit 3–14, when y changes by 100 BPs in either direction, the estimated price change is very close to the actual price change. For yield changes greater than 100 BPs in either direction, the estimated price changes become less accurate. The degree to which the estimated price diverges from the actual price is a function of the level of convexity of the underlying bond.

Negative Convexity

In some cases, the price–yield line is not convex to the origin at every yield. This occurs when a bond price and yield move in the same direction. In general, prepayment provisions on a bond will cause this kind of price reaction. Bonds that are subject to call prior to maturity will be priced in the market to the call date and redemption price any time the yield falls below the coupon rate. For example, a $100, 30-year municipal bond that is issued at 6.00 percent and can be called in five years at $102 will be priced as a five-year bond with a redemption price of $102 when market rates fall below 6.00 percent. When rates are below 6.00 percent, it is advantageous for the issuer to call these bonds and refinance at the lower market rates. For this reason, the market views this bond as having a maturity coincident to the call date. Whenever rates are at or above 6.00 percent, the bond will be priced as a 30-year bond.

This tendency for bond prices to move in the same direction as yields, when the yield is below the coupon rate on the bond, gives rise to what is called *negative convexity*. Negative convexity exists when the modified duration estimate is above some or all of the price–yield line. When this occurs, the price–yield line is said to be concave to the origin. The change in price due to convexity in this area is *negative*.

As shown in Exhibit 3–15, the price–yield line for a callable bond follows a different pattern than the one shown in Exhibit 3–14. In particular, when the yield on the callable bond falls below the coupon of 6.00 percent, the price–yield line bends back toward

EXHIBIT 3–15
Negative Convexity Example

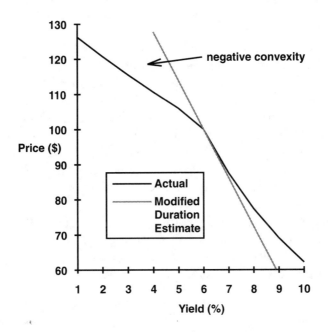

the price axis. This is due to the increased probability that the bond
will be called for refinancing at rates below the coupon. For this
reason, when yields are below the bond coupon rate, the bond will
be priced to the call date with a redemption price of $102 in five
years. The region where yields are below the coupon is where the
bond is said to exhibit negative convexity. In this area, the
price–yield line is concave to the origin. The measures of convexity
are negative in this region due to the pricing aberration. When
rates are above the 6.00 percent level, the bond is priced as a typical, 30-year, 6.00 percent bond; the bond exhibits concavity in this
region.

SUMMARY

In this chapter, we explained the mathematics involved with municipal securities. We also discussed the concept of price volatility
and the measures of duration and convexity. Acquiring an understanding of all these concepts is important for investors, so that
they will be able to fully assess the risks and returns of municipal
securities.

The value of a municipal security, like the value of any other
financial asset, equals the present value of the expected cash flows
over the life of the security. The coupon, the maturity, and the discount rate are the main determinants of a bond price.

A full-coupon bond is easy to value because its cash flows are
known over the life of the bond. The price of a full-coupon bond is
the discounted present value of the expected coupon payments
and the principal over the life of the bond. Similarly, the value of a
zero-coupon bond is simply the present value of the principal payment expected at maturity.

Because municipal derivative securities generally have unknown cash flows, their valuation is more difficult. In the chapters
that follow, we use the techniques developed in this chapter and
expand upon them to develop pricing models for municipal derivative securities.

CHAPTER 4

EXPECTATIONAL ANALYSIS

INTRODUCTION

The value of a derivative security, like that of any other financial asset, equals the present value of its *expected* cash flows. That seems like a simple enough statement! What's so confusing here?

For many people, the source of the confusion surrounding the understanding and valuation of debt-based derivative securities is that their *cash flows* are dependent upon *unknown* future interest rate levels. Because their future cash flows are *uncertain*, the valuation of derivative securities is a little more complex than the discounting of a known cash flow on a handheld calculator or a bond calculator. To understand and value derivative securities, market participants must expand their skill set to learn *three basic concepts.* The first concept is *expectational analysis*—how today's yield curve works to quantify current expectations regarding future unknown interest rates. This chapter addresses expectational analysis. The second concept is the *building blocks of derivative securities,* a subject which is examined in Chapters 5, 6, and 7. The third concept is the *derivative asset pricing model,* also called the *DAP model,* which is examined in Chapter 8.

The valuation of a security with cash flows that depend upon unknown future interest rates is a problem that has been addressed in the corporate derivatives market. Since the introduction of interest rate swaps in the early 1980s, and the recent trading of interest rate cap and floor options, market participants have had to develop valuation models that attempt to project levels of future interest rates. As a basis for these projections, these models generally incorporate the yield curve, which depicts the term structure of interest rates.

The various theories that describe the yield curve and the information the yield curve is supposed to convey to market participants are discussed in the next section. Next comes a description of the mathematics underlying the term structure of interest rates— how *implied zero-coupon bond rates* and *implied forward interest rates* can be derived from the taxable par Treasury yield curve. Examples of trading strategies are cited, to show how market participants, given the assumptions of *perfect capital markets,* can use existing Treasury coupon and zero-coupon bonds to *lock in* the zero-coupon rates and the forward rates implied in the Treasury par yield curve. This is an important step for bond market participants to understand; this exercise is not just academic theory. This type of procedure, in a very simplistic manner, is similar to the trading strategies used by Wall Street's premier derivatives and arbitrage groups. An important set of relationships between the par yield curve, zero-coupon rates, and implied forward rates is the focus of a number of arbitrage trading strategies.

In the final section of the chapter, we focus on the tax-exempt yield curve and the derivation of *implied tax-exempt forward rates.* The valuation of municipal derivative securities is crucially dependent upon implied tax-exempt forward rates. The various market imperfections associated with the tax-exempt yield curve are discussed, and the derivation of implied tax-exempt forward rates is explained.

THEORIES OF THE YIELD CURVE

The yield curve, otherwise known as the *term structure of interest rates,* describes the relationship between the *yield* on a security and its *duration* or *maturity.* In an examination of the yield curve, it is important that the securities represented differ only in duration or maturity and not in other factors—particularly not in risk of default. Typically, the shape of the taxable yield curve is determined by noncallable, risk-free, highly liquid US Treasury securities. The Treasury yield curve will be the one focused upon in this section. It should be noted that many participants in the taxable debt derivatives marketplace focus on the London Interbank Offered Rate (LIBOR) yield curve and that many taxable derivative products and some tax-exempt derivative products are pegged to this marketplace. However, to reduce *rate confusion,* we will use the more familiar default-free Treasury yield curve as the basis for estimates of expectational analysis.

Several academic hypotheses attempt to explain term structure of interest rates, as well as the information that it conveys to the marketplace. The three most common explanations are known as the *pure expectations hypothesis,* the *liquidity preference hypothesis,* and the *preferred habitat hypothesis* or the *market segmentation hypothesis.*

The Pure Expectations Hypothesis

The *pure expectations hypothesis* explains the yield curve as a function of a series of expected forward rates. As such, the yield curve can be decomposed into a series of expected future short-term rates that will adjust in such a way that investors will receive equivalent holding period returns. In its traditional form, this hypothesis implies that the expected average annual return on a long-term bond is the geometric mean of the expected short-term rates. For example, the two-period spot rate can be thought of as the one-year spot rate and the one-year rate expected to prevail one year hence. Under the pure expectations theory, the expected future short-term spot rates *equal* the forward rates implied in the yield curve.

Under this theory, an upward-sloping yield curve (see Exhibit 4–1, Panel A) means that investors expect higher future short-term interest rates, whereas an inverted yield curve (see Exhibit 4–1, Panel C) implies expectations of lower future short-term rates. Since expected short-term rates are implied in the yield curve, investors are assumed to be indifferent about whether they hold a 20-year investment, a series of 20 consecutive 1-year investments, or 2 consecutive 10-year investments. Based on this theory, we can calculate the series of expected short-term (e.g., one-year) spot rates, which over any given period will, in aggregate, reproduce the observed market rates expressed in the yield curve. This set of forward rates is known as the *implied forward yield curve* and is the basis for the valuation of derivative securities.

The more modern continuous-time version of the pure expectations hypothesis posits that, regardless of maturity, the expected

EXHIBIT 4–1
Sample Yield Curves

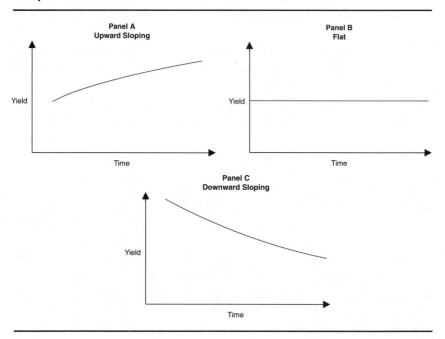

one-year holding period return is the same on all bonds as on a one-year bond.[1] Under the pure expectations hypothesis, investors are assumed to be risk-neutral with regard to interest rate risk preferences. This theory implies a flat yield curve when investors expect that short-term rates will remain constant (see Exhibit 4–1, panel B).

The Liquidity Preference Hypothesis

The *liquidity preference hypothesis* is an extension of the pure expectations hypothesis. It states that long-term rates are composed of expected short-term rates *plus a liquidity premium*. The theory posits that most investors prefer to hold short-term maturity

---

[1]See J. Cox, J. Ingersoll, and S. Ross, "A Theory of the Term Structure of Interest Rates," *Econometrica*, vol. 53, 1985, pp. 385–407.

securities. In order to induce investors to hold bonds with longer maturities, the issuer must pay a liquidity premium. For example, an investor who prefers a bond with a two-year maturity can purchase a bond with a three-year maturity and sell the bond after two years; however, this strategy incurs additional risk. The liquidity premium is risk compensation for investors who would otherwise invest in shorter maturities. The amount of the liquidity premium is the extra yield demanded by the market to stretch its maturity a specified number of years.

The liquidity premium increases with time to maturity. The observed yield curve under the liquidity preference hypothesis is always higher than the yield curve predicted solely by the pure expectations hypothesis (see Exhibit 4–2, panels A and B). The liquidity preference hypothesis assumes that investors are risk-averse. This theory implies an upward-sloping yield curve even when investors expect that short-term rates will remain constant. Further, if liquidity premiums increase with term to maturity, as many market participants believe they do, the yield curve will have a tendency to exhibit a positive upward slope. An upward-sloping yield curve is consistent with the majority of observations of the Treasury yield curve over the last three decades.

Under the liquidity preference hypothesis, the expected future short-term spot rates are generally less than the forward rates implied in the yield curve.

The Preferred Habitat Hypothesis

The *preferred habitat hypothesis*—also called the *market segmentation hypothesis*—recognizes that the market is composed of diverse investors with differing investment requirements. Some investors, such as corporations that have temporary funds to invest prior to the use of these funds for longer-term capital investment in their businesses, prefer to invest in bonds at the short end of the yield curve, and to avoid the potential capital losses associated with selling longer bonds prior to maturity. Others, such as insurance companies and pension funds, desire bonds with longer maturities, the term and cash flows of which coincide with their obligations under insurance policies and pension programs. All investors prefer to invest so that the life of their assets matches the life of their liabilities.

EXHIBIT 4–2
Yield Curve Shapes: Liquidity Preference Hypothesis

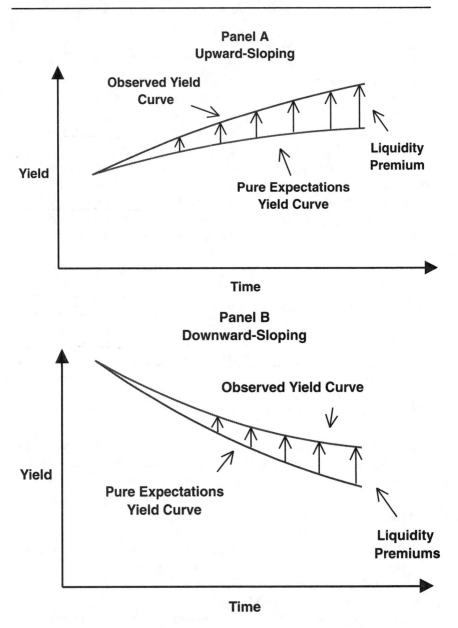

Panel A
Upward-Sloping

Observed Yield Curve

Liquidity Premium

Yield

Pure Expectations Yield Curve

Time

Panel B
Downward-Sloping

Observed Yield Curve

Yield

Pure Expectations Yield Curve

Liquidity Premiums

Time

In order to induce investors to move away from their preferred position on the yield curve, an issuer must pay a premium. For this reason, the preferred habitat hypothesis predicts that any maturities that do not have a balance of supply and demand will sell at a premium or discount to their expected yields.

Under the preferred habitat hypothesis, there is no formal relationships between expected future short-term spot rates and implied forward rates; rather, the shape of the yield curve is a function of supply and demand.

The Yield Curve as a Predictor of Short-Term Rates

To our knowledge, no market participants or even ivory-tower academicians truly believe that the yield curve, or the term structure of interest rates, accurately predicts the future course of short-term interest rates. There is academic evidence of liquidity premiums in the yield curve. However, the ability to quantify these liquidity premiums and to determine how they shift over time and over different interest rate scenarios has eluded academicians and practitioners.

Further, based on empirical evidence, the yield curve has been a particularly poor predictor of future short-term interest rates. If the pure expectations hypothesis of the yield curve efficiently incorporated information about future short-term rates of interest into the term structure of interest rates, there should not be another method which would provide a better forecast of future short-term rates. In 1976, Eugene Fama compared[2] the forecasting ability of forward rates implied by the yield curve with a simple alternative forecasting model—an assumption that short-term rates will remain *constant* for the next observation period. Fama observed that this assumption provided forecasts *superior* to the results obtained by using the forward rates implied by the yield curve.

Because of liquidity premiums, and probably for other unknown reasons, the forward rates implied by the yield curve do not equal the expectations of the future short-term rate of interest.

---

[2] See E Fama, "Short-Term Interest Rates as Predictors of Inflation," *American Economic Review*, June 1975, pp. 269–82.

In fact, most of the time, implied forward rates probably *overesti-mate* expected future short-term rates.

If Fama's alternative assumption is indeed valid, why do we continue to use zero-coupon yield curves (which are described in the next section) and implied forward rates derived from the pure expectations model of the yield curve? Here are some reasons for their extreme importance:

1. Theoretically, arbitrage activity can lock in implied zero-coupon rates and implied forward rates.
2. The implied zero-coupon yield curve can provide the yields or discount rates used to value the cash flows associated with debt securities (see Chapter 5).
3. Most of the models used by market participants in valuing any derivative product incorporate the forward rates implied by the pure expectations hypothesis of the yield curve.

THE MATHEMATICS OF EXPECTATIONAL ANALYSIS[3]

In an effort to *objectively* value contingent interest derivative securities, continuous-time models have been developed that describe the yield curve in terms of one variable—the short-term, risk-free interest rate, the *spot rate*. Therefore, any long-term bond yield may be described by the current spot rate and a series of expected future short-term spot rates. Most of the valuation models used by practitioners, in order to present an objective valuation without regard to individual risk preferences, incorporate the pure expectations theory of the yield curve, which implies interest rate risk neutrality.

State-of-the-art, continuous-time valuation models are beyond the scope of this book, but the sections that follow provide a simple description of the theory and mathematics underlying the expectations associated with these models. The example described below

---

[3]This section in large part follows T Campbell and W Kracaw, "The Term Structure of Interest Rates," in *Financial Risk Management*, Harper Collins, New York, 1993.

takes a full-coupon yield curve and calculates the series of *implied forward interest rates* that act as the basis for valuing contingent interest derivative securities—forwards, swaps, and options.

Definitions and Notation

First, let's focus on some definitions and notation that will make the mathematics a little simpler to understand.

Time

n = years to maturity of a cash flow or bond
t = time measured in semiannual periods

Bond Characteristics

P = price of a bond or cash flow
C = annual full-coupon bond rate, in dollars
F = principal or face amount of a bond

Rates

r_t = zero-coupon interest rate from time 0 to t
$_{t-1}r_t$ = zero-coupon interest rate from period $t-1$ to t
$_{t-1}f_t$ = implied forward taxable rate for period $t-1$ to t
$_{t-1}f_t^*$ = implied forward tax-exempt rate from period $t-1$ to t
y = market yield
c = annual full-coupon interest rate in percentage

All yields and rates, unless otherwise stated, are bond equivalent yields (BEYs), which assumes semiannual compounding and discounting of cash flows.

Implied Zero-Coupon Rates

Most graphs of the yield curve depict the yield of par, full-coupon bonds as a function of term to maturity, t. This depiction assumes that each of the semiannual coupon payments, $C/2$, will be reinvested in a manner that will give an amount at maturity such that the bond yields y. In effect, the yield to maturity on coupon bonds depends significantly on the reinvestment rates. Because of this reinvestment dependency in calculating yield, there is significant *reinvestment risk* associated with coupon-bearing bonds.

The zero-coupon yield is the yield to maturity, or discount rate, on a bond or investment with only one cash flow, which occurs on a specific date or maturity. Recall from Chapter 3 that the value of a zero-coupon bond, P, that has a cash flow F in year n with p compounding periods per year is:

$$P = \frac{F}{(1 + y/p)^{np}}$$

Example.
Let:

$F = \$1000$
$n = 10$ years
$p = 2$
$y = 10.00\%$

Then:

$$P = \frac{\$1000}{(1 + 0.10/2)^{20}} = \$376.89$$

Implied zero-coupon rates are the set of discount rates implied in the par yield curve that equates the cash flows of a full-coupon-bearing bond to those of a set of zero-coupon bonds. Since a zero-coupon bond makes no interest payments until maturity, there is no reinvestment risk. The theoretical implied zero-coupon rate adjusts the full-coupon rate for the loss or gain associated with the periodic reinvestment of the semiannual interest payments.

We can directly derive an implied zero-coupon curve from a full-coupon curve. Assume that a full-coupon bond makes a payment of $C/2$, for time periods $t = 1, 2, 3, \ldots 2n$. At time $t = 2n$, the maturity of the bond, the full-coupon bond also pays the $100 face value.

Let:

C = coupon rate on bond in dollars
F = face value or principal at maturity
r_t = implied zero-coupon rate for time 0 to t

Then:

$$100 = \left[\sum_{t=1}^{2n} \frac{(C/2)}{(1 + r_t/2)^t} \right] + \frac{100}{(1 + r_t/2)^{2n}}$$

The rates that solve this expression represent the set of implied zero coupon discount rates. Columns 3 and 4 of Exhibit 4–1 depict examples of full-coupon annual and semiannual yield curves, respectively. As a starting point, the zero-coupon discount rate for the first time period is equal to the spot rate of 0.0220 (2.2 percent semiannually, 4.4 percent annually). This result is intuitive because a six-month full-coupon bond is identical to a six-month zero-coupon bond. To calculate the one-year implied zero-coupon discount rate, we discount the known semiannual coupon payments by the known six-month zero rate and solve for the remaining one-year zero rate, as follows:

$$100 = \frac{2.25}{1.022} + \frac{102.25}{(1 + r_2/2)^2}$$

Solving for r_2 gives us an implied one-year zero rate of 0.022505 (a semiannual rate of 2.2505 percent and an annual BEY of 4.501 percent). Similarly, using the implied one-year zero-coupon rate from above, we can solve for the 1.5-year implied zero-coupon rate, as follows:

$$100 = \frac{2.30}{1.022} + \frac{2.30}{1.022505^2} + \frac{102.30}{(1 + r_3/2)^3}$$

The zero-coupon rate that solves this equation is 0.023015. In this manner, we continually solve for the zero-coupon rate and use the results to calculate the next implied zero-coupon discount rate. Column 5 of Exhibit 4–3 summarizes the implied zero-coupon yield curve for three years (six semiannual periods).

From the above calculations, we can see that the derivation of the implied zero-coupon discount rates from the full-coupon yield curve is an iterative and simple (albeit messy) procedure that is relatively easy to program into a spreadsheet. Exhibit 8–1 in Chapter 8 presents a printout of a spreadsheet showing a 30-year par yield curve, an implied zero-coupon curve, and implied forward curves for January 3, 1994, as printed in *The Wall Street Journal* on January

EXHIBIT 4–3
Sample Yield Curve: Implied Zero-Coupon Rates

Period	Years	Annual Full-Coupon Rates	Semiannual Full-Coupon Rates	Implied Zero-Coupon Rates
t	n	C	$C/2$	$r_t/2$
1	0.5	4.400%	2.200%	2.2000%
2	1.0	4.500	2.250	2.2506
3	1.5	4.600	2.300	2.3015
4	2.0	4.800	2.400	2.4049
5	2.5	4.900	2.450	2.4565
6	3.0	5.000	2.500	2.5088

4, 1994 (see Exhibit 4–4). *The Wall Street Journal* has also begun giving zero-coupon yields directly for certain US government securities, which allows the reader to observe these yields rather than deriving them from the full-coupon yield curve. It is important to understand that, theoretically, the zero-coupon discount rates implied in the yield curve can be attained through arbitrage transactions by efficient market participants.

EXHIBIT 4–4
***The Wall Street Journal:* Taxable Yield Curve (January 3, 1994)**

Year	Full Coupon	Implied Zero	Implied Forward	Year	Full Coupon	Implied Zero	Implied Forward
1994	3.710	3.710	3.71	2009	6.300	6.572	7.67
1995	4.300	4.319	4.93	2010	6.350	6.648	7.88
1996	4.680	4.713	5.51	2011	6.400	6.729	8.11
1997	5.050	5.109	6.30	2012	6.450	6.814	8.36
1998	5.310	5.389	6.52	2013	6.500	6.904	8.63
1999	5.470	5.562	6.43	2014	6.510	6.906	6.95
2000	5.670	5.793	7.19	2015	6.520	6.912	7.03
2001	5.750	5.876	6.46	2016	6.530	6.920	7.09
2002	5.870	6.020	7.18	2017	6.540	6.930	7.15
2003	5.960	6.128	7.10	2018	6.550	6.941	7.22
2004	6.020	6.197	6.89	2019	6.560	6.954	7.29
2005	6.080	6.271	7.09	2020	6.570	6.969	7.36
2006	6.140	6.349	7.29	2021	6.580	6.986	7.44
2007	6.200	6.431	7.50	2022	6.590	7.005	7.53
2008	6.250	6.499	7.46	2023	6.600	7.025	7.62

Implied Forward Rates

Many market participants are perplexed by forward rates. They understand how a par yield curve is constructed, and they understand the underlying cash, or spot, interest rates associated with a given security. They can observe the spot rates: they can see them, smell them, almost taste them! However, they don't quite understand that the yield curve, with a very minor mathematical manipulation, can also tell them all they need to know about implied forward interest rates, which cannot be directly observed.

Underlying the yield curve, which depicts the relationship between short-term and long-term interest rates, is a relationship between the current short-term spot rate, implied forward interest rates, and the current long-term rate. On the *forward market*, or the *futures market*, investors can contract for an interest rate or yield on a bond or a loan that will begin at a point in the future and will run for a predetermined period of time. Through arbitrage procedures implied forward rates, theoretically, can be locked in today. Only time will tell whether an implied forward rate is a good estimate of future spot rates.

To understand implied forward rates, it is helpful to use an arbitrage argument. Two assets that have the same expected risk-free payoffs at the same time, from a risk–reward perspective, must have the same price. This arbitrage relationship is known as the *law of one price*. If the two assets do not have the same price, arbitrageurs will initiate arbitrage trading strategies to exploit the differential, which will eventually move asset prices into equilibrium. For a simple example, we can reexamine the yield curve shown in the previous section, and derive the implied forward rates. Using the semiannual rates shown in Exhibit 4–3, the implied 6-month forward rate of 2.2506 percent equals the 6-month investment or loan rate that can be contracted for today and that will begin 6 months hence. Implied forward rates can be calculated easily, using the zero-coupon yield curve calculated in the previous section.

Graphically, the calculation of implied forward rates can be depicted as shown in Exhibit 4–5.

Arbitrage conditions require that the relationship between zero-coupon rates, $_0r_t$, and implied forward rates be as follows:

EXHIBIT 4–5

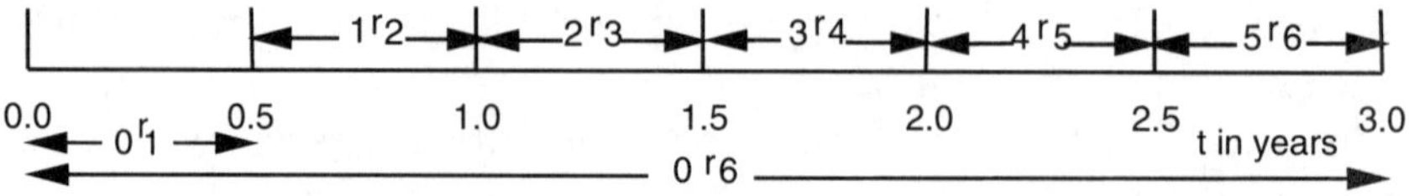

Let:

r_t = implied zero coupon rate for period 0 to t

$_{t-1}f_t$ = implied forward rate for period $t-1$ to t

Then:

$$\left(1 + \frac{r_t}{2}\right)^t = \left(1 + \frac{r_1}{2}\right)(1 + {}_1f_2)(1 + {}_2f_3) \ldots (1 + {}_{t-2}f_{t-1})(1 + {}_{t-1}f_t)$$

Rearranging this equation gives the implied forward rate for period $t-1$ to t as:

$$_{t-1}f_t = \left[\frac{(1 + r_t/2)^t}{(1 + r_1/2)(1 + {}_1f_2)(1 + {}_2f_3) \ldots (1 + {}_{t-2}f_{t-1})}\right] - 1$$

Example. Let's look at the zero-coupon curve from Exhibit 4–1. The implied forward rates can be derived as follows:

$$r_1 = {}_0f_1 = 0.022000$$

$$_1f_2 = \frac{1.022506^2}{1.022000} - 1 = 0.023012$$

$$_2f_3 = \frac{1.023015^3}{(1.022000)(1.023012)} - 1 = 0.024036$$

$$_3f_4 = \frac{1.024049^4}{(1.022)(1.023012)(1.024036)} - 1 = 0.027155$$

$$_4f_5 = \frac{1.024565^5}{(1.022)(1.023012)(1.024036)(1.027155)} - 1 = 0.026633$$

$$_5f_6 = \frac{1.025088^6}{(1.022)(1.023012)(1.024036)(1.027155)(1.026633)} - 1 = 0.027706$$

Even more simply, implied forward rates can be expressed by the following equation:

$$_{t-1}f_t = \frac{(1 + r_t/2)^t}{(1 + r_{t-1}/2)^{t-1}} - 1$$

Example.   To calculate the 2.0-year ($t = 4$) forward rate from above, proceed as follows:

$$_3f_4 = \frac{(1 + r_4/2)^4}{(1 + r_3/2)^3} - 1 = \frac{1.024049^4}{1.023015^3} - 1 = 0.027155$$

Now that we know how to derive implied *taxable* forward rates, how does that help in the valuation of derivative *tax-exempt* securities? How are expectations of future short-term tax-exempt rates incorporated? We answer these questions in the following section.

THE TAX-EXEMPT YIELD CURVE[4]

This section explores the eccentricities of the tax-exempt yield curve and the derivation of tax-exempt forward rates. *The implied tax-exempt forward rates are the crucial inputs underlying expectational analysis and the valuation procedures for tax-exempt derivative securities.*

Comparison to the Taxable Yield Curve

The overwhelming attraction of tax-exempt bonds for investors is the exemption of their interest from federal and certain state and local income taxes. Therefore, one would expect the tax-exempt yield curve to be derived from the Treasury yield curve on an after-tax basis, adjusting for the reduction in taxes associated with the purchase of municipal obligations. Compared to Treasury securities, municipal bonds have higher default risks, less liquidity, and more unusual redemption features—hence, increased uncertainty about future cash flows. Due to these characteristics of municipal

---

[4]This section in large part follows pp. 7–12 of G Gray and K Engebretson, "Residual Interest Bonds (RIBS)," *Municipal Finance Journal*, (vol. 13, no. 1, Spring 1992, pp. 1–29.

securities, assuming all else is equal, an investor would expect to receive a larger expected yield (on an after-tax basis) on municipal securities than on comparable Treasury securities. Otherwise, why would a rational investor endure the added risks and uncertainties?

Since the decision to invest in tax-exempt bonds is based upon an after-tax comparison, US tax policy and investors' individual tax rates are critical determinants of the shape of the tax-exempt yield curve. Also important are investors' analyses of potential default risk, liquidity risk, redemption risk, and tax law risk (i.e., future changes in tax policy governing municipal bonds).

Because of the great diversity among issuers, varying types of credit risks, and complex redemption features, the tax-exempt yield curve is not as *pure*, from the perspective of term structure of interest rates, as the Treasury yield curve. Indeed, there is no single tax-exempt yield curve; rather, a series of individual yield curves are purported to be the *benchmark* for municipal bonds with varying features. Tax-exempt yield curves for issues of varying credit quality are published by Delphis-Hanover Corporation on a daily basis in *Range of Yield Curve Scales*. Also, investment-grade tax-exempt yield curves for differing types of issues (general obligation credits, revenue bonds, and securities subject to the alternative minimum tax (AMT) and eligible for bank qualification) are published daily in *The Bond Buyer*. These tax-exempt yield curves reflect not only the various theories of the future course of short-term rates inherent in the Treasury yield curve but also the influences, over time, of potential default risk, lower liquidity, uncertain redemption features, and potential tax law changes.

To look at the general relationship between the Treasury yield curve and the tax-exempt yield curve, we compared short-term rates (the 91-day BEY Treasury bill rates versus the Kenny 30-day Short-Term Index adjusted to a BEY basis) and long-term rates (the 30-year Treasury bond rate versus the Bond Buyer Revenue Bond Index) for 624 weekly observations during the period September 1981 to September 1993. Exhibit 4–6 shows comparisons of short-term Treasury yields and short-term municipal yields for the period September 1981 to September 1993. Short-term municipal yields were consistently below short-term Treasury yields, with the exception of three observations which occurred at the end of the year, when there is usually a surge of issuance to beat year-end tax

EXHIBIT 4–6
A Comparison of Short-Term Rates in Municipal and Treasury Markets

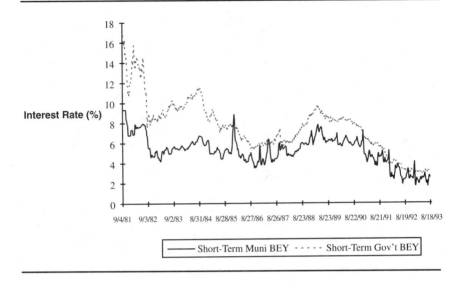

Interest Rate (%)

9/4/81   9/3/82   9/2/83   8/31/84   8/28/85   8/27/86   8/26/87   8/23/88   8/23/89   8/22/90   8/21/91   8/19/92   8/18/93

——— Short-Term Muni BEY   - - - - - Short-Term Gov't BEY

law changes, and one observation on April 15 (the payment date for individual income taxes), when short-term municipal rates have historically spiked, due to tax-payment disintermediation by individuals through withdrawals from tax-exempt money market funds.

The average short-term municipal yield for the period was 5.20 percent (the range was from 1.63 to 9.31 percent) while the average short-term Treasury yield was 7.61 percent (with a range of 2.74 to 17.36 percent).

Exhibit 4–7 shows comparisons of the long-term, 30-year Treasury yield and the long-term municipal yield for the same 624 observations. The exhibit shows that long-term municipal yields were very similar to the Treasury yields. The average long-term municipal yield was 8.27 percent (with a range of 5.45 to 13.44 percent) while the average long-term Treasury yield was 9.55 percent (with a range of 6.35 to 15.08 percent).

Exhibit 4–8 compares the ratios of short-term municipal to short-term Treasury yields and long-term municipal to long-term Treasury yields. This comparison shows a very interesting relationship. The

EXHIBIT 4–7

A Comparison of Long-Term Rates in Municipal and Treasury Markets

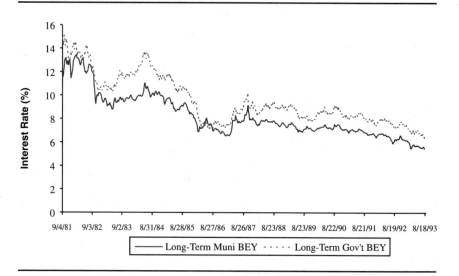

EXHIBIT 4–8

Ratios of Short- and Long-Term Rates in Municipal and Treasury Markets

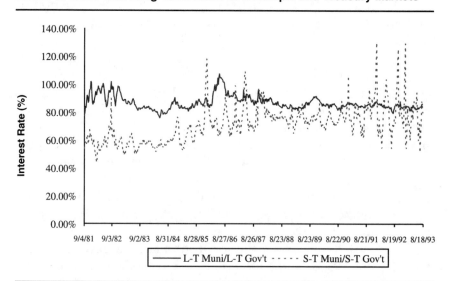

average ratio of long-term municipals to long-term Treasuries is a relatively high 86.6 percent, while the average ratio of short-term municipals to short-term Treasuries is a more modest 70.9 percent. The reasons for this differential are discussed in the next section.

Exhibit 4–9 shows another interesting comparison, which we use as a proxy for the slope of the yield curve. This exhibit compares the differences between short- and long-term rates in tax-exempt versus Treasury markets. The difference between the average short-term (5.20 percent) and the long-term (8.27 percent) municipal yields during the period was a substantial 3.07 percent, while the difference between the average short-term (7.61 percent) and the long-term (9.55 percent) Treasury yields was a more modest 1.94 percent.

Reasons for the More Pronounced Upward Slope of the Tax-Exempt Yield Curve

The above data describing the Treasury and tax-exempt yield curves suggest that the tax-exempt yield curve is consistently positive and more steeply sloped (with a 3.07 percent average differ-

EXHIBIT 4–9

Differences between Long- and Short-Term Rates in Municipal and Treasury Markets

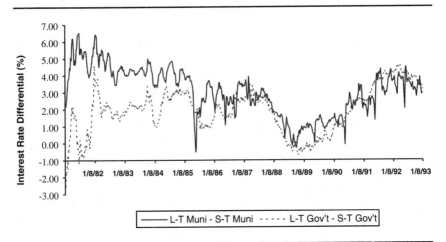

L-T Muni - S-T Muni · · · · · L-T Gov't - S-T Gov't

ence) than the Treasury yields (with a 1.94 percent average difference). What is the reason for this, and will these relationships continue? We believe that the steeper slope is principally due to the several differential risks inherent in municipal bonds which are not present in the US Treasury market (discussed above), and also due to the preferred habitat approach of investors in the tax-exempt market. Given current tax policy, particularly the recent increase to 39.6 percent in the maximum federal income marginal tax rates under the Omnibus Budget Reconciliation Act of 1993, we expect that this relationship will continue.

Academicians who are more familiar with the capital asset pricing model (CAPM) than with the municipal marketplace may doubt that participants in the tax-exempt market actually behave consistently with either the market segmentation theory or the preferred habitat theory. Underlying the CAPM are assumptions regarding perfect capital markets.[5] In the real world, however, market imperfections do exist—and these imperfections may move asset prices away from their theoretical values under CAPM. The imperfections are even more significant in relation to the tax-exempt market, as discussed below. One of the most important assumptions relating to the theories underlying the taxable yield curve is that investors can borrow and lend freely at the risk-free rate of interest. This assumption allows arbitrageurs to take advantage of pricing disparities along the yield curve to arbitrage discrepancies in Treasury bond prices into alignment. Another assumption inherent in CAPM is a neutral tax policy—that is, either that there are no taxes or that taxes on interest, dividends, and capital gains are equal.

The two perfect capital market assumptions stated above do not hold true for the municipal bond market. The interest payments associated with tax-exempt bonds are free from federal and certain state and local income taxes, while interest, dividend, and capital gains payments on most other investments are subject to taxation at rates of up to 39.6 percent. Also, investors are not allowed, under Section 265 of the Internal Revenue Code of 1986, to

---

[5] See C Haley and L Schall, Chapter 7 in *The Theory of Financial Decisions*, McGraw-Hill, New York, 1973.

deduct interest paid on borrowed monies invested in tax-exempt bonds. Therefore, not only is tax policy not neutral but arbitrageurs in the market must borrow at higher costs than the rates at which they can invest.

The strict regulation of tax-exempt money market funds (TEMMFs) also encourages behavior by participants in the tax-exempt market consistent with the preferred habitat theory. TEMMFs are restricted by Rule 2a-7 of the Investment Company Act of 1940 from owning tax-exempt securities that have a maturity or liquidity facility of longer than 397 calendar days. TEMMFs are also required to hold a dollar weighted average portfolio maturity not in excess of 90 days. These severe restrictions force them to bid aggressively for a relatively small percentage of instruments. According to the Federal Reserve Board in its 1993 *Third Quarter Flow of Funds Account*, there was approximately $1.2395 trillion in outstanding tax-exempt debt. Of that amount, $99.4 billion (8.02 percent of outstanding municipals) was held by approximately 200 TEMMFs. Therefore, this major investor base may participate only in the short-term municipal market.

Other short-term buyers in the tax-exempt market, principally corporations and investment advisers, look primarily at one concern: their tax-exempt return relative to after-tax returns on comparable taxable investments. The principal purchasers of SAVRS, for example, are corporations looking to invest excess cash on a short-term basis at the highest available after-tax return. The current maximum corporate tax rate of 35 percent, under the 1993 Tax Act, is therefore an important consideration in investors' evaluation of alternatives. Default, liquidity, prepayment, and tax law risks are of minimal concern to an investor who is buying short-term, AAA-rated securities. All else equal, short-term municipal rates can be expected to average slightly above 65 percent of comparable taxable instruments. The analysis in the previous section, showing an average ratio of 70.9 percent, is close to the predicted ratio for risk-free, liquid short-term securities.

Buyers of long-term tax-exempt securities, including individuals, insurance companies, and bond funds, have more pronounced concerns about default, liquidity, redemption, and tax law risks. The maximum individual income tax rate of 39.6 percent is still an important consideration. The analysis in the previous section shows an average ratio of long-term municipal rates to long-term Treasury rates of 86.6 percent. The difference in the average ratios between short- and long-term municipals and Treasuries is evidence for an additional upward bias in the municipal yield curve—even in a flat Treasury yield curve environment.

Implied Tax-Exempt Forward Rates

Earlier in this chapter, we addressed the derivation of implied forward rates from a full-coupon taxable Treasury yield curve. Under the pure expectations model of the yield curve, which most market participants use in valuing derivative securities, implied forward rates equal expected future short-term spot rates. However, our intention in this book is to address the valuation of *tax-exempt* derivative securities. Our focus in this section will be on the derivation of implied forward tax-exempt interest rates.

As previously discussed, because of a great diversity of issues, credit risk, and redemption features, the tax-exempt yield curve is not as pure as the Treasury yield curve is for the purpose of forecasting future expected short-term interest rates. Compared to Treasury securities, tax-exempt bonds have higher default risk, less liquidity, and more embedded redemption features, creating an increased uncertainty of future cash flow.

Because of the above-described uncertainties inherent in the municipal yield curve, participants in the municipal securities market generally have used *taxable yield curves* (e.g., LIBOR or Treasury) to derive implied forward taxable rates and, by multiplying them by a conversion ratio (e.g., 70 to 75 percent), to convert them to tax-exempt equivalent rates. Exhibit 4–10 summarizes sample implied tax-exempt forward rates, which are calculated by multiplying the implied taxable forward rates by a conversion ratio of 71 percent for the six-period, semiannual yield curve described above.

In the valuation analysis that follows in the rest of this book (Chapters 5 through 8), the Treasury yield curve will be used to derive implied taxable forward rates, $_{t-1}f_t$, and will be converted to implied tax-exempt forward rates, $_{t-1}f_t^*$, by multiplying by 71 percent. *The implied tax-exempt forward rates are the crucial inputs that are used in the valuation procedures for the hedging and option components*

EXHIBIT 4–10
Sample Yield Curve: Implied Tax-Exempt Forward Rates

(1)	(2)	(3)	(4)	(5)	(6)	(7)
		Annual Full-Coupon Rates	Semiannual Full-Coupon Rates	Implied Zero-Coupon Rates	Implied Taxable Forward Rates	Implied Tax-Exempt Forward Rates
Period t	Years n	C	$C/2$	$r_t/2$	$_{t-1}f_t$	$_{t-1}f_t^*$
1	0.5	4.400%	2.2000%	2.2000%	2.2000%	1.5620%
2	1.0	4.500%	2.2500%	2.2506%	2.3012%	1.6338%
3	1.5	4.600%	2.3000%	2.3015%	2.4036%	1.7065%
4	2.0	4.800%	2.4000%	2.4049%	2.7155%	1.9280%
5	2.5	4.900%	2.4500%	2.4565%	2.6633%	1.8909%
6	3.0	5.000%	2.5000%	2.5088%	2.7706%	1.9671%

of municipal derivative securities. These hedging and option components are valued in Chapters 6 and 7.

SUMMARY

In this chapter, we described the first basic concept, called *expectation analysis*, that is essential for understanding and valuing derivative securities. Expectational analysis is based upon the *pure expectations hypothesis* of the term structure of interest rates.

The *term structure of interest rates* refers to the relationship between yield and maturity for debt securities that are alike in all other respects. Yield versus maturity is the operative comparison. All other aspects of debt securities—default risk, tax treatment, liquidity, and embedded options—are held constant. The yield curve that many market participants use in quantifying the interest rate risks associated with the term structure of interest rates is the Treasury yield curve.

There are several theories regarding the yield curve and what the relationship between yield and maturity is supposed to explain. The theory that most market participants use in pricing and valuing derivative securities is the *pure expectations hypothesis*. According to the classical version of this theory, expected holding period returns for a debt security over multiple periods should be the same, regardless of whether an investor rolls over a sequence of short-maturity bonds or holds a long-term zero coupon bond. In other words, the yield curve reflects today's expectations of future short-term rates.

The yield curve that market participants observe is the *par yield curve*. This gives the yield to maturity on coupon-bearing bonds, where the coupon rates are the same as the yield to maturity. The par yield curve assumes that semiannual coupon payments are constantly reinvested at the bond's yield. Embedded in the par yield curve is coupon reinvestment risk—a natty problem that can be overcome by deriving a zero-coupon yield curve.

We showed how implied zero-coupon rates can be derived from a par yield curve. Implied zero-coupon rates are the set of discount rates that equates the cash flow of a full-coupon-bearing bond to the cash flow of the set of zero-coupon bonds. The *zero-coupon yield curve* is constructed by using yields to maturity on zero-coupon bonds, each of which has only a single cash flow.

Underlying the pure expectations model of the term structure of interest rates, or the yield curve, is a relationship between the current long-term rate and the rates on current (or spot) loans and expected future (or forward) short-term loans. On the *forward market,* a participant can contract for rates on loans or investments that begin at some time in the future. Using the zero-coupon yield curve and the law of one price arbitrage constraint, we showed how implied forward rates can be derived.

Next, we discussed the various eccentricities of the tax-exempt yield curve and noted that there are various reasons why it has a more pronounced upward slope than the Treasury yield curve. Most, if not all, municipal derivatives market participants use *taxable yield curves* (e.g., LIBOR or Treasury) to derive implied forward rates and, by multiplying by a conversion ratio (e.g., 70 to 75 percent), to convert them to implied tax-exempt forward rates. We emphasized that the implied tax-exempt forward rates are the crucial inputs that are used in the valuation procedures for the hedging and option components of municipal derivative securities.

CHAPTER 5

THE BUILDING BLOCKS—
DEBT COMPONENTS

INTRODUCTION

Complex derivative securities can be analyzed as a package of simpler securities, or *building blocks,* the value of which is dependent upon the sum of the underlying components. For the purposes of valuing municipal derivative securities, these building blocks can be broadly grouped into three categories:

1. *Debt or credit extension components:* fixed-rate bonds, zero-coupon bonds, and mortgage-style level amortizing debt. Only *positive* values are associated with these debt components. Typically, the relative value of the debt components at the time of issuance of the derivative security accounts for between 90 percent and 100 percent of the offering price of the security.

2. *Hedging or price-fixing components:* interest rate forward and future contracts, and interest rate swap contracts. The value of these components may be *positive* or *negative,* depending on movements of and shifts in the yield curve. These components are usually designed and priced such that their relative value at the time of issuance of the derivative security is zero. As interest rates shift, the relative values of hedging components typically range from +10 percent to −10 percent.

3. *Option or price insurance components:* interest rate floor and interest rate cap options. *Zero or positive* values are associated with these components, for the *owner* of the option,

whereas *zero or negative* values are associated with them, for the *writer* of the option. These components are usually designed and priced such that their relative value at the time of issuance of the derivative security ranges from -5 percent to $+5$ percent. Naturally, the value of these components will change as interest rates move.

In this chapter, we deal with the debt components, and in Chapters 6 and 7, we address the hedging and option components.

TYPES OF DEBT COMPONENTS

Debt components of a derivative security consist of the cash-flow obligations that may be thought of as the repayment of the *principal* plus the *normal payment* or accretion of *interest* on the derivative security. The three types of debt components considered below are: a fixed-rate bond component with semiannual interest payments; a zero-coupon bond component that pays, at maturity or redemption, the original principal along with interest that has accreted on a compounded semiannual basis; and a level-amortizing bond component that involves a set semiannual payment of both interest and principal.

Fixed-Rate Bond Component

A fixed-rate bond component of a municipal derivative security is analogous to a fixed-rate municipal bond, in which the fixed-rate bond component has a specified maturity date, a specified redemption price, and a fixed rate of interest payable semiannually, as well as any issuer-triggered early redemption features that may exist.

The issuer of the derivative security is obligated to make its semiannual interest and principal payments in accordance with its bond contract. As with a $5000 fixed-rate bond, interest is paid semiannually in arrears, on the $5000 principal amount outstanding. When the $5000 principal amount is retired in a lump principal repayment, interest stops accruing on the bond. Likewise, in the event of a payment default, the $5000 outstanding principal amount plus accrued interest generally are due immediately; the default accelerates the issuer's obligation to repay its debt.

Most of the derivative securities that we examine—such as RIBS, inverse floaters, cap bonds, and BEAR Floaters—most easily accommodate a fixed-rate bond approach in valuing their debt components. Graphically, the cash flows associated with a three-year, 4 percent fixed-rate ($100 in interest paid semiannually) par bond are as shown in Exhibit 5–1.

Zero-Coupon Bond Component

A zero-coupon bond component of a municipal derivative security is analogous to a zero-coupon municipal bond in which an issuer offers the zero-coupon bond at a specified price. Interest compounds, or accretes, semiannually on the zero-coupon bond at the offering yield (e.g., 4 percent) along a compound accreted value schedule. The zero-coupon bond has a specified maturity date (e.g., three years) and a specified maturity price (e.g., 100 percent), and any issuer-triggered early redemption features have a redemption price based on the compound accreted value schedule. The issuer is obligated by the bond contract to make a one-time payment of the maturity price on the maturity date to the holder of the zero-coupon bond component.

EXHIBIT 5–1
Three-Year Fixed-Rate Bond

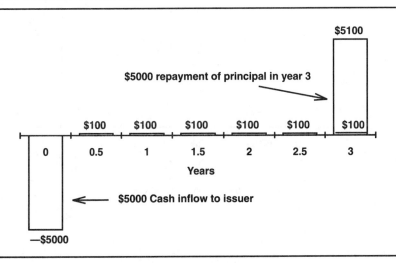

In the event of a default under the bond documents, the accreted value of the zero-coupon bond generally is due immediately and the issuer's obligation to repay its debt is accelerated.

Some derivative securities, such as Bond Payment Obligations, on which certain cash flows associated with the BPOs can be *stripped* and sold separately (see Chapter 8), easily accommodate a zero-coupon bond approach in valuing their debt components. An example of a zero-coupon bond with a $5000 maturity amount, a three-year maturity date, and a 4 percent offering yield would have an initial offering price of $4439.86. Graphically, its cash flows would be as shown in Exhibit 5–2.

Level-Amortizing Bond Component

A level-amortizing bond component of a municipal derivative security is analogous to a semiannually payable, level-debt mortgage payment in which the level-amortizing bond component has a series of semiannual interest and *principal* payments (e.g., $892.63); a specified final payment date (e.g., three years); a fixed rate of interest (e.g., 4 percent) payable semiannually, in arrears, based on the principal then outstanding; and any issuer-triggered early redemption features.

EXHIBIT 5–2
Three-Year Zero Coupon Bond

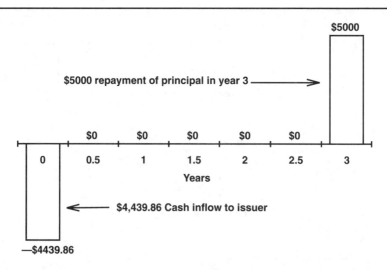

In the event of a payment default, the remaining principal amount outstanding of a level-amortizing bond component generally becomes due and the issuer's obligation to repay its debt is accelerated.

Certain BPOs, such as BULL and BEAR Annuity Coupons (see Chapter 8) easily accommodate a level-amortizing bond approach in valuing their debt components. For example, a level-amortizing bond with a $5000 initial offering price, a 4 percent interest rate, and a three-year final maturity would have a $892.63 semi-annual payment. Graphically, its cash flows would be as shown in Exhibit 5–3.

VALUATION OF DEBT COMPONENTS

The valuation process of these debt components is similar to the valuation process of any debt security. A characteristic of all fixed-income securities is that the present value of the debt component will decrease as the discount rate, or the set of discount rates, increases. Likewise, the value of the debt component will increase as the relevant discount rates decrease (see Exhibit 5–4).

EXHIBIT 5–3
Three-Year Level-Amortizing Bond

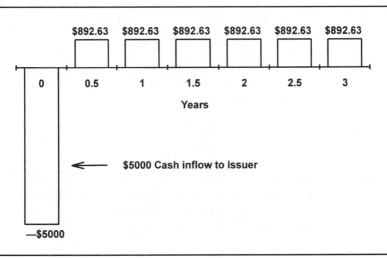

EXHIBIT 5–4
Present Value of Debt Components

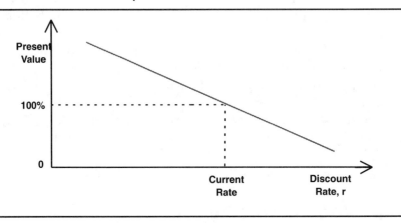

Basic Valuation Framework

Most practitioners in the bond markets are familiar with the calculation of yield to maturity, or internal rate of return, associated with bond pricing. You may recall the following equation, which was first given in Chapter 3.

Let:

$$P = \text{price of the bond}$$
$$C = \text{annual coupon payment}$$
$$F = \text{principal or face value}$$
$$y = \text{market discount rate}$$
$$t = \text{time}$$
$$n = \text{number of years to maturity}$$

Then:

$$P = \sum_{t=1}^{2n} \frac{C/2}{(1 + y/2)^t} + \frac{F}{(1 + y/2)^{2n}}$$

This equation is appropriate for valuing a fixed-rate bond, or the fixed-rate debt component of many municipal derivative securities, such as inverse floaters, RIBS, BEAR Floaters, cap bonds, and BULL Forward BPOs. In fact, its familiarity to municipal practitioners makes it easier to use than the method described below, which is technically more correct. We believe that the use of this equation is appropriate in most cases when valuing debt components of municipal derivatives, and we will use this method in valuing the five securities in Chapter 8.

However, the yield curve (particularly the municipal yield curve) is rarely flat, and standard bond valuation uses the same discount rate to value all expected future cash flows. When the focus is on the valuation of *strippable securities*, where distinct cash flows can be stripped and sold at the investor's option through a preset CUSIP mechanism, an adjustment must be made. Examples of strippable securities include certain strippable BPOs, derivative security cash-flow streams that resemble a series of zero-coupon payments, and level-amortizing debt services such as BULL and BEAR Floater BPOs. The way we will handle the valuation of the debt components of strippable and annuity, level-debt-style derivative securities is similar to the approach we used in Chapter 4, in which an implied zero-coupon curve was derived. We will start with an *issue-specific* full-coupon municipal yield curve for the bonds being offered. From the full-coupon municipal yield curve, an implied zero-coupon issue-specific yield curve will be derived. Then, the zero-coupon discount rates, r_t, will be used to price each of the individual expected semiannual cash flows. The individual cash flows will then be summed to determine a market value for the debt component.

For example, in Exhibit 5–5, an implied zero coupon yield curve is derived from a full-coupon tax-exempt yield curve in the manner described above.

Valuation of Zero-Coupon and Level-Amortizing Bond Components

Using the implied semiannual zero-coupon yield curve from column 5 of Exhibit 5–5, let's now value the cash flows associated with the zero-coupon bond component and the level-amortizing bond component examples shown above. To include the set of zero-coupon discount rates, $r_t/2$, instead of only one blended yield, y, the bond price equation is altered to the following:

EXHIBIT 5–5
Example of a Tax-Exempt Yield Curve

(1)	(2)	(3)	(4)	(5)	(6)
		Annual Full-Coupon Rates	Semiannual Full-Coupon Rates	Implied Semiannual Zero-Coupon Rates	Implied Annual Zero-Coupon Rates
Period t	Year n	C	$C/2$	$r_t/2$	r_t
1	0.5	3.500%	1.750%	1.750%	3.500%
2	1.0	3.600%	1.800%	1.801%	3.602%
3	1.5	3.700%	1.850%	1.851%	3.702%
4	2.0	3.800%	1.900%	1.902%	3.804%
5	2.5	3.000%	1.950%	1.954%	3.908%
6	3.0	4.000%	2.000%	2.006%	4.012%

$$P = \sum_{t=1}^{2n} \frac{C/2}{[1 + (r_t/2)]^t} + \frac{F}{[1 + (r_t/2)]^{2n}}$$

Each cash flow, $C/2$, is now discounted by the implied semiannual zero-coupon rate associated with the time it is expected to be received, $r_2/2$, as opposed to being discounted by a blended yield, y, which should represent a present-value weighted average of the individual zero-coupon spot rates.

Why are we suggesting this implied zero-coupon discounting approach for zero-coupon and level-amortizing bond components but not for fixed-rate bond components? The principal reasons for using two different approaches are:

1. The durations of the cash flows of the three different debt components are vastly different—2.86 years for the fixed-rate bond component, 3.0 years for the zero-coupon bond component, and 1.72 years for the level-amortizing bond component. Using an approach that does not take this difference in duration into consideration would give incorrect valuations relative to risk or price volatility levels.

2. It is *easier* for market participants that are familiar with yield calculations to plug in one discount rate, y, to their bond calculator or handheld calculator to value derivative

securities. Since the duration of a fixed-rate bond component equals the duration of a comparable fixed-rate bond,
using the standard bond equation for these municipal debt
components will give valuation results that are close
enough for government work.

Let's now value our zero-coupon and level-amortizing bond
components using the implied zero discount rate approach.

Assume that the zero-coupon bond component of a municipal derivative security has a $5000 maturity amount and a 3-year
maturity date, and that it is priced in accordance with the implied
semiannual zero-coupon yield curve of column 5 of Exhibit 5–5.
There is only one cash flow—$5000 in period $t = 6$. In this exam-
ple, the cash flow, F, is discounted at the six-period, implied semiannual discount rate, $r_6/2 = 2.006$ percent (at a 4.012 percent
annual rate).

Let:

$F = \$5000$

$r_6 = 2.006\%$

$n = 3$ years

$$P = \frac{\$5000}{(1.02006)^6} = \$4438.29$$

The valuation of $4438.29 is slightly different from the
$4439.86 value of the zero-coupon bond shown in Exhibit 5–2. This
difference is due to the use of different discounting rates, 4.012 percent versus 4.000 percent. The higher rate reflects the *implied zero-
coupon yield*. In an upward-sloping yield curve, the difference
between full-coupon rates and implied zero-coupon rates will increase with increasing time to maturity.

Let's now examine the valuation of an annuity or level-amortizing bond component. Assume that the level-amortizing bond
component makes six semiannual payments of $892.63, and that
the implied semiannual zero-coupon yield curve is that of column
5 of Exhibit 5–5. There are six cash flows, $892.63 in periods 1
through 6, to discount at the appropriate rates, $r_t/2$. The value of
this debt component is as follows:

$$P = \frac{892.63}{1.01750} + \frac{892.63}{1.01801^2} + \frac{892.63}{1.01851^3} + \frac{892.63}{1.01902^4}$$
$$+ \frac{892.63}{1.01954^5} + \frac{892.63}{1.02006^6}$$

$P = 877.28 + 861.33 + 844.84 + 827.83 + 810.30 + 792.35$

$P = \$5013.93$

The valuation of $5013.93 is significantly different from the $5000 value of the level-amortizing bond shown in Exhibit 5–3. This difference in valuation also is due to the different discount rates employed in using an implied zero-coupon curve.

Duration of Debt Components

In Chapter 3, we discussed the price and maturity measures of duration. The standard measure for fixed rate bonds is Macaulay's duration or modified duration. Recall that these measures of duration assume a flat yield curve or constant discount rate over the life of the bond. We use the same assumption of a constant discount rate when we value fixed-rate bond components. To be consistent with the valuation techniques of fixed-rate bonds, we calculate the duration of fixed rate components with the standard duration measures from Chapter 3. Remember, the time duration measure, D_t^*, and the price duration, D_p^*, are approximately equal for fixed-rate bonds. In Chapter 8, we value several derivative securities and calculate both the time and price duration measurements of the debt components of each of the securities using modified duration.

USE OF DEBT COMPONENTS IN MUNICIPAL DERIVATIVE SECURITIES

All the municipal derivative securities that have been marketed contain debt components that represent the greatest percentage in value (usually 90 to 100 percent) of the derivative security. Most of the derivative securities that recently have been marketed have debt components that may be easily valued. Naturally, the value of the debt component, like the value of any fixed-rate bond, will be dependent upon and inversely related to movements in yields of comparable fixed-rate municipals.

As you will see when each security is described in depth in Chapter 8, the fixed-rate bond component for the derivative securities can be analyzed as described below.

RIBS

The interest rate formula (on a bond equivalent basis) for the RIBS can be derived as follows:

RIBS rate + SAVRS rate = 2(6.25%)
RIBS rate = 2(6.25%) − SAVRS rate
RIBS rate = 6.25% + (6.25% − SAVRS rate)

We will analyze the RIBS as a combination of a fixed-rate debt component at 6.25 percent and an interest rate swap hedging component, which will be described in Chapter 6, of 6.25 percent minus the SAVRS rate. The AA-rated RIBS matures on August 1, 2014, and is callable on August 1, 2003, at a price of 104 percent. The fixed-rate bond component will be valued using these parameters. On January 3, 1994, according to the data in Exhibit 2–3, a comparable-maturity fixed-rate, AA-rated bond should be valued at a yield of 5.25 percent. We will value the RIBS to maturity and to the earlier call dates in Chapter 8.

Inverse Floater

The interest rate formula for the inverse floater is:

c = 6.15% + (4.70% − Kenny Index) prior to 8/15/1999

c = 6.15% from 8/15/1999 until maturity on 8/15/2012

We will analyze the inverse floater as a combination of a fixed-rate debt component at 6.15 percent and an interest rate swap component, also described in Chapter 6, of 4.70 percent minus the Kenny Index. The AA-rated inverse floater matures on August 15, 2012, and is callable on August 15, 2002, at a price of 102 percent. According to Exhibit 2–3, on January 3, 1994, a comparable-maturity fixed-rate, AA-rated bond should be valued at a yield of 5.20 percent. We will value the inverse floater in Chapter 8.

Cap Bond

The interest rate formula for the cap bond is:

$c = 6.60\% + MAX$ (0%, PSA Index $- 3.50\%$) prior to 10/1/1997
$c = 6.60\%$ from 10/1/1997 until maturity on 10/1/2016

We will analyze the cap bond as a combination of a fixed-rate debt component at 6.60 percent and an interest rate cap option component, described in Chapter 7, of MAX (0%, PSA Index $- 3.50\%$). The Baa-1-rated cap bond matures on October 1, 2016, and is callable on October 1, 2002, at a price of 101.5 percent. According to Exhibit 2–3, a comparable-maturity, fixed-rate A-rated (no Baa-1 rating) should be valued at approximately a yield of 5.60 percent. We will value the cap bond in Chapter 8.

BEAR Floater

The interest rate formula for the BEAR Floater is:

$c = 6.10\% + 2$ (Kenny Index $- 5.00\%$) prior to 8/15/2002
$c = 6.10\%$ from 8/15/2002 until maturity on 8/15/2012

The minimum (4 percent) and maximum (8.2 percent) rates on the BEAR Floater will be addressed in Chapter 7. We will analyze the BEAR Floater as a combination of a fixed-rate debt component at 6.10 percent and hedging and option components. The AAA-rated (insured) BEAR Floater matures on August 15, 2022, and is callable on August 15, 2002, at a price of 102 percent. According to Exhibit 2–3, an AAA (insured) bond maturing in 2022 should be valued at a yield of 5.45 percent. We will value the BEAR Floater in Chapter 8.

BULL Forward BPO

The interest rate formula for the BULL Forward BPO is:

$c = 5.20\%$ prior to 6/15/1994
$c = 5.20\% + 3$ (interest rate adjustment) from 6/15/1994 until maturity on 6/15/2005

The interest rate adjustment is explained in Chapter 8. We will analyze the BULL Forward BPO as a combination of a fixed-rate debt component at 5.20 percent and hedging and option components. The AAA-rated (insured) BULL Forward matures on June 15, 2005. According to Exhibit 2–3, an AAA (insured) bond maturing in 2005 should be valued at a yield of 4.75 percent. We will value the BULL Forward BPO in Chapter 8.

SUMMARY

In this chapter, we began to describe the process of valuing a complex derivative security as a package of simpler securities, or building blocks, and we focused on the debt component building blocks.

The debt component consists of the cash-flow obligations of a derivative security, which may be thought of as the repayment of principal plus the normal payment or accretion of interest. The debt component represents the largest percentage, usually 90 to 100 percent at issuance, of the value of a municipal derivative security. The three types of debt components that we considered were a fixed-rate bond component, a zero-coupon bond component, and a level-amortizing bond component.

We also discussed the valuation of debt components. As with any fixed-income security, the present value of a debt component will decrease as yields increase. We saw that standard debt valuation procedures work very well in valuing the fixed-rate debt components of the five municipal derivative securities that we will value in Chapter 8. We also discussed, however, the special cases involved in valuing certain *strippable* or *level-amortizing* debt components. We found that, in these cases, each cash flow should be discounted at the implied zero-coupon rate associated with the time when it is expected to be received.

CHAPTER 6

THE BUILDING BLOCKS— HEDGING COMPONENTS

Forwards, Futures, and Swaps

INTRODUCTION[1]

The *hedging component building blocks* of municipal derivative securities consist of financial instruments with interest payments contingent upon future levels of interest rates or upon an interest rate index. They are called *hedging* components because financial instruments with similar payment characteristics often are used to hedge or offset price changes of other financial assets or liabilities held in a portfolio. The nature of a hedge instrument is that its value reacts to a change in interest rates in a manner *opposite* to the change in value of the asset or liability that is being hedged.

Two types of hedging components have been used in municipal derivative securities and will be examined in this chapter. These are payment instruments that resemble forwards and futures, and payment instruments that resemble interest rate swaps. As with any financial asset, the present value of a forward contract, a futures contract, or an interest rate swap contract equals the discounted value of its expected future cash flows. The *amount of the expected future cash flows* used in the valuation of these hedging

---

[1]For an in-depth description of forwards, futures, and interest rate swaps, see one of the following books: T Campbell and W Kracaw, *Financial Risk Management*, Harper Collins, New York, 1993; R Kolb, *Financial Derivatives*, Kolb Publishing Company, Miami, FL, 1993; or J Hull, *Introduction to Futures and Options Markets*, Prentice-Hall, Englewood Cliffs, NJ, 1991).

components is based upon *implied forward rates*. The *present values* of the expected future cash flows are calculated by *discounting* each cash flow at the appropriate *implied zero-coupon rate*. Depending on the yield curve, the implied forward rates, and the implied zero-coupon rates, the value of the hedging components of municipal derivative securities may be positive, zero, or negative.

The valuation of hedging components is primarily dependent on the level and movement of interest rates—*interest rate risk*. An additional concern is credit risk, which effects the likelihood that an obligor, or counterparty, in a derivative security will make the payments that it has contractually promised to pay. To handle credit risk, numerous methods have been used, including marking to market of margin accounts, credit insurance, collateralization, and third-party guarantees. The valuation procedures that we will focus on in this chapter and in Chapter 7 relate solely to interest rate risk and assume that counterparty credit concerns have been adequately addressed.

In the sections that follow, we examine these hedging components—the payment streams embedded in municipal derivative securities which resemble forwards and futures, as well as those which resemble interest rate swaps. Careful attention is paid to the techniques that are used to value the components. These techniques use expectational analysis and implied forward rates.

FORWARD-LIKE AND FUTURE-LIKE COMPONENTS

Many derivative securities have the characteristics of forwards and futures. For this reason, understanding the structure, valuation and use of these contracts is important to understanding municipal derivative securities. In this section, we describe common interest rate futures contracts and the theory behind their valuation. We also describe the use of forwards and how they appear in the municipal market.

Introduction

A *forwards or futures contract* is a *two-sided agreement* between a buyer and a seller, in which the settlement price of an asset or an index is agreed upon in advance. The parties agree to the delivery of an asset, or the settlement of a price differential based on an index, at some time in the future. The term "two-sided" implies that both parties are obligated to fulfill the contractual agreement whether prices go up or down. In a *spot transaction,* the trade occurs *immediately* and is settled in accordance with normal settlement procedures (usually two to seven days). With a *forwards* or *futures* contract, the price and terms of the trade are set, but the settlement date is *delayed* for a predetermined period of time (usually from one month to two years). The buyer or owner of a forwards or futures contract is *long* the contract. This party receives delivery of the asset, the financial instrument, or the fixed index versus the floating-rate payment. The seller or writer of the forwards or futures contract is *short* the contract. This party delivers the asset, financial instrument, or the fixed index versus the floating-rate payment.

Forwards and futures contracts are similar in terms of their price performance and their valuation. However, in the financial marketplace a *futures contract* is a highly standardized forwards contract that has a standard contract size, standard settlement procedures, and a limited number of settlement dates. In contrast, a *forwards contract* is a specially tailored financial arrangement that may be designed to meet a particular transactional objective. Futures contracts are traded on certain commodity exchanges; they have an advantage over forwards contracts both because of their greater liquidity and because of their more established settlement and margin procedures, which reduce counterparty default risk.

Since our interests lie in interest rate sensitivity and price performance characteristics of securities, as opposed to institutional and settlement differences, the terms "forwards" and "futures" will be used interchangeably. In addition, the focus of this book is on forwards and futures contracts that are based on a financial instrument or a financial index, as opposed to tangible commodities (e.g., pork bellies). Below, we present three examples of financial futures contracts that are traded on exchanges. The Treasury bond futures contract is designed such that the change in value of the contract over time should approximately equal the change in value of a 20-year, 8 percent Treasury bond. The change in value of the municipal bond futures contract should approximately mimic the change in value of a comparable similar-term municipal bond. The change in value of a three-month Eurodollar futures contract is designed to approximate the change in three-month rates that is expected in the Eurodollar market on each forward delivery date. Eurodollar futures rates are very similar to implied forward rates.

Treasury Bond Futures Contract

The Treasury bond futures contract that we will examine has a $100,000 face value and is quoted in terms of a *hypothetical* 20-year-maturity Treasury bond with an 8 percent current coupon. The price and yield on the contract vary with market conditions: as long-term Treasury rates rise, the price of the contract falls proportionately to the change in the price of a 20-year, 8 percent bond. For example, if the spot interest rate on a 20-year Treasury bond goes from 7.5 percent to 7.75 percent, and the spot Treasury price falls from 105.138 percent to 102.521 percent, we will expect the Treasury futures price to have an *approximately* equal magnitude of price change. If comparable Treasury interest rates fall, the price of the Treasury bond futures contract will be expected to rise commensurately. Delivery options and complex conversion factors are associated with the delivery of the securities to fulfill the seller's obligation under the contract, but they are not germane to our discussion (see footnote 3 on page 144). The Treasury bond futures contract has been very successful; in fact, it is the most popular long-term interest index futures contract. Settlement dates for the contract extend out 18 months, and there is significant activity from market participants for both hedging and speculating purposes. Exhibit 6–1 shows trading results in Treasury bond contracts for the Chicago Board of Trade (CBOT) on January 3, 1994.

Exhibit 6–1

TREASURY BONDS (CBT)—$100,000; pts. 32nds of 100%							
					Yield		Open
	Open	High	Low	Settle	Chg	Settle	Chg	Interest
Mar	114-16	114-18	113-13	113-20	– 28	6.749	+ .073	275,879
June	113-10	113-11	112-11	112-18	– 28	6.838	+ .074	12,371
Sept	112-08	112-08	111-14	111-19	– 28	6.921	+ .075	18,341
Dec	112-04	112-04	111-04	111-08	– 29	6.950	+ .077	13,192
Mr95	110-26	110-26	110-12	11-014	– 29	7.021	+ .079	62
Est vol 400,000; vol Fri 63,670; op int 319.724, + 1,231.							

Source: *The Wall Street Journal*, Jan. 4, 1994, Page C–14.

Municipal Bond Futures Contract

The municipal bond futures contract that we will discuss is an interest rate futures contract the value of which is based on the value of *The Bond Buyer 40-Bond* Index. The BBI-40 is the average converted price for long-term municipal revenue and general obligation bonds that have certain size, term, call, and liquidity characteristics. The BBI-40 was designed as a proxy for the movement in prices of municipal bonds with changes in interest rates. The municipal bond futures index has a contract size equal to $1000 multiplied by the BBI-40. As municipal bond interest rates rise, the BBI-40 declines. The converse relationship also holds. There is no delivery of an underlying commodity associated with municipal bond futures. Settlement amounts are based solely upon the price at which a participant buys and sells the contract. For example, a market participant who bought the March 1994 municipal bond futures contract on October 25, 1993, at 103 + 12/32, and sold the contract on January 3, 1994, at 102 + 8/32, would have lost $(1 + 4/32) \times \$1000 = \$1125$ on the single contract. Settlement dates for the municipal bond futures contract currently extend out only six months. Exhibit 6–2 shows trading results in municipal bond contracts for the CBOT, on January 3, 1994.

Eurodollar Futures Contract

The Eurodollar futures contract is an interest rate futures contract with a $1 million face value. Its value and settlement price are based upon the three-month Eurodollar deposit rate. The Eurodollar futures contract was designed as a proxy for expectations of changes in future short-term interest rates. The futures price is equal to 100 percent minus the annualized yield for three-month

Exhibit 6–2

MUNI BOND INDEX (CBT)—$1,000; times Bond buyer MBI							
	Open	High	Low	Settle	Chg	High	Low	Open Interest
Mar	103-06	103-06	102-07	102-08	– 30	105-22	99-22	24,074

Est vol 3,500; vol Fri 789; open int 24,115, +53.
The Index; Close 103-18; Yield 5.65.

Source: *The Wall Street Journal*, Jan. 4, 1994, Page C-14.

Eurodollar time deposits. For example, if the three-month Eurodollar time deposit rate were 4.55 percent, the futures price for the nearest contract would equal approximately 100 percent minus 4.55 percent, or 95.45 percent. As Eurodollar deposit rates rise, the futures price declines. A 1-BP change in the futures price equals a change in value of the futures contract of $1 million × 0.0001 × 0.25 year = $25. As with the municipal bond futures contract, there is no delivery of an underlying commodity. Settlement amounts are based solely upon the price at which a participant buys and sells the contract. Settlement dates for the Eurodollar futures contract currently extend seven years, with four settlement months (March, June, September, and December) per year. These contracts are extremely popular with market participants in the interest rate swap market who need to hedge the short end of the yield curve by undertaking transactions in the Eurodollar futures market. Exhibit 6–3 shows trading results in Eurodollar futures contracts for the Chicago Mercantile Exchange (CME) on January 3, 1994.

Exhibit 6–3

EURODOLLAR (CME)—$1 million; pts of 100%

	Open	High	Low	Settle	Chg	Yield Settle	Chg	Open Interest
Mar	96.48	96.50	96.45	96.46	− .03	3.54 +	.03	399,366
June	96.14	96.14	96.08	96.10	− .05	3.90 +	.05	328,494
Sept	95.83	95.83	95.75	95.78	− .06	4.22 +	.06	250,654
Dec	95.42	95.42	95.43	95.36	− .07	4.64 +	.07	175,151
Mr95	95.26	95.26	95.19	95.21	− .07	4.79 +	.07	186,557
June	95.02	95.02	94.95	94.97	− .07	5.03 +	.07	126,661
Sept	94.83	94.83	94.76	94.77	− .07	5.23 +	.07	112,073
Dec	94.51	94.52	94.45	94.46	− .07	5.54 +	.07	85,648
Mr96	94.49	94.49	94.41	94.41	− .08	5.59 +	.08	82,034
June	94.30	94.30	94.24	94.24	− .08	5.76 +	.08	62,950
Sept	94.17	94.17	94.11	94.10	− .09	5.90 +	.09	55,929
Dec	93.92	93.92	93.84	93.84	− .09	6.16 +	.09	44,279
Mr97	93.90	93.90	93.83	93.84	− .09	6.16 +	.09	42,419
June	93.77	93.77	93.70	93.71	− .09	6.29 +	.09	34,639
Sept	93.67	93.67	93.61	93.61	− .09	6.39 +	.09	32,673
Dec	93.45	93.45	93.39	93.39	− .09	6.61 +	.09	25,548
Mr98	93.45	93.45	93.41	93.42	− .09	6.58 +	.09	21,845
June	93.35	93.35	93.31	93.32	− .09	6.68 +	.09	16,829
Sept	93.29	93.29	93.25	93.25	− .10	6.75 +	.10	9,505
Dec	93.12	93.12	93.08	93.08	− .10	6.92 +	.10	6,563
Mr99	93.17	93.17	93.13	93.13	− .10	6.87 +	.10	3,014
June	93.07	93.09	93.06	93.06	− .10	6.94 +	.10	2,976
Sept	93.04	93.05	93.02	93.03	− .10	6.97 +	.10	2,831
Dec	....	....	....	92.88	− .10	7.12 +	.10	2,251
Mr00	92.95	92.96	92.94	92.94	− .10	7.06 +	.10	1,943
June	92.90	92.91	92.89	92.89	− .10	7.11 +	.10	2,244
Sept	92.88	92.89	92.87	92.87	− .10	7.13 +	.10	1,599
Dec	92.75	92.75	92.73	92.73	− .10	7.27 +	.10	334
June01	....	....	....	92.71	− .10	7.29 +	.10	207
Sept	....	....	....	92.68	− .10	7.32 +	.10	140

Est vol 231,298; vol Fri 71,650; open int 2,116,982, −557.

Source: *The Wall Street Journal*, Jan. 4, 1994, Page C-14.

The Relationship between Spot Prices and Futures Prices[2]

We use the following notation:

P = spot price of a bond

$E(P_t)$ = expected price of a bond at time t

B_t = current price of a futures contract that settles at time t

t = time in semiannual periods

There are three basic relationships between spot prices (or cash market prices), futures prices, and expected spot prices that, because of arbitrage considerations, generally hold in the marketplace. These relationships are:

1. The current price of a futures contract, B_t, with a settlement date of t, should have a relationship to the expected spot price of the asset at time t, $E(P_t)$.

2. The current price of the futures contract, B_t, should be related to the current spot price of the asset, P. Any difference between the spot price, P, and the futures price, B_t, is associated with the *cost of carry*—the cost of storing, holding, and/or financing the underlying asset.

3. When the settlement date, t, is reached, the futures price, B_t, must equal the spot price, P, due to arbitrage constraints. Further, the *property of convergence* states that futures and spot prices will move toward each other as the futures contract approaches its settlement date.

Exhibit 6–4 shows the relationship between price and time for spot and futures prices. In panel A, as time passes and the settlement date, t, approaches, the futures price approaches the spot price from above. This movement is consistent with the theory of *contango*, which associates futures pricing predominantly with the hedging of the purchase of an asset with futures contracts that are expensive compared to spot market prices. In panel B, the futures price approaches the spot price from below, which posits an excess demand for short positions in the futures contract. This type of

---

[2]The discussion in this section and the next follows pages 124–135 of Campbell and Kracaw, *Financial Management*.

EXHIBIT 6–4
Property of Convergence

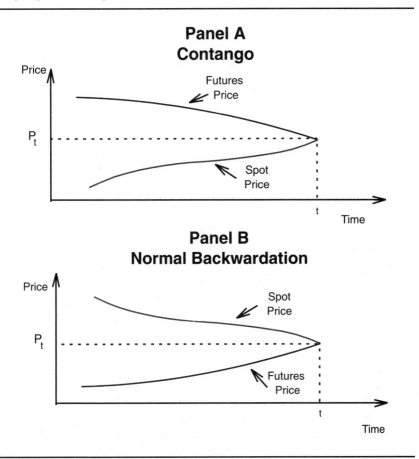

Panel A
Contango

Panel B
Normal Backwardation

pricing mechanism generally is seen in the pricing of Treasury bond futures, municipal bond futures, and Eurodollar futures (see Exhibits 6–1, 6–2, and 6–3). This pricing relationship is consistent with the theory of *normal backwardation* of interest rates, which posits a tendency toward an upward-sloping yield curve.

Because of arbitrage constraints, as described in the next section, in equilibrium there is a necessary triangular relationship between an assets spot market price, P, the current price of a futures contract, B_t, with settlement date of t, and the expected spot price, $E(P_t)$, at time t, that can be thought of as shown in Exhibit 6–5.

EXHIBIT 6–5
Equilibrium Condition for Prices in Spot and Futures Markets

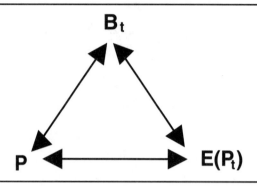

The relationship involves a simultaneous balance between the three variables P, B_t, and $E(P_t)$. A change in one variable involves a necessary change in the other two variables to maintain a three-way equilibrium. The key to these relationships, and to the price changes of the three variables for the interest rate forwards and futures hedging components of municipal derivative securities, is *implied forward rates*.

Arbitrage and the Cost of Carry Condition

According to the *cost of carry condition*, the difference between the spot price, P, of a commodity and its price for future delivery, B_t, at time t, is determined by the costs associated with carrying the commodity until the settlement date of the transaction. Carrying costs for commodities include the costs of transportation, insurance, storage, and financing. For physical commodities (such as soybeans, gold, and wheat) transportation, insurance, and storage costs are significant, whereas, for financial futures and forwards contracts, the only significant cost is the *financing cost*.

Perfect Capital Markets and Non-Coupon-Bearing Spot Commodities
The cost of carry condition defines the relationships between spot prices and forwards or futures prices such that risk-free arbitrage profits are not possible. To keep things simple, we initially will

look at prices for forwards delivery contracts on zero-coupon bonds. The cost of carry equation for financial futures and forwards contracts is:

$$B_t = P(1 + r_t)^t$$

where r_t is the zero-coupon discount rate for the period from time 0 to the settlement date, t, of the contract.

If the equilibrium price relationship does not hold, in perfect capital markets it is possible to execute trades that lock in arbitrage profits. Trading will tend to drive the spot–futures price relationship back to equilibrium. For instance, if:

$$B_t < P(1 + r_t)^t$$

the asset is trading at a premium in the spot market. An arbitrage opportunity exists whereby a participant can buy the futures contract, sell short the spot commodity, and invest the proceeds from the short-sale at r_t until settlement of the futures contract. This type of transaction is described in the example shown in Exhibits 6–6 and 6–7.

In perfect capital markets, the transactions shown in Exhibit 6–6 do not require any net money to execute. The proceeds of the short sale of the spot asset are reinvested at r_t, and no money is required on the futures contract until settlement.

EXHIBIT 6–6
Opening Transaction (Day 0)

1. Sell short spot asset at P and receive P.
2. Invest proceeds of short sale, P, at r_t.
3. Buy futures contract at B_t.

Net proceeds = 0

EXHIBIT 6–7
Closing Transactions (Day N)

1. Receive spot asset for price, B_t.
2. Repay short position by delivering spot asset.
3. Receive proceeds of investment, $P(1 + r_t)^t$.

Net proceeds = $P(1 + r_t)^t - B_t$

The close-out portion of the arbitrage transaction (Exhibit 6–7) is accomplished on day t by receiving the spot asset for payment of price B_t, repaying the short position by delivering the spot asset that cost B_t, and receiving the proceeds of investment, $P(1 + r_t)^t$.

If it is possible to conduct transactions in which no net proceeds are required on day 0 (Exhibit 6–6) and a guaranteed profit is generated on day t (Exhibit 6–7), market participants will buy undervalued futures contracts and will short the spot asset until the price equilibrium is reestablished.

Similar market transactions will occur if forwards and futures contracts are priced at a premium to spot prices, as follows:

$$B_t > P(1 + r_t)^t$$

In this situation, risk-free arbitrage profits can be generated by buying the spot asset at P and financing the purchase for t days at r_t, and selling the futures contract at B_t (see Exhibit 6–8).

Closing out this arbitrage transaction on day t involves receiving B_t for the delivery of the spot asset, and repaying the loan P plus interest of r_t (see Exhibit 6–9).

To the extent that B_t exceeds $P(1 + r_t)^t$, market participants will buy the undervalued spot commodity and sell the overvalued futures contracts on day 0 until the price equilibrium is reestablished.

EXHIBIT 6–8
Opening Transaction (Day 0)

---

1. Buy spot asset at P and pay P.
2. Borrow amount P at interest rate r_t for t days.
3. Sell futures contract B_t.

Net proceeds = 0

EXHIBIT 6–9
Closing Transaction (Day N)

---

1. Receive B_t for the delivery of the spot asset.
2. Repay loan $P(1 + r_t)^t$.

Net proceeds = $B_t - P(1 + r_t)^t$

The Cost of Carry Condition and Implied Forwards Rates

As seen above, the cost of carry condition is based on arbitrage opportunities and the action of market participants to undertake transactions to drive market prices back into equilibrium. In perfect capital markets, the price of an asset at settlement date t should be the same whether it is bought today in the spot market and *carried* until settlement date, or purchased through a futures contract with delivery on the settlement date. Embedded in this arbitrage approach is a relationship between spot and forwards prices and the *forwards rate implied* by the term structure of interest rates.

We will now present a simple example of this relationship using zero-coupon bonds and forwards contracts on zero-coupon bonds. Assume that a one-year, zero-coupon bond with semiannual compounding yields 8 percent; a two-year, zero-coupon bond yields 10 percent; and the price of a forwards contract on a $1000 zero-coupon bond with one year to maturity and a delivery date one year from today is $870.00. Using the implied forwards yield calculations described in Chapter 4, the relationships shown in Exhibit 6–10 in the spot and futures markets hold.

The one-year implied forwards yield, assuming semiannual compounding, from period $t = 2$ (year 1) to period $t = 4$ (year 2) is computed as 12.380 percent. The implied futures yield, $_2b_4$, based on a price of $870 at time $t = 2$ (year 1) is 14.943 percent. The price of the one-year, zero-coupon bond deliverable in one year, implied by the yield curve in the spot market, is ($1000/1.12380) = $889.83. The price of the one-year, zero-coupon bond deliverable in one year in the futures market is $870.00—a difference of $19.83. Is there an arbitrage opportunity here? As Rocky Mountain State inhabitants would say, "You bet!"

EXHIBIT 6–10

Spot Market	Futures Market
$r_2 = 8.00\%,\ r_4 = 10.00\%$	$B_2 = \$870.00$
$_2f_4 = \dfrac{(1 + r_4/2)^4 - 1}{(1 + r_2/2)^2}$	$_2b_4 = \dfrac{\$1000.00}{\$870.00} - 1$
$_2f_4 = 12.380\%$	$_2b_4 = 14.943\%$

The cash-and-carry arbitrage opportunity is to buy one-year, zero-coupon bonds deliverable in one year in the futures market at $870.00, and then to sell them in the cash market and arbitrage the yield curve opportunity. This strategy is shown in Exhibit 6–11.

In perfect capital markets, for financial forwards and futures contracts, there is a necessary triangular relationship between the spot market price, P, the futures price, B_t, and the expected spot price, $E(P_t)$, at time t. This relationship is driven and determined by implied forwards interest rates.

Coupon-Bearing Spot Commodities

We now introduce a complicating element into the spot–futures price relationships: The underlying spot commodities in financial futures and forwards contracts make periodic interest payments. For instance, the spot commodity that underlies the Treasury bond futures contract is a hypothetical 8 percent, 20-year Treasury bond that pays interest every 6 months.[3] The municipal bonds underlying the municipal bond futures contract pay interest every six months. How should this interest payment affect the spot–futures price relationship?

The cost of delivering an asset on the settlement date, t, should be the same whether the asset is delivered through the futures market with futures price, B_t, or through the spot market with cost of carry $P(1 + r_t)^t$. This is the basic principle underlying the cash-and-carry condition.

We can continue to follow the cost of carry arbitrage approach and see how the receipt of coupon payments on the spot commodity affects the relationship. Assume that the spot commodity (Trea-

---

[3]Although prices and yields on Treasury bond futures contracts are quoted in terms of a hypothetical 20-year, 8 percent bond, the CBOT allows a seller of the Treasury bond futures contract to deliver many different specific Treasury bonds to satisfy the seller's obligation under the contract. A deliverable Treasury bond must have at least 15 years to the shorter of its maturity or first call date. Depending on the coupon rate, maturity date, and call date of the Treasury bond, the CBOT determines a *conversion factor* that estimates the price that the particular Treasury bond would sell for at the beginning date of the month of delivery if the *yield* on the Treasury bond were 8 percent. The Treasury bond futures contract calls for delivery of a $100,000 face amount of 20-year, 8 percent bonds. If the conversion factor on a high-coupon Treasury bond were 1.2, the seller of a Treasury bond futures contract could deliver $83,333.33 ($100,000/1.2) principal amount of that bond to fulfill the contractual obligation.

EXHIBIT 6–11
Cash-and-Carry Arbitrage Example

Day 0

1. Buy one-year futures contract at $870 for settlement in year (1).
2. Invest $822.70 at 8% for 1 year (with semiannual compounding).
3. Borrow $822.70 at 10% for 2 years (with semiannual compounding).

Net proceeds = $0

Year 1

1. Purchase one-year, zero-coupon spot asset at $870.
2. Receive proceeds of investment of $822.70 $(1 + 0.08/2)^2 = 889.83.

Net proceeds = $19.83

Year 2

1. Receive maturity of one-year, zero-coupon bond = $1000.
2. Pay off $822.70 borrowing that compounded to $1000.

Net proceeds = $0

---

sury bonds or municipal bonds) yields y and pays interest semiannually. Also assume that it is possible to borrow or invest for the term of the forwards or futures contract, t, at the fixed-rate c, also paid semiannually. Note that the maturity date of the spot commodity (e.g., 20 years) is significantly longer than the settlement date of the futures contract (e.g., 1 month to 2 years).

Market participants have the option of buying the spot commodity and immediately receiving the yield, y, or buying the futures contract for delivery on date t at price B_t and investing P at a fixed yield of c until day t. The cost of carry condition in perfect capital markets states that these two date t delivery options should be equal. This means that on day 0, the futures–spot price relationship should be:

$$B_t(1 + y)^t = P(1 + c)^t$$

If we divide both sides of this equation by $(1 + y)^t$, we can isolate the relationship among the theoretical futures price, B^t, the yield of the spot commodity, y, and the cost of financing the position until settlement date c. The result is:

$$B_t = P\,\frac{(1 + c)^t}{(1 + y)^t}$$

This result provides an important relationship between spot and futures prices and yields for the spot commodity, y, and the financing cost, c. The yield associated with the spot commodity, 20-year Treasury bonds or municipal bonds, is a long-term yield. The yield associated with the financing cost, c, is coincident with the settlement date, t, and generally is a short-term yield (one year or less). *Therefore this is essentially a yield curve relationship.* If $y > c$, the spot commodity long-term yield is greater than the financing cost and the futures price should be less than the spot commodity price.

Example.
Let:

$P = 100$
$y = 6.00\%$, paid semiannually
$c = 3.00\%$, paid semiannually
$t = 2$ semiannual periods

Then:

$$B_2 = 100\,\frac{(1 + 0.03/2)^2}{(1 + 0.06/2)^2}$$

$$B_2 = \frac{1.030225}{1.0609}$$

$$B_2 = 97.1086$$

In an upward-sloping yield curve in which the spot yield is greater than the financing rate, the futures price is typically at a discount to the spot price. The futures price generally trades at a discount to the spot price. The discount is a function of the difference between the financing cost and the spot commodity yield and the amount of time to the settlement of the contract.

The converse relationship also holds. Futures prices are at a premium to spot prices when there is an inverted yield curve.

Example.
Let:

$P = 100$
$y = 6.00\%$

$$y = 6.00\%$$

$t = 2$ semiannual periods

Then:

$$B_2 = 100 \; \frac{(1 + 0.08/2)^2}{(1 + 0.06/2)^2}$$

$$B_2 = 101.9512$$

Likewise, if there were a flat yield curve and if $y = c$, we would expect that the theoretical futures price would equal the spot price.

The equations developed above are used in valuing embedded forwards and futures contracts in municipal derivative securities.

Imperfect Capital Markets

As previously discussed, perfect capital markets represent an *idealized version* of the marketplace. Market imperfections exist which make the arbitrage-free cash-and-carry condition merely a theoretical calculation and the law of one price effectively an approximation. Market imperfections that are particularly relevant to the forwards and futures markets are the existence of transactions costs, restrictions on use of proceeds from short sales, and unequal borrowing and investment rates. We refer to the sum of the market imperfections as *market costs*.

The existence of market costs to market participants means that there will be a *band* around the theoretical futures price, B_t, in which the futures price can move without creating an arbitrage opportunity. The band exists because the market costs must be overcome before arbitrage opportunities are possible. If the futures price stays within this band, risk-free arbitrage is not possible. Once the futures price leaves this band, market participants can and will exploit arbitrage opportunities.

For example, assume market costs of 2 percent and a theoretical futures price of $100 (see Exhibit 6–12). The band around the futures price, B_t, which no arbitrage would be possible is:

$$100 \, (1 - .02) \le B_t \le 100 \, (1 + 0.02)$$

$$98 \le B_t \le 102$$

Not all market participants face the same market costs. For instance, large banks and broker-dealers that are members of the exchanges have market costs that are a fraction of the costs incurred by a retail investor. Big institutional players have an arbitrage band

EXHIBIT 6–12
Arbitrage Boundaries

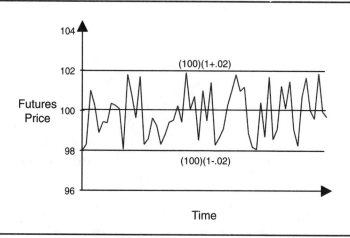

that is very narrow, whereas an individual investor's arbitrage band will be many times wider. The large market players will drive futures prices to within the arbitrage bands of the lowest-cost market players. Thus, the existence of market imperfections and market costs, as long as they are relatively insignificant for the major players, should do little to negate the spot–futures price relationship dictated by the cost of carry condition.

Use of Forward-Style Structures in
Municipal Derivative Securities

At the time of this writing, pure forwards- and futures-style payoff structures have been incorporated as hedging components into a relatively few number of municipal derivative securities.

In early 1989, The First Boston Corporation introduced a hybrid municipal security called *Refunding Escrow Deposits (REDs[SM])*.[4] This product involves the paired issuance by a tax-exempt entity of a taxable security and a forward agreement to issue tax-exempt

---

[4]Refunding Escrow Deposits[SM] and REDs[SM] are service marks of The First Boston Corporation.

bonds. The tax-exempt bonds have specified coupon, maturity, interest payment dates, and call provisions and are to be delivered on the forward delivery date. The taxable security pays interest at a predetermined rate until it matures on the forward delivery date, at which time the investor in the REDs receives the tax-exempt bonds. An investor purchases the REDs at a negotiated price, usually close to par at issuance, and can buy and sell these hybrid securities in the secondary market. This product was designed to effect an advanced refunding for certain private-purpose bonds that otherwise could not be advance-refunded on a tax-exempt basis under the Tax Act of 1986.

Similar to REDs was a product that was introduced by Goldman Sachs in 1989, called *Municipal Forwards*[SM].[5] Municipal Forwards are long-term forwards contracts obligating an investor to purchase a tax-exempt bond for future delivery on the forward delivery date. The coupon, maturity, interest payment dates, and redemption provisions are specified in the contract. The main difference between Municipal Forwards and REDs is that there is no interim taxable investment involved in Municipal Forwards or in similar products introduced by other investment banks. However, many of these products require that the investors, who are obligated to take delivery of the tax-exempt bonds on the forward delivery date, enter into an *escrow agreement* and deposit with a custodian bank cash or securities as collateral. If the investor fails to purchase the tax-exempt bonds, the collateral can be sold and liquidated damages paid to the issuer.

The REDs and Municipal Forwards programs have been used in a number of transactions. In order to entice investors to purchase these products, yields that are well above current spot yields for immediately deliverable comparable bonds are generally offered. A major problem is that the yields associated with the offerings are significantly higher than would have been predicted by a cash-and-carry analysis of futures prices, making it undesirable for issuers to offer these securities. This higher yield requirement may be due to the lack of liquidity of the instruments, the complexity of the transactions, certain concerns about the effects of changing tax

---

[5]Municipal Forwards[SM] is a service mark of Goldman Sachs & Company.

law on an issuer's ability to deliver the tax-exempt securities, and accounting and regulatory aspects of investment in these contracts by regulated investment companies.[6]

A second type of forward-style payoff structure that has been embedded in municipal derivative securities was introduced in August 1993 by Lehman Brothers for a City of Philadelphia transaction, which included BEAR Forward BPOs and BULL Forward BPOs. These securities allow investors to enter into what amounts to a one-year forwards contract on municipal bond rates, with a payoff on a tax-exempt basis. These are different from municipal bond futures contracts which have taxable payoffs. BULL and BEAR forwards are semiannually payable, stepped-coupon, mirrored securities that, when added together, result in a fixed borrowing cost (a linked coupon) for the issuer. There are two categories of cash flows associated with each BPO, as follows:

1. Interest cash flows, which are initially fixed (e.g., at 5.20 percent) and subsequently recalculated based on a one-time fixed-rate adjustment for the remaining term of the BPOs (this is the interest rate adjustment). The interest cash flows are divided between BULL and BEAR Forward BPO holders in amounts determined by the level of an interest rate index (the yield to maturity on the BBI-40) at the contract settlement date (IAD).
2. Principal cash flow, which is a lump-sum $5000 principal payment at the maturity date.

The present value of the payments of the BEAR Forward BPO interest rate adjustment is designed to replicate, *on a tax-exempt basis*, the cash payoff from short-selling the municipal bond futures contract with a contract settlement date equal to the IAD. BEAR Forward BPO owners benefit if the yield to maturity on the BBI-40 is greater on the IAD than on the date of issuance. Conversely, the payments on the BULL Forward BPO replicate, *on a tax-exempt basis*, the cash payoff from owning a municipal bond futures con-

---

[6]For an in-depth description of Municipal Forwards, see A Gurwitz, A Miller, and M Deligiannis, "The Valuation of Municipal Forwards," *Municipal Market Research*, August 1989. (*Municipal Market Research* is a publication of Goldman Sachs & Company.)

tract with a contract settlement date equal to the IAD. Decreasing bond yields and higher bond prices with lower BBI-40 yields to maturity benefit the BULL Forward BPO owner.

The pricing of BPOs incorporates cost of carry condition pricing concepts for Treasury futures which take into account the upward-sloping nature of the municipal yield curve. This transaction is more fully described in Chapter 8. Whether this type of transaction will become popular in the marketplace is yet to be determined, and market participants currently are digesting the complexity and the various moving pieces of the forward BPO structure.

INTEREST RATE SWAP-LIKE COMPONENTS

Interest rate swaps are an important part of the municipal market. In some new issues, derivatives containing swaps are issued to give the issuer a synthetic fixed rate. In others, swaps are implicitly structured in the payments. In either case, these components are an important part of municipal derivative valuation. This section describes the use of interest rate swaps in the municipal market.

Introduction

Since the introduction of Residual Interest Bonds (RIBS) in March 1990, there have been numerous types of municipal derivative securities with embedded hedging components that incorporate an interest rate swap-like payment mechanism. To properly model and value these hedging components, it is helpful to have an understanding of the general features of interest rate swaps.

Interest rate swaps are contractual agreements under which two parties, a *floating-rate payer* and a *fixed-rate payer,* agree to make or receive net payments at a series of future points in time. There is a *term* associated with an interest rate swap, typically 3 to 10 years, and net payments are made semiannually or quarterly. Each net payment is calculated by multiplying a *notional principal amount* (e.g., $1000) times the difference in the level of an interest index (e.g., the Kenny Index) versus a prespecified fixed *reference rate* (e.g., 4.00 percent), times the number of days in the period (e.g., 0.5

year). For example, if the Kenny Index averaged 5.00 percent over the 0.5-year period and the reference rate equaled 4.00 percent, the floating-rate payer would pay to the fixed-rate payer the following amount:

Notional amount × period length × (Kenny Index − reference rate)

= net payment

$$\$1{,}000 \times 0.5 \; year \times (5.00\% - 4.00\%) = \$5.00$$

In an interest rate swap contract, payments are made on a series of specified future dates during a specified term and may be thought of and analyzed as a series of forwards contracts. For example, a three-year interest rate swap can be characterized as six forwards contracts (six semiannual payments), with net payments based upon the Kenny Index minus the reference rate of 4.00 percent. In an interest rate swap, there is no exchange of principal between the two parties, which are also known as *counterparties,* and only net payments relating to an interest rate differential are transferred between the counterparties.

Interest rate swaps, which are custom-tailored contracts, are not traded on an exchange as futures contracts are; rather, they are arranged and structured by swap dealers. Swap dealers are financial intermediaries that generally are investment or commercial banks. The swap dealer takes a risk position by acting as a counterparty to the two ultimate parties—the fixed- and floating-rate payers. If one party defaults on its obligations, the swap dealer is obligated to make the required payments. The swap dealer may take the position of the ultimate fixed- or floating-rate payer in a transaction or may successfully find two ultimate counterparties. The swap dealer earns profits by having a pays–receives spread differential for swaps of different terms.

In the taxable interest rate swap marketplace, the pricing convention is to quote a taxable interest index, usually the LIBOR versus the *on-the-run* (meaning the continuously quoted Treasury bond rates on Treasury dealers' computer screens) full-coupon Treasury bond yields. The price quotes include a bid–ask spread differential, called the *Pays–Receives rate,* in basis points (BPs) (0.01 percent) over the comparable Treasury yield. The swap dealer makes the pays–receives spread quoted on the fixed-rate portion of the LIBOR flat swap. For a sample swap quotation run, on which the swap dealer expects to receive an 8- to 11-BP spread per year on the swap, see Exhibit 6–13.

For example, for a market participant that wished to swap five-year fixed-rate exposure to *receive* floating-rate LIBOR, the dealer would *pay* a five-year fixed reference rate of 5.31 percent and the market participant would pay the dealer LIBOR on each payment date. Conversely, for a market participant that wished to receive a floating-rate LIBOR from the dealer and pay a five-year fixed-rate exposure, the dealer would *receive* a fixed-rate of 5.40 percent and would pay LIBOR. The five-year pays–receives spread in this example would be 9 BPs.

Although interest rate swap prices are quoted for convenience against full-coupon *on-the-run* Treasury bonds, market makers *calculate* swap rates by using *implied forward rates* discounted to the present, with the appropriate *zero-coupon yield curve*.

In the tax-exempt swap marketplace, swap dealers quote a tax-exempt interest rate index, such as the Kenny Index or the Public Securities Association (PSA) Index versus a derived fixed-rate schedule that is a function of maturity and of implied forward rates in the tax-exempt marketplace. Swap dealers in the tax-exempt market also generally quote a pays–receives spread similar to the one seen in Exhibit 6–13.

An interest rate swap contract generally can be terminated through negotiation with the swap dealer and a *buyout* of the swap. Depending on the movement of interest rates and the slope of the yield curve, the buyout may result in a payment from the counterparty to the swap dealer, or in the receipt of money by the counterparty from the swap dealer. The calculation of the buyout

EXHIBIT 6–13
Pricing Structure for LIBOR—Flat Swaps

On the-Run Treasury	Treasury Rate	Pays Spread	Dealer Pays Rate	Receives Spread	Dealer Rec. Rate
2-year	3.72%	+.60	4.32%	+.68	4.40%
3-year	4.08%	+.62	4.70%	+.70	4.78%
5-year	4.66%	+.65	5.31%	+.74	5.40%
7-year	4.98%	+.67	5.65%	+.77	5.75%
10-year	5.34%	+.69	6.03%	+.80	6.14%

amount is based upon the level of implied forward rates at the time of the buyout versus the contractual reference rate over the remaining term of the swap, and upon the bids–receives spread. Generally, if interest rates have risen since the swap contract was entered into, the fixed-rate payer will receive money in the event of termination. This amount is equal to the discounted value of the swap's expected future cash flows based on the then-current yield curve. If interest rates have fallen since the swaps inception, the fixed-rate payer generally will have to pay money, in the event of termination.

Typically, most of the swap-like hedging components of municipal derivative securities have semiannual settlement dates that are coincident with the interest rate payments of the municipal bond. For example, assume that there is a three-year, semiannually payable Kenny Index based swap with a reference rate of 4.00 percent and a notional principal amount of $1000. During any period in which the Kenny Index averages greater than 4.00 percent, the floating-rate payer will make a payment to the fixed-rate payer in accordance with the interest rate swap equation. Conversely, when the Kenny Index averages less than 4.00 percent, the fixed-rate payer will make a payment to the floating-rate payer as calculated by the same equation. In general, when we analyze complex municipal derivative securities with embedded interest rate components that perform similarly to the interest rate swap equation, we value them as interest rate swaps.

Valuation—Implied Forward Rates

The valuation of an interest rate swap equals the discounted value of its expected future cash flows. Participants in the marketplace estimate the expected cash flows of the hedging and option components of a derivative security by using the implied forward rates associated with the pure expectations theory of the yield curve. The expected cash flows are then discounted at the relevant implied zero-coupon discount levels associated with each cash flow. This is the valuation technique underlying expectational analysis; it is used to value *at market* and *off-market* swaps. In an at-market swap, the swap rate is set at the current market rate and has a present value equal to zero. The swap rate of an off-market swap is set above or below the current market swap rate and has a present value equal to a positive or negative number. We value an at-market swap and an off-market swap, below.

The valuation of hedging components should be *solely* dependent on an assessment of interest rate risk—not on credit risk. Credit risk or counterparty payment risk can be addressed through collateralization of the parties obligations under the hedging contract.

Valuation of an Off-Market Interest Rate Swap

For illustrative purposes, we use the yield curve shown in Exhibit 4–10 to value a three-year, semiannually payable, Kenny Index-based interest rate swap with a reference rate of 3.4 percent, or 1.7 percent semiannually. We assume that the conversion ratio used to convert from Treasury-based taxable forward rates to Kenny Index-based tax-exempt forward rates is 71 percent. From the standpoint of a fixed-rate payer, we develop Exhibit 6–14.

Exhibit 6–15 shows a graph of the three-year, six-period, taxable full-coupon curve, the taxable implied zero-coupon curve, $r_t/2$, the taxable implied forward curve, $_{t-1}f_t$, and the tax-exempt implied forward curve, $_{t-1}f^*_t$, all on a semiannual basis. In this hypothetical interest rate environment, the fixed-rate payer expects *today* to make payments in periods 1 through 3 and to receive payments in periods 4 through 6. The value of each payment is dependent upon

EXHIBIT 6–14
Net Present Value of a $1000 Notional Swap to a Fixed-Rate Payer

(1)	(2)	(3)	(4)	(5)	(6)	(7)	(8)
			Implied Taxable	Implied Tax-Exempt		Present	$1,000x
		Implied	Forward	Forward		Value	Present
Period	Year	Zero Rates	Rate	Rate	Reference	of	Value
t	n	$r_t/2$	$_{t-1}f_t$	$_{t-1}f^*_t$	Rate	[(5) - (6)]	Difference
1	0.5	2.200%	2.200%	1.562%	1.700%	(0.135)	($1.35)
2	1.0	2.251%	2.301%	1.634%	1.700%	(0.063)	($0.63)
3	1.5	2.302%	2.405%	1.708%	1.700%	(0.007)	($0.07)
4	2.0	2.402%	2.702%	1.918%	1.700%	0.198	$1.98
5	2.5	2.454%	2.662%	1.890%	1.700%	0.168	$1.68
6	3.0	2.507%	2.772%	1.968%	1.700%	0.231	$2.31
							$3.92

EXHIBIT 6–15
Yield Curve (Semiannual Basis)

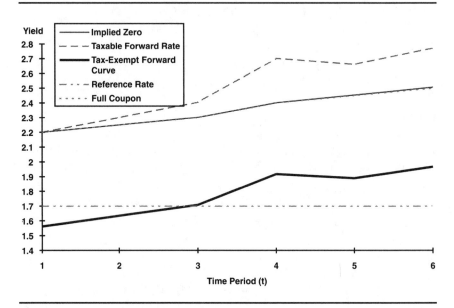

the difference between the implied tax-exempt forward rate and the known reference rate. The net present value of these payments, discounted at the relevant implied zero-coupon rates, is $3.92.

For the fixed-rate payer (the floating-rate receiver) the interest rate swap is said to be *in the money,* in periods when the fixed-rate payer expects to receive payments, when the tax-exempt implied forward rate is above the reference rate. The swap shown in Exhibit 6–15 is expected to be in the money for the fixed-rate payer in periods 4, 5, and 6. It is important to keep in mind that, depending on future short-term interest rate levels, the fixed-rate payer may or may not actually receive payments during these periods.

Calculation of the At-Market Interest Rate Swap Rate
Most interest rate swap structures embedded in a municipal derivative security have a term of 10 years or less. Generally, at the time an interest rate swap is entered into, the reference rate is set in accordance with the length of time of the swap, such that the swap has a discounted present value of zero. This rate is known as the *at-*

market swap rate. *This means that the sum of the discounted individual expected swap cash flows is zero—not that each expected cash flow is zero.* In fact, in an upward-sloping yield curve, the fixed-rate payer will expect to have negative swap payments in the early years and positive swap payments in the later years. The converse relationship is true for the floating-rate payer.

A question frequently raised by many municipal market participants is, "Where do these swap rates come from?" Simplistically, the procedure that many derivatives market participants use to set the *at-market swap rate* is to take the implied tax-exempt forward rates, $_{t-1}f_t^*$, over the term of the swap (see column 5 in Exhibit 6–16), discount them at the appropriate zero-coupon yields, $r_t/2$ (the zero-coupon yields are shown in column 3 and the discount factors are shown in column 6 of Exhibit 6–16), sum the present value implied tax-exempt foward rates (see column 7 in Exhibit 6–16) and divide the result by the sum of the discount factors to arrive at the *at-market* (or *mid-market*) *swap rate*. To that mid-market swap rate, dealers add a bids–receives spread.

For illustrative purposes, we will again use the six-period yield curve shown in Exhibit 4–10 to get the calculation of at-market swap rate of 3.55 percent annually (1.775 percent semiannually), as shown in Exhibit 6–16.

EXHIBIT 6–16
Calculation of At-Market Swap Rate

(1)	(2)	(3)	(4)	(5)	(6)	(7)
						Present Value of
			Implied Taxable	Implied Tax-Exempt		Implied Tax-Exempt
		Implied	Forward	Forward	Discount	Forward
Period	Year	Zero Rates	Rate	Rate	Factor	Rate
t	n	$r_t/2$	$_{t-1}f_t$	$_{t-1}f_t^*$	$1/(1+r_t/2)^t$	(5) x (6)
1	0.5	2.200	2.200	1.562%	0.978	1.528%
2	1.0	2.251	2.301	1.634%	0.956	1.563%
3	1.5	2.302	2.404	1.707%	0.934	1.594%
4	2.0	2.405	2.716	1.928%	0.909	1.753%
5	2.5	2.457	2.663	1.891%	0.886	1.675%
6	3.0	2.509	2.771	1.967%	0.862	1.695%
					5.526	9.808%
	9.808%/5.526=1.775% semiannual swap rate					

Forward Delivery Interest Rate Swaps[7]

Most long-term fixed-rate municipal bonds have a redemption option that allows the issuer, usually after 10 years, to call the bonds at a predetermined redemption price (e.g., 102 percent of par value). The 1986 Tax Act (see Chapter 2) severely restricted the ability of issuers to refund, in advance of the first redemption date, certain municipal bond issues. If interest rates have fallen since the issuance of the bond, the call option may have significant value for an issuer. This value is approximately equal to the difference between the current market price of the callable bond and the market value of an otherwise identical noncallable bond. The value of the call option will fall if municipal interest rates rise. The issuer's goals are to preserve the current value of the call option and to hedge against higher interest rates.

An interest rate swap with a delayed delivery date (a *forward swap*), coupled with floating- and/or fixed-rate municipal debt issuance strategies on the call date, is an approach that investment banking firms are recommending as an appropriate hedge against the risks associated with higher future interest rates. Another question we have frequently heard from municipal market participants is, "Where do the interest rate swap rates on forward delivery swaps come from?"

To illustrate how forward delivery interest rate swap rates are calculated, assume that we are facing the six-period yield curve shown in Exhibit 6–15. We have seen in Exhibit 6–15 that the calculated *three-year at-market swap rate* is 3.55 percent annually (1.775 percent semiannually). Using the same calculation procedures, we can compute the *at-market swap rate one year forward* by taking the average of the present value of the tax-exempt implied forward rates over the one-year period, as follows:

$$\frac{1.528\% + 1.563\%}{2} = 1.546\% \text{ semiannually, } 3.092\% \text{ annually}$$

Further assume that there is no swap dealer bids–receives spread and that there is a market participant (the issuer) who desires to be a fixed-rate payer in a two-year forward delivery swap with a

[7]The discussion in this section follows pp. 59–62 of K Brown and D Smith, "Forward Swaps, Swap Options, and the Management of Callable Debt," *The Journal of Applied Corporate Finance*, winter 1990, pp. 59–71.

dealer. The swap is to begin at the end of year 1 (the end of period 2) and to end at the end of year 3 (the end of period 6).

To get the desired swap payment characteristics, the issuer can enter simultaneously into two swap transactions with the dealer. The two transactions will involve the same notional principal amount but will have different terms. The first will be a one-year swap in which the issuer receives the one-year fixed swap rate (e.g., 3.092 percent annually) and pays the dealer the Kenny Index, and the second will be a three-year swap in which the issuer pays the three-year fixed swap rate (e.g., 3.55 percent annually) and receives the Kenny Index from the dealer. Economically, this is the basic idea. Operationally, however, there is only one transaction; one swap agreement combines the swap cash flows and terms.

The net cash flows resulting from these two transactions are as follows:

1. The Kenny Index cash flows offset each other in year 1.
2. A small *stub* payment (3.55% − 3.092% = 0.458% annually, or 0.229% semiannually) is owed to the dealer during the first year.
3. An at-market fixed-rate swap rate of 3.55 percent annually (1.775 percent semiannually) is set for years 2 and 3.

Effectively, the at-market swap rates used for forward delivery swaps should equal the swap rates for the comparable-term, current-pay swap, with adjustments for handling the stub payments. To accommodate the desire of issuers, most dealers *future-value* the stub payments to the forward swap start date and apportion the payments over the term of the swap. The zero-coupon and forward rates implied in the yield curve are used in this procedure.

In a greatly simplified version of this procedure, which you can check on a handheld calculator, we use a uniform discount rate, ignore the dealers bids–receives spreads, and compute the at-market forward swap rate. If we future-value, at an annual rate of 3.55 percent (1.775 percent semiannually), the 0.229 percent (22.9-BP) semiannual stub payment to the forward swap start date at the end of year 1, we have a future stub value of 0.462 percent (46.2-BPs). The semiannual annuity payment, discounted at an annual rate of 3.55 percent (1.775 percent semiannually), over the two-year swap period (which has, of course, four semiannual periods) necessary to amortize the 46.2-BP stub value is .112 percent per semiannual period (the stub adjustment). The forward swap rate equals the current *at-market* swap rate plus the *stub adjustment*. This swap rate is 1.775% + 0.112% = 1.887% semiannually, or 3.774 percent annually

In reality, the stub adjustment will be much higher than in the example above, due to dealer bids–receives spreads, dealer taxable borrowing costs, longer delayed delivery periods, and generally larger differences between the issuers pays-fixed, shorter-term swap rates and the receives-fixed, longer-term swap rates.

Swaptions

Another development of the 1980's in the swaps market was the introduction of options on swaps, or "swaptions." A *swaption* gives its owner the right, but not the obligation, to enter into an interest rate swap at some time in the future. Essentially, a swaption allows a buyer to exchange a variable-rate debt instrument for a fixed-rate obligation at some future date.

Consider, for example, an individual who plans to borrow at a variable rate one year in the future and wishes to swap the loan to a fixed rate at that time. In order to *lock in* a desired rate and avoid the interest rate risk associated with the fixed-rate swap, the borrower can buy a swaption, or an option to enter into a swap at a given rate. The swaption assures the borrower of achieving a rate at or below the strike rate on the option. If, when the loan begins one year in the future, the current market swap rate is above the swaption rate, the borrower will exercise the swaption and receive a below-market fixed rate. Otherwise, the borrower will let the swaption expire, unexercised.

Changes in Value of Hedging Components

As interest rates move and/or as the yield curve shifts, the present value and expected cash flows on a derivative product change. As implied forward interest rates, $_{t-1}f_t$, rise, the value of an outstanding interest rate forwards or a swap contract to a fixed-rate payer also rises. Conversely, as implied forward interest rates fall, the value of an interest rate forwards or a swap contract to a fixed-rate payer also falls. The change in value–change in interest rate payoff profile of interest rate swaps and forwards is shown in Exhibit 6–17.

Duration of an Interest Rate Swap

As was discussed in Chapter 3, duration is a measure of either the weighted average time to maturity or the change in price for a given change in interest rates. The time duration, D_t^*, of an interest rate swap is the weighted average time to maturity of the expected cash flows. The expected cash flows can be measured using the expectational analysis techniques developed in Chapter 4. When a derivative security is issued, the present value of the total expected cash flows on the swap will approximately equal zero and the time duration D_t^* of the interset rate swap portion will be small. For bullish derivatives, positive up-front cash flows will be offset by expectations of negative cash flows in the future. For bearish

EXHIBIT 6–17
Payoff Profile of Swaps and Forwards

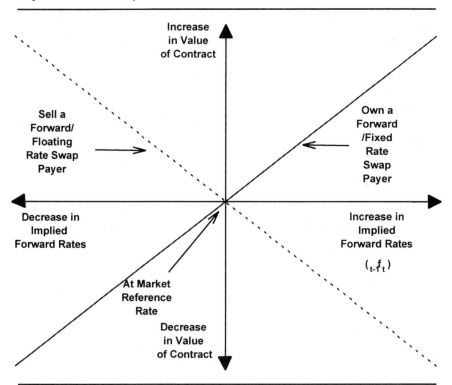

derivatives, negative up-front cash flows will be offset by positive future cash flows. Using expectational analysis, we can estimate the total expected cash flow on the derivative, which includes the cash flow from the swap. In Chapter 8 we measure the time duration for several derivative securities using this methodology.

The price duration, D_p^*, is an estimate of the change in price of a security for a small parallel shift in interest rates. For the floating-rate payer (fixed-rate receiver), an interest rate swap can be analyzed as a combination of a long position in a fixed-rate bond and a short position in a floating-rate bond. The price duration of the swap is measured as the duration of the fixed-rate bond minus the duration of the floating-rate bond. Generally, the price duration, D^{swap}, of an interest rate swap for a floating-rate payer will be positive. For the fixed-rate payer (floating-rate receiver), an interest rate swap can be analyzed as a combination of a short position in a fixed-rate bond and a long position in a floating-rate bond. The price duration of the swap in this case is measured as the duration of the floating-rate bond minus the duration of the fixed-rate bond. Generally, the price duration, D^{swap}, of an interest rate swap to a fixed rate payer will be negative.

The duration of a floating-rate bond is assumed to be the same as the periodic interest reset on the bond. For example, a floating-rate bond that has a semiannual interest reset has a duration of .5 years. The duration of the fixed-rate bond is measured below using Macaulay's duration and modified duration.

Example. Consider a swap with a maturity of 5 years, a semiannual fixed rate payment of 5.00%, a floating rate payment of LIBOR, and, for simplicity, assume a flat yield curve with a uniform discount rate of 5.50%. We begin by calculating the duration, D, of a 5.00% fixed-rate bond:

Let:

$C = \$5.00$
$y = 5.50\%$
$F = \$100$
$P = \$100$
$t = 1,2,3,...,10$
$n = 5$

$$D = \sum_{t=1}^{10} \left[\frac{5.00/(1.0275)^t}{100} \left(\frac{t}{2} \right) \right] + \left(\frac{100/(1.0275)^{10}}{100} \right) (10) = 4.479$$

The fixed-rate bond portion of the swap has a duration of 4.479 years and a modified duration of 4.359 years. The floating-rate bond portion of the swap has a duration of .5 years and a modified duration of .487 years. Therefore, the price duration of this swap to the floating-rate payer is:

$$D^{swap} = 4.359 \text{ years} - .487 \text{ years} = 3.872 \text{ years}$$

And the duration of this swap for the fixed-rate payer is:

$$D^{swap} = .487 \text{ years} - 4.359 \text{ years} = -3.872 \text{ years}$$

We use this duration to calculate the price duration of a derivative security that includes an interest rate swap component. It is evident that the price duration of a swap is of greater importance than its time duration. In Chapter 8 we calculate the duration of each of the individual components and cumulate these durations to arrive at a total duration for the security.

Use of Swap-Like Structures in Municipal Derivative Securities

The majority of the municipal derivative securities introduced in the 1990s include a hedging component that has a price performance profile similar to the profile of an interest rate swap. The floating-rate payment is determined either by an auction-rate security, such as SAVRS, or by a formula based on the Kenny Index, the PSA Index, or another tax-exempt or taxable index. For example, some municipal bond interest rate formulas are based on the 10-year constant maturity Treasury index or on LIBOR.

In structural terms, municipal derivative securities have taken two forms: *bull market* products, such as RIBS, inverse floaters, BULL Floaters, and BULL Forwards, and *bear market* products, such as BEAR Floaters, BEAR Forwards, and cap bonds. Bull market products benefit either from an upward-sloping yield curve with a slope that either remains unchanged over time or becomes steeper, or from a yield scenario in which interest rates, in general, are declining. Bear market products benefit when the yield curve starts to flatten or invert, or when interest rates, in general, are increasing.

Let's look at the interest rate formulas for the bull products that we value in Chapter 8, to see how the hedging components should be analyzed. For each of the bull products below, the return improves in a bullish bond market (i.e., when there is a decline in the interest rate index relative to a fixed reference rate).

Residual Interest Bonds

Consider a bond issue that consist of equal amounts of RIBS and SAVRS that mature on August 1, 2014, and has a *linked-rate* BEY of 6.25 percent. The interest rate formula for the RIBS can be derived as follows:

$$\text{RIBS rate} + \text{SAVRS rate} = 2\,(6.25\%)$$
$$\text{RIBS rate} = 2\,(6.25\%) - \text{SAVRS rate}$$
$$\text{RIBS rate} = (6.25\%) + (6.25\% - \text{SAVRS rate})$$

The SAVRS rate is equal to the Dutch auction rate on the companion SAVRS security plus auction expenses, which typically total 28 BPs. The interest on both RIBS and SAVRS is paid every 35 days in most transactions. The interest on SAVRS is paid on an actual/360-day basis, which is consistent with other money market instruments. In fact, the interest rate is paid every 35 days at 2 times the linked coupon of 6.173 percent, which is a BEY of 6.25 percent. This interest is divided between the SAVRS and RIBS holders. For ease of analysis, assume that the linked 35-day coupon payment is a comparable 6.25 percent semiannual BEY payment. The RIBS may be thought of as a 6.25 percent fixed-rate bond plus an interest rate swap, with a term equal to the maturity of August 1, 2014. In this analogy, the RIBS owner is the floating-rate payer, who pays the SAVRS rate, and is also the recipient of a fixed-rate swap payment or *reference rate* of 6.25 percent.

Effectively, the SAVRS fulfill the role of a *floating-rate counterparty*. The spread between the SAVRS rate and the reference rate of 6.25 percent generates the positive or negative interest rate swap payment.

Inverse Floater

The interest rate formula for the inverse floater is as follows:

$$c = 6.15\% + (4.70\% - \text{Kenny Index}) \text{ prior to } 8/15/1999$$
$$c = 6.15\% \text{ from } 8/15/1999 \text{ until maturity on } 8/15/2012$$

The hedging component of this municipal derivative security is a semiannual payment interest rate swap, with a term until August 15, 1999. The inverse floater owner is the floating-rate payer and the recipient of a fixed-rate swap payment of 4.70 percent.

BULL Forward BPO

The interest rate formula for the BULL Forward BPO is as follows:

c = 5.20% prior to 6/15/1994

c = 5.20% + 3 (interest rate adjustment) from 6/15/1994 until maturity on 6/15/2005

There is no embedded swap-like hedging component in this security. The three embedded forward-style hedging components are further explained in Chapter 8.

Let's now look at the interest rate formulas for the bear products that we value in Chapter 8, to see how these hedging components should be analyzed.

BEAR Floater

The interest rate formula for the BEAR Floater is as follows:

c = 6.10% + 2 (Kenny Index − 5.0%) prior to 8/15/2002

c = 6.10% from 8/15/2002 until maturity on 8/15/2022

The minimum and maximum interest rates on the BEAR Floater are addressed in Chapter 7, in the discussion of interest rate options. The hedging components embedded in this municipal derivative security are two semiannually payable interest rate swaps, with a term of August 15, 2002. The BEAR Floater owner is the fixed-rate payer and the recipient of a floating-rate swap payment based on the Kenny Index.

Cap Bond

The interest rate formula for the cap bond is as follows:

c = 6.60% + MAX (0%, PSA Index − 3.50%) until 10/1/1997

c = 6.60% from 10/1/1997 until maturity on 10/1/2016

Note that, in contrast to the interest rate on the BEAR Floater, the interest rate on the cap bond will never decline below the initial rate. Instead, it will rise with increases in short-term rates, prior to

October 1, 1997. There is no embedded swap-like hedging component in this security. There is an embedded interest rate cap-like
payment structure until October 1, 1997. This payment structure
will be more closely examined in Chapter 7.

Other Formulas

Some interest rate formulas in the derivatives marketplace may
seem confusing, and it is not immediately obvious how they
should be analyzed. One example is a 1993 inverse floater transaction with the following payment structure:

$c = 12.25\% - 2$ (Kenny Index), prior to $7/1/2000$

$c = 4.95\%$ from $7/1/2000$ until maturity on $9/1/2003$

To break this formula down so that it may be analyzed more
easily, it is helpful to think of the inverse floater as a combination
of a fixed-rate bond, in this example equal to 4.95 percent, and two
hedging components. If we subdivide the 12.25 percent into 4.95
percent plus 7.30 percent, the interest rate formula can be derived
as follows:

$c = 4.95\% + 7.30\% - 2$ (Kenny Index)

$c = 4.95\% + 2 (3.65\% -$ Kenny Index) prior to $7/1/2000$

$c = 4.95\%$ from $7/1/2000$ until maturity on $7/1/2003$

This inverse floater can be analyzed and valued as a combination of a 4.95 percent fixed-rate bond that matures on July 1, 2003,
and two interest rate swaps with a maturity of July 1, 2000. The inverse floater holder pays the Kenny Index, and the recipient receives a fixed-rate swap payment of 3.65 percent.

In general, when we see formulas in municipal derivative securities that look like "floating index–fixed rate" or "fixed
rate–floating index," we analyze the hedging components in terms
of fixed-to-floating or floating-to-fixed interest rate swaps.

SUMMARY

In this chapter, we have continued to describe the process of valuing a complex derivative security as a package of simpler securities,

with a focus on the understanding and valuation of the hedging component building blocks.

The hedging component building blocks consist of financial instruments with interest payments that are contingent upon future levels of interest rates or upon an interest rate index. These instruments are called *hedging components* because financial instruments with similar payment characteristics are often used to offset price changes of other financial assets or liabilities held in a portfolio. The valuation of hedging components is primarily dependent on the level and movement of interest rates—*interest rate risk.*

The first two types of hedging components that we examined were forwards and futures contracts. Forwards and futures contracts are two-sided agreements between a buyer and a seller, in which the settlement price of an asset or an index is agreed upon in advance, and in which the parties agree to the delivery of the asset at some time in the future. In other words, the settlement date of the transaction is *delayed* for a predetermined period (usually one month to two years).

In examining the relationship between spot prices, future prices, and expected spot prices, we found equilibrium conditions between the three variables that result from arbitrage conditions or the *law of one price*. The key to the relationship between these three variables, at least for the interest rate forward and future hedging components of municipal derivative securities, is *implied forward rates*. We discussed the *cost of carry condition* of future pricing, which states that the difference between the spot price, P, of a commodity and its price for future delivery, B_t, at time t, is determined by, in the case of financial contracts, the cost of financing the asset, and that the relationship is driven and determined by implied forward rates. We also examined the use of forward-style structures in municipal derivatives securities.

The next type of hedging component that we examined was the interest rate swap contract, a two-sided agreement under which two parties, a *floating-rate payer* and a *fixed-rate payer* (jointly called the *counterparties*), agree to make or receive net payments at a series of future points in time. There is a *term* associated with the swap (usually 3 to 10 years), and each net payment is based upon a *notional principal amount*. An interest rate swap may be thought of as a series of forwards contracts.

We looked at the pricing structure of interest rate swaps, and we also valued an off-market interest rate swap. In Exhibit 6–16, we showed how to calculate the at-market swap rate, a procedure that has puzzled many market participants, and we also discussed the setting of a forward swap rate. Finally, we examined the use of swap-style structures in municipal derivative securities.

CHAPTER 7

THE BUILDING BLOCKS— OPTION COMPONENTS

Interest Rate Caps and Floors

INTRODUCTION TO OPTIONS[1]

Investors in the municipal market are familiar with certain options that are embedded in municipal bonds. The most common municipal bond option is the *early redemption*, or the *call option*, on the bond. The call option allows an issuer of a bond to buy or *call* it on or after a predetermined date, the *call date*, at a predetermined call price. Investors that have been stung by having 12 percent tax-exempt bonds called in a six percent municipal bond market understand the pain associated with call risk. In this chapter, we provide an overview of the mechanics and the valuation of options. The option valuation techniques, as they apply to municipal derivatives, are important for the valuations discussed in Chapter 8.

General

Investors in callable bonds, effectively, *sell* a call option to the bond issuer. Because the actual redemption date of the bond is unknown, the future cash flows on a callable bond are uncertain. Investors in callable bonds are willing to accept this added uncertainty and *risk*

---

[1]For a good general description of options, see one of the following books: T Campbell and W Kracaw, *Financial Risk Management*, Harper Collins, New York, 1993; R Kolb, *Financial Derivatives*, Kolb Publishing Company, Miami, FL, 1993; or J Hull, *Introduction to Futures and Options Markets*, Prentice-Hall, Englewood Cliffs, NJ, 1991).

only if it is compensated for by an interest rate, or yield, *above* that of an otherwise comparable noncallable bond. The valuation of the call option has been examined and modeled extensively both by the academic community and by capital market participants. Therefore we will not formally address it in this book.

Another option with which municipal participants are familiar is the *put option*, which allows an investor in a bond to sell or *put* it on a specific date, or set of dates, at a predetermined put price, usually par value. Investors in *puttable* bonds, effectively, *buy* the put option from the issuer. If interest rates move up and the value of the puttable bond falls below the put price, the investor will exercise the put option. From an investor's perspective, the effective maturity of the bond has been shortened by the put option, which acts to shorten the duration of the bond. There is less risk for the investor in a bond that contains a put option than in an otherwise comparable bond that does not have this option. Because there is *lower risk*, investors in puttable bonds are willing to compensate the issuer for the sale of the put option with an interest rate, or yield level, *below* that of an otherwise comparable noncallable bond.

Interest rate options, which are less common in the tax-exempt market than in the taxable market, are *interest rate cap options* and *interest rate floor options* that have recently been embedded in municipal derivative securities. Interest rate cap and floor options are valued and analyzed, at length, in this chapter.

Before we get ahead of ourselves, let's first define the option terminology that will be used in this chapter.

A *call option* is the right to *buy* an underlying asset, such as a share of stock, a Treasury bond, or a futures contract on a Treasury bond, at a predetermined price, the *strike or exercise price*, for a predetermined time, the *term* of the option. The buyer of the call option, the *call owner*, pays a fee, the call premium, to the entity that sells the call option, the *call writer*.

S = current market price of the security underlying the option

X_c = exercise price or strike price on the call option

A call option is *in the money* if the current price of the underlying security, S, is greater than the exercise price, X_c. For example, if you own an International Business Machines (IBM) call option with a strike price of $45, and IBM is trading at a current price of $50, then the call is in the money in the amount of $5.

A *put option* is the right to *sell* or put an underlying asset at the strike price on or prior to the exercise date. The *put owner,* or *buyer,* pays a fee, the *put premium,* to the entity that sells the put contract, the *put writer.*

X_p = exercise price or strike price on the put option

A put option is in the money if S, the market value of the asset, is less than the *exercise price,* X_p.

Options may be limited as to when they can be exercised. Options that may be exercised only upon maturity are called *European* options. Most options associated with fixed-income securities are European options. Options that can be exercised at any time prior to or including maturity are called *American* options. Most common stock options are American options.

The *owner* of an option is *long* the option. The value of an option to an owner can be positive or zero but never negative. That is because, if at expiration the option is *out of the money,* a rational option owner will choose not to exercise it. The *writer* of the option is *short* the option, and will receive a fee to write the option. The amount of this fee will be set such that the option writer believes that the option fee income is in excess of the probable loss if the option is *in the money* and is exercised. The value of an option to an option writer can be negative, if the present value of the payments to the option owner exceeds the option fee income to the option writer.

The *price,* or value, of a put or a call option has two components. The first, called the *intrinsic value,* is the difference between the current asset price and the strike price of the option. In the IBM stock example described above, the intrinsic value is $50 - $45 = $5. The second component of an option's price, called the *time value,* reflects expectations of an option's profitability associated with exercising it at a future point in time. Whereas the option's intrinsic value is easily observable, the time value is derived by subtracting the intrinsic value from the observed market price of the option.

The option or price insurance components of municipal derivative securities, like the hedging components, consist of financial instruments with interest payments contingent upon unknown future levels of interest rates. However, the *value* of the option components is also heavily dependent upon the *volatility* of the interest rates, while the value of the hedging components is not dependent upon volatility. Another difference between hedging contracts (such as futures and forwards) and option contracts is that an option contract involves a *choice* rather than *obligation*. An option is a *one-sided obligation* unlike the two-sided obligation associated with hedging contracts. With interest rate futures contracts, there is a two-sided commitment to deliver or to purchase an asset, or to settle on the difference in the asset price, at a specific time and dollar price whether the price has gone down or up. In contrast, an option contract gives the owner of the option a choice about whether or not to finalize a transaction at a prespecified time and price.

Payoff Profiles of Options

Exhibit 7–1, which is presented in four panels, shows the payoffs to both owners and writers of call and put options at the *expiration date*. Panel A shows the gross and net payoffs to a call owner. The *gross payoff* at the expiration date of the option is the asset price, S, minus the exercise price, X_c. The *net payoff* is simply the gross payoff minus the cost of the option, the *call premium*. If $S > X_c$ at the expiration of the call option, the option is in the money and a rational investor will exercise it. If $S < X_c$ at the exercise date, the option is out of the money and a rational investor will not exercise it.

Panel B shows the gross and net payoffs from owning a put option with a gross payoff of $X_p - S$, where X_p is the exercise price on the put, and a net payoff is equal to the gross payoff, $X_p - S$, minus the cost of the option, the *put premium*. Again, a rational investor will exercise the put option at expiration when $X_p < S$ and will not exercise the option when $X_p > S$. Option owners can lose no more than the cost of their put and/or call premiums if the option expires out of the money.

Panel C shows the gross and net payoffs to a put writer. A basic relationship in the options market is that the combined payoffs of an owner and a writer of a call option or an owner and a writer of a put option with the same exercise price and expiration date will always net out to zero. This is commonly referred to as a

EXHIBIT 7–1
Gross Payoffs to Option Parties

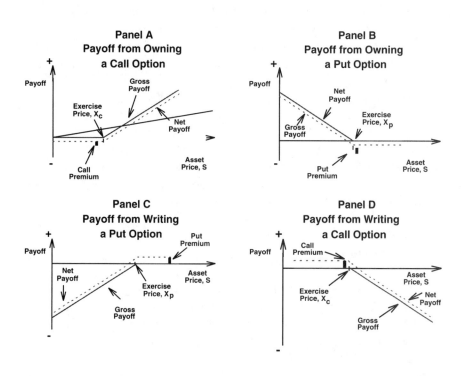

zero-sum game. A put writer's gain is a put owner's loss, and a call owner's gain is a call writer's loss, etc. Since a rational put owner will only exercise the option if it is at or in the money, when $S \leq X_p$, the gross payoff to the put writer is $S - X_p$, which is a *negative* number. If the put option expires out of the money, when $S > X_p$, the gross payoff to the put writer is 0. The net payoff to the put writer is the gross payoff *plus* the put premium.

Without a cash payment or some other form of compensation, no investor would *write* an option. The option premium is the *maximum* amount of compensation that an option writer will receive for the option contract. Panel D shows the gross and net payoffs to a call writer. Since a rational call owner will exercise the option only if it is at or in the money, when $S \geq X_c$, the gross payoff to the put writer is $S - X_c$, which is a *negative* number. If the call option expires out of the money, when $S < X_c$, the option will expire and the gross payoff to the call writer will be zero. The net payoff to the call writer will be the gross payoff *plus* the call premium.

Algebraically, the gross payoff to the various option parties, where *MAX* denotes the maximum of the numbers in the parentheses and *MIN* denotes the minimum of the numbers in the parentheses, can be expressed shown in Exhibit 7–2.

The net payoffs at expiration date to the various option parties are shown in Exhibit 7–3. The net payoffs to call owners and call writers are shown in panel A, and the net payoffs to put owners and put writers are shown in panel B. At all the possible asset prices at expiration, the aggregate value of profit and loss of option owners and option writers is equal to zero.

Relationship between Option Contracts and Futures or Forwards

As previously discussed, there is a major difference between hedging contracts, such as futures and forwards, and options contracts, such as puts and calls. For a futures owner, there is a *two-sided payoff* and cash flows can be positive or negative. For an option owner, there is a *one-sided payoff*, neglecting fees. However, if we look closely at panels A and C of Exhibit 7–1, we see an interesting relationship. If we combine the two panels and the exercise prices on the two contracts are equal ($X_c = X_p$) the combination represents owning a call option plus writing a put option. In this case, the payoff profile at the option expiration date (see Exhibit 7–4, panel A) is identical to the payoff profile of owning a futures or forward contract with a settlement price equal to the exercise price (see Exhibit 7–4, panel B).

EXHIBIT 7–2
Gross Payoffs to Option Parties

	Owner	Writer
Call Option	MAX [X_c-S, O]	MIN [X_c-S, O]
Put Option	MAX [S-X_p, O]	MIN [S-X_p, O]

EXHIBIT 7–3

Panel A
Net Payoffs on Call Options

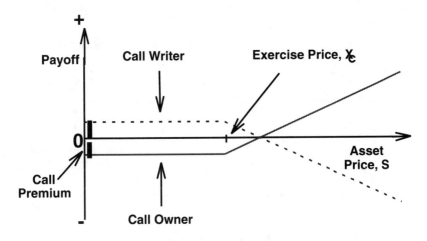

Panel B
Net Payoffs on Put Options

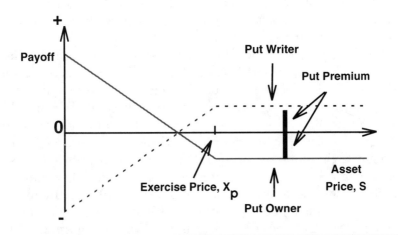

EXHIBIT 7–4

Options Strategy Replicating the Buying of a Long Futures Contract

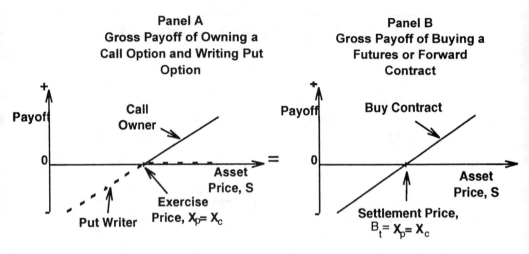

Panel A	Panel B
Gross Payoff of Owning a Call Option and Writing Put Option	Gross Payoff of Buying a Futures or Forward Contract

There is a similar relationship between panels B and D of Exhibit 7–1. If we own a put option and write a call option with equal exercise prices (e.g., $X_c = X_p$). The payoff profile at the option expiration date from this combined option position (see Exhibit 7–5, panel A) is identical to a payoff profile from selling a futures or forward contract with a settlement price equal to the option exercise price (see Exhibit 7–5, panel B).

We are sure that the above discussion about the relationship between the payoff profiles of options and futures contracts is at least mildly interesting to a participant in the municipal marketplace. But what is the real significance of these relationships? The goal of this discussion is to show that all the contingent cash flow obligations, their payoff profiles, and their values are *related*. We can create the same payoff profile on a municipal derivative security by embedding an interest rate swap, a series of forward contracts, or the right combination of options contracts. In addition, we can *value* the embedded portion derivative security as if it were a combination of these hedging and/or option contracts. Partici-

EXHIBIT 7–5
Options Strategy Replicating the Selling of a Futures Contract

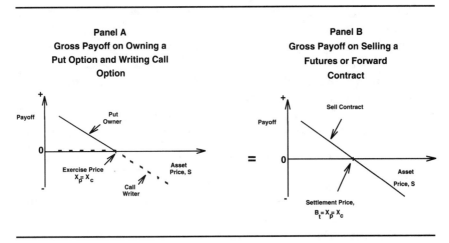

pants have choices about how to approach the valuation of municipal derivative securities. They can choose the valuation option with which they are most comfortable; the same result should be obtained, no matter which one they choose.

VALUATION OF OPTIONS

We'll now turn to the valuation of options and will focus first on the valuation of a call option. Then, we will use *put–call parity* to derive the value of a put option. After we develop valuation techniques for call options and put options, we extend the analysis to include interest rate caps and interest rate floors. The valuation and duration of interest rate options is an important part of the derivative valuations in Chapter 8.

Variables That Influence Option Value

For an option owner, an option is a financial instrument that gives its owner the *right* to buy or to sell an asset at a predetermined price within a specified period of time.

To simplify the option valuation process, let's assume that the underlying asset on which the option is written is not expected to make any payments during the life of the option. Therefore, though we will list (below) six variables that affect the price of an option, the sixth of these variables will not be a concern in this example. The higher the value of the underlying asset, all else equal, the greater the value of the option. At the expiration date of the option, when the asset price, S, is greater than the strike price, X_c, the intrinsic value of the option is positive and the option should be exercised. The relation described by the following equation is relevant.

$$\text{Call value (at expiration)} = S - X_c$$

Now let's look at the value of an option prior to maturity. Clearly, this value will still be greatly dependent on the intrinsic value of the option—the relationship between the asset value and the strike price. However, an option owner does not have to pay the strike price, X_c, until the option is exercised, which may be as far away as maturity, t. Therefore, it is possible to approximate the current value of a call option by the *difference between the current asset price minus the strike price discounted from its maturity date, t, at an appropriate risk-free interest rate.*

Let:

V_c = value of a call option

S = price of the security underlying the option

X_c = exercise price or strike price on the call option

$\tilde{r}$ = risk-free rate of interest

$f(t,\tilde{r})$ = a functional relationship among the variables

Then:

$$V_c \approx S - X_c f(t,\tilde{r}); \; 0 \le f(t,\tilde{r}) \le 1$$

This is the basic idea underlying option valuation. As you can see from this equation, the call value is a function of the asset price, S, the strike price, X_c, the time to maturity of the option, t, and the risk-free rate, $\tilde{r}$.

The equation is adjusted to introduce the volatility of the underlying asset, σ^2, and statistical distribution functions, $N(d_1)$ and $N(d_2)$, that assure that the option's value never becomes negative. In fact, as the price volatility of an asset increases, as measured by changes in the volatility of the asset's price—the variance of its return, the probability increases that the asset will be *in the money* at some point during the life of the option. This increased probability means that the option value increases with higher volatility.

As with hedging components, the valuation of option components is solely dependent on an assessment of interest rate risk— not on credit risk. Again, credit risk or counterparty (floor writer or cap writer) payment risk can be addressed through collateralization of a party's obligations under the option contract.

As we mentioned above, there are six variables that may affect the value of an option, as follows:

S = the current price of the underlying asset. The higher the price of the asset, the greater the option value.

X_c = the strike or exercise price of the option. The higher the strike price of the call option, the lower the option value.

σ^2 = the price volatility of the underlying asset. The greater the volatility, the greater the option value.

t = the time to maturity of the option, measured in years. The greater the time to maturity, the greater the option value.

$\tilde{r}$ = the risk-free interest rate. The greater the risk-free rate, the greater the option value.

C = the interest payments or dividend payments on the underlying asset during the life of the option. The greater those payments, the lower the value of a call option (the higher the value of a put option).

The relationship between the call value and the variables that influence it are shown in Exhibit 7–6.

The Black-Scholes Option Pricing Model

In this section, we describe the valuation of call options on common stock, using the pathbreaking Black-Scholes option pricing model. We attempt to explain, in simple terms and using a simple example, that you don't need a degree in astrophysics to use this model. Although the model may be used to value call and put options on long-term fixed-rate treasury and municipal bonds, it has some assumptions, particularly constant interest rates, that make it inappropriate for valuing interest rate options based on movements in short-term

EXHIBIT 7–6
Variables that Influence Call Value

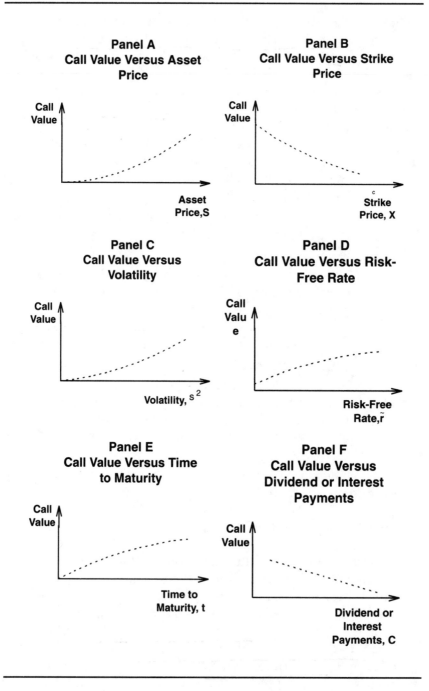

Panel A
Call Value Versus Asset Price

Panel B
Call Value Versus Strike Price

Panel C
Call Value Versus Volatility

Panel D
Call Value Versus Risk-Free Rate

Panel E
Call Value Versus Time to Maturity

Panel F
Call Value Versus Dividend or Interest Payments

interest rates on bonds. A more appropriate model for valuing interest rate caps and floors is Black's model, which we will describe later in this chapter. This section is designed to get you comfortable, in general, with option pricing. In fact, the Black-Scholes model has fairly broad applications. The authors have seen the model empirically proved in a wide array of situations, ranging from deciding between full-day and half-day ski-lift passes in Aspen, Colorado, to valuing the á la carte versus the prix fixe menus at Le Cirque.

F. Black and M. Scholes in the early 1970s[2] developed an option pricing model for use in valuing European call options on non-dividend-paying stock. In developing this model, they used an arbitrage pricing approach which compared the returns associated with buying a call option on a stock to the returns from buying a share of the stock and borrowing a portion of the cost of the stock at the risk-free rate of interest. Using this arbitrage model and assuming perfect capital markets, the returns from owning the call option position and from holding a properly hedged leveraged position in the underlying asset should be identical. In this approach, there is a need to constantly adjust the hedge position to create a perfectly arbitraged position. The Black-Scholes equation given below replicates this hedged approach.

Let:

V_c = value of the call option

S = current asset price

X_c = call strike price

$\tilde{r}$ = risk-free rate of interest

t = time to maturity of option measured in years

e = 2.7182, the base for natural logarithms and the discounting factor for continuous time

σ^2 = variance of the rate of return on the underlying asset, a measure of volatility

$N(\cdot)$ = cumulative normal probability density function, the probability that a normally distributed random variable will be less than or equal to the value in parenthesis

[2]See F Black and M Scholes, "The Valuation of Option Contracts and a Test of Market Efficiency," *Journal of Finance,* May 1972, pp. 399–417; and F Black and M Scholes, "The Pricing of Options and Corporate Liabilities," *Journal of Political Economy,* vol. 81, May–June 1973, pp. 637–654.

<u>Then:</u>

$$V_c = S\,N(d_1) - X_c e^{-rt} N\,(d_2)$$

where

$$d_1 = \frac{1n\,(S/X_c) + (\tilde{r} + \sigma^2/2)t}{\sigma\sqrt{t}}$$

$$d_2 = d_1 - \sigma\sqrt{t}$$

Although these equations may seem formidable at first, they are relatively simple equations that depend on only five variables, which are easily observed or estimated. The formula states that the *value of a call option* is equal to the investment in the underlying asset of S times a probability function, $N(d_1)$, minus a borrowing of an amount equal to $X_c e^{-rt}$ times a probability function, $N(d_2)$.

Interest rates used in option pricing models are generally compounded on a continuous time basis. Recall, from Chapter 3, that the present value of a cash flow is found by dividing the cash flow by a discount factor, in this case composed of $1 + \tilde{r}$. As the number of compounding periods increases, we must divide the interest rate, in this case $\tilde{r}$, by the number of compounding periods, p, and increase the power of the discount factor accordingly.

Let:

PV = present value of X_c

X_c = exercise price of the call option

$\tilde{r}$ = risk-free rate of interest

n = number of years

p = number of compounding periods

Then:

$$PV = \frac{X_c}{(1 + \tilde{r}/p)^{np}}$$

As the number of compounding periods per year increases to a infinity, the value in the denominator mathematically approaches e^{rt}. Therefore, we can rewrite this equation as:

$$PV = \frac{X_c}{e^{rt}} = X_c e^{-rt}$$

The purpose of e in the equation is to provide for continuous compounding, which is a standard assumption in option pricing.

Although the entire derivation is quite complex, it is not necessary to understand the derivation in order to apply the model. The most difficult aspect of the model to understand is the role of the normal cumulative probability functions and d_1 and d_2, which are analogous to z values from a standard normal probability function. The Black-Scholes formula requires inputs equal to the percentage area under the curve that lies to the left of the appropriate d value. The reason for this is that the model assumes that asset prices underlying the option follow a normal distribution. This assumption greatly assists in the valuation process because it allows us to place probability estimates on the movement of the underlying asset price based solely on the estimated volatility of the price.

Exhibit 7–7 shows a graph of the normal probability function, and Exhibit 7–8 shows the cumulative distribution function for the standard normal random variable.

Example.   To see how the Black-Scholes model is used, let's look at an example. Let's assume we're valuing a call option on a non-dividend-paying stock.

EXHIBIT 7–7
Normal Probability Function

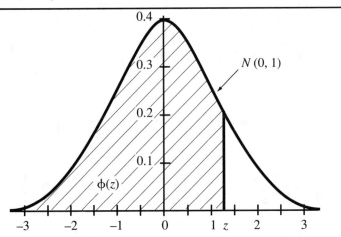

EXHIBIT 7–8

Cumulative Distribution Function for the Standard Normal Random Variable

	0.00	0.01	0.02	0.03	0.04	0.05	0.06	0.07	0.08	0.09
0.0	0.5000	0.5040	0.5080	0.5120	0.5160	0.5199	0.523 9	0.5279	0.5319	0.5359
0.1	0.5398	0.5438	0.5478	0.5517	0.5557	0.5596	0.563 6	0.5675	0.5714	0.5753
0.2	0.5793	0.5832	0.5871	0.5910	0.5948	0.5987	0.602 6	0.6064	0.6103	0.6141
0.3	0.6179	0.6217	0.6255	0.6293	0.6331	0.6368	0.640 6	0.6443	0.6480	0.6517
0.4	0.6554	0.6591	0.6628	0.6664	0.6700	0.6736	0.677 2	0.6808	0.6844	0.6879
0.5	0.6915	0.6950	0.6985	0.7019	0.7054	0.7088	0.712 3	0.7157	0.7190	0.7224
0.6	0.7257	0.7291	0.7324	0.7357	0.7389	0.7422	0.745 4	0.7486	0.7517	0.7549
0.7	0.7580	0.7611	0.7642	0.7673	0.7704	0.7734	0.776 4	0.7794	0.7823	0.785
0.8	0.7881	0.7910	0.7939	0.7967	0.7995	0.8023	0.805 1	0.8078	0.8106	0.8133
0.9	0.8159	0.8186	0.8212	0.8238	0.8264	0.8289	0.831 5	0.8340	0.8365	0.8389
1.0	0.8413	0.8438	0.8461	0.8485	0.8508	0.8531	0.855 4	0.8577	0.8599	0.8621
1.1	0.8643	0.8665	0.8686	0.8708	0.8729	0.8749	0.877 0	0.8790	0.8810	0.8830
1.2	0.8849	0.8869	0.8888	0.8907	0.8925	0.8944	0.896 2	0.8980	0.8997	0.9015
1.3	0.9032	0.9049	0.9066	0.9082	0.9099	0.9115	0.913 1	0.9147	0.9162	0.9177
1.4	0.9192	0.9207	0.9222	0.9236	0.9251	0.9265	0.927 9	0.9292	0.9306	0.9319
1.5	0.9332	0.9345	0.9357	0.9370	0.9382	0.9394	0.940 6	0.9418	0.9429	0.9441
1.6	0.9452	0.9463	0.9474	0.9484	0.9495	0.9505	0.951 5	0.9525	0.9535	0.9545
1.7	0.9554	0.9564	0.9573	0.9582	0.9591	0.9599	0.960 8	0.9616	0.9625	0.9633
1.8	0.9641	0.9649	0.9656	0.9664	0.9671	0.9678	0.968 6	0.9693	0.9699	0.9706
1.9	0.9713	0.9719	0.9726	0.9732	0.9738	0.9744	0.975 0	0.9756	0.9761	0.9767
2.0	0.9772	0.9778	0.9783	0.9788	0.9793	0.9798	0.980 3	0.9808	0.9812	0.9817
2.1	0.9821	0.9826	0.9830	0.9834	0.9838	0.9842	0.984 6	0.9850	0.9854	0.9857
2.2	0.9861	0.9864	0.9868	0.9871	0.9875	0.9878	0.988 1	0.9884	0.9887	0.9890
2.3	0.9883	0.9896	0.9898	0.9901	0.9904	0.9906	0.990 9	0.9911	0.9913	0.9916
2.4	0.9918	0.9920	0.9922	0.9925	0.9927	0.9929	0.993 1	0.9932	0.9934	0.9936
2.5	0.9938	0.9940	0.9941	0.9943	0.9945	0.9946	0.994 8	0.9949	0.9951	0.9952
2.6	0.9953	0.9955	0.9956	0.9957	0.9959	0.9960	0.996 1	0.9962	0.9963	0.9964
2.7	0.9965	0.9966	0.9967	0.9968	0.9969	0.9970	0.997 1	0.9972	0.9973	0.9974
2.8	0.9974	0.9975	0.9976	0.9977	0.9977	0.9978	0.997 9	0.9979	0.9980	0.9981
2.9	0.9981	0.9982	0.9982	0.9983	0.9984	0.9984	0.998 5	0.9985	0.9986	0.9986
3.0	0.9987	0.9987	0.9987	0.9988	0.9988	0.9989	0.998 9	0.9989	0.9990	0.9990

Let:

$S = \$50$

$X_c = \$45$

$t = 1$ year

$\tilde{r} = 6.00\%$

$\sigma = 8.00\%$ or 0.08

$\sigma^2 = 0.64\%$ or 0.0064

First, let's calculate the values for d_1 and d_2, as follows:

$$d_1 = \frac{1n(S/X_c) + (\tilde{r} + \sigma^2/2)^t}{\sigma \sqrt{t}}$$

$$d_1 = \frac{1n(50/45) + (0.06 + 0.0064/2)^1}{0.08 \sqrt{1}}$$

$$d_1 = \frac{0.105361 + 0.0632}{0.08}$$

$$d_1 = 2.107013$$

$$d_2 = d_1 - \sigma \sqrt{t}$$

$$d_2 = 2.107013 - 0.08\sqrt{1}$$

$$d_2 = 2.027013$$

Using Exhibit 7–8, we get the following values:

$$N (d_1) = N (2.107) = 0.9826$$

$$N (d_2) = N (2.027) = 0.9788$$

Now we have:

$$V_c = SN(d_1) - X_c e^{-rt} N(d_2)$$

$$= 50 (0.9826) - 45 (e^{-(0.06)(1)}(0.9788))$$

$$= 50 (0.9826) - 45 (0.9417) (0.9788)$$

$$= 49.13 - 41.48$$

$$= \$7.65$$

In the event that either d_1 or d_2 were negative, then the z value would be to the left of 0 in Exhibit 7–7 and $N(d_1)$ or $N(d_2)$ would equal $1 - N(d)$. For example, if $d_1 = -0.07$, $N(d_1) = 1 - 0.5279 = 0.4721$.

Remember that the Black-Scholes formula is a simple algebraic equation that is not difficult to use, with a little practice.

Through the concept of *put–call parity*, the Black-Scholes formula can also be used to price put options. Again an arbitrage pricing approach is used, this time with a three-asset portfolio consisting of a share of stock, a call option with strike price, X_c, and a put option with strike price, $X_p = X_c$. Using put-call parity, we can replicate the expected cash flows on a put by buying a call, selling the underlying asset and borrowing the present value of the strike price. Since the portfolio of these three assets has the same expected cash flows as a put, we can value a put by summing the values of each of the assets.

With this information, we can formulate the value of a put option as shown below.

Let:

V_p = value of a put option
V_c = value of a call option
S = value of the underlying asset
X_c = strike price on the call option
e^{-rt} = continuous time discount function

Then:

$$V_p = V_c - S + X_c e^{-rt}$$

Example.   Using the variables from the example above, we can calculate the value of a put as follows:

$$V_p = 7.65 - 50 + 45\, e^{-0.06)(1)}$$
$$= 7.65 - 50 + 42.3765$$
$$= \$0.028$$

Delta of an Option

An important concept in option valuation is the measure of the change in the option value for a given change in the value of the underlying asset. This measure is commonly referred to as the delta of the option.

Let:

Δ_c = delta of a call option
Δ_p = delta of a put option
ΔV_c = change in the value of the call

ΔV_p = change in the value of the put

ΔS = change in the value of the underlying asset

Then

$$\Delta_c = \frac{\Delta V_c}{\Delta S}$$

and

$$\Delta_p = \frac{\Delta V_p}{\Delta S}$$

For a European call option with no dividends or coupon payments on the underlying asset, the delta can be estimated for small changes in the price of the underlying asset as simply:

$$\Delta_c = N\,(d_1)$$

The delta of a call option is always positive and falls between 0 and 1. This positive relationship means that as the price of the underlying asset increases, the value of the call option increases proportionately. (See Exhibit 7–6, Panel A for a graphical representation of the relationship between the value of a call and the price of the underlying asset.)

Similarly, for a European put option with no dividends or coupon payments on the underlying asset, the delta can be estimated for small changes in the price of the underlying asset as:

$$\Delta_p = N\,(d_1) - 1$$

The delta for a put option is always negative and falls between 0 and −1. This negative relationship means that as the price of the underlying asset increases, the value of the put option decreases.

Delta serves as a measure of the movement of the value of the option relative to the underlying asset. For example, consider a call option with a delta of 0.45 ($N(d_1) = 0.45$). A \$1.00 increase in the price of the underlying asset should approximately result in a \$0.45 increase in the price of the call option. The concept of delta is generally used as a hedge ratio in option hedging strategies. However, as we will show in Chapter 8, the delta of interest rate contingent options, is also a good measure of its price duration.

INTEREST RATE CAP AND FLOOR OPTIONS

Interest rate caps and floors can be analyzed as a series of European options that have periodic payments, depending upon interest rate levels on a series of predetermined future dates. For interest rate caps and floors, *payments depend on levels of an interest rate index*, not on the *price or value of a specific asset*, such as a stock option. In this section, we look closely at the payoff profiles associated with caps and floors, and at how they vary with interest rates.

Next, we discuss, in depth, Black's interest rate cap option pricing model which is used by many participants in the market place. We use this model to value a one-year, Kenny-based, 3 percent interest rate cap option, assuming the yield curve shown in Exhibit 4–10. We then use put–call parity to derive the value of a one-year, 3 percent interest rate floor option. Finally, we show how interest rate caps and floors are embedded, and how they should be valued in each of the five municipal derivative securities that are being examined in this book.

Overview

The two types of option components that have frequently been embedded in municipal derivative securities are interest rate cap and floor options. An interest rate *cap is a call* option, and an interest rate *floor* is a *put* option. The periodic payments of both are based on a notional principal amount and on the level of interest rates as compared to a predetermined strike price. As with hedging components, the future cash flows associated with these instruments depend on unknown future levels of interest rates. The valuation of these option components depends not only on expectations of future interest rates but also on the volatility of the rates. Interest rate caps are bearish instruments that allow cap owners to protect themselves against, or benefit from, higher interest rates. Interest rate floors are bullish instruments that allow their owners to protect themselves against, or benefit from, lower interest rates. It is important to recognize that caps and floors function as option contracts, rather than as hedging contracts like forwards or futures, because they are one-sided obligations. Periodic payments are made under the interest rate cap only if the interest index is above the strike price. Likewise, payments are made on the interest rate floor only if the interest index is below the strike price.

An *interest rate cap* is an obligation designed to provide insurance against the possibility that the rate of interest, such as the Kenny Index or the PSA Index, will go above a specified level, called the *cap rate*, X_c. It is a contract between two parties, the *cap writer* and the *cap owner*. The cap writer, in consideration of an upfront payment or some other form of consideration, agrees to make periodic payments to the cap owner if the Kenny Index exceeds the cap rate (e.g., 4.00 percent) for a period of time. An interest rate cap can be thought of as a portfolio of European call options on the level of an interest rate, such as the Kenny Index. The settlement date on an individual cap option generally coincides with an interest payment date on the municipal bond in which it has been embedded.

The payment profile to an owner of an interest rate cap for any settlement date is the greater of either $0 or the product of a notional dollar principal amount (e.g., $5000) times the amount of time in the payment period (e.g., 0.5 years) times the excess of the average Kenny Index minus the cap rate of 4.00 percent. For example, if the Kenny Index averaged 4.00 percent or less during the six-month interest period, the cap owner would receive $0. If the Kenny Index averaged 5.00 percent during the interest period, the cap owner would receive from the cap writer the amount expressed by the following equation.

$$\text{Payment to cap owner} = \text{notional amount} \times \text{period length}$$
$$\times MAX[0, (\text{Kenny Index} - \text{cap rate})]$$
$$\$25.00 = \$5000 \times 0.5 \text{ year}$$
$$\times MAX[0, (5.00\% - 4.00\%)]$$

The gross and net payoff profiles for a cap owner and a cap writer are shown in Exhibit 7–9, panels A and B, respectively. Whatever the cap owner receives, the cap writer must pay; this is a zero-sum game. It is assumed that the cap owner pays a cap premium or gives some other kind of compensation, such as a reduction in annual interest on the bond or writes an interest rate floor, to the cap writer for making the contingent cap interest payments, as described in the equation above. If the Kenny Index exceeds the cap rate, 4.00 percent, the cap owner will receive payments in accordance with Exhibit 7–9.

An *interest rate floor* is an obligation that is designed to provide insurance against the possibility that the rate of interest (i.e., the Kenny Index) will go below a specified level, called the *floor rate,* X_p. It is a contract between two parties, the *floor writer* and the *floor owner.* The floor writer, in consideration of an up-front payment or some other form of consideration, agrees to make periodic payments to the floor owner in the event that the Kenny Index is below the floor rate (i.e., 4.00 percent) for a period of time. An in-

EXHIBIT 7–9

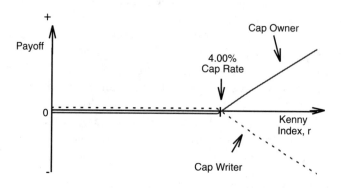

Panel A
Gross Payoff on Cap Options

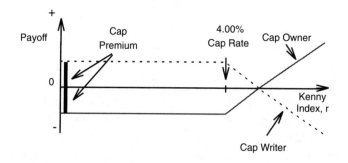

Panel B
Net Payoff on Cap Options

terest rate floor can be thought of as a portfolio of European put options on the level of an interest rate, the Kenny Index, versus the floor rate, P. The payment profile of an owner of an interest rate floor for any settlement date is opposite to the payment profile of an owner of an interest rate cap, in that the floor owner receives $0 if the Kenny Index averages greater than or equal to the floor rate during the interest period. If the Kenny Index averages 3.00 percent during the period, the floor owner will receive the following amount from the floor writer:

$$\text{Payment to floor owner} = \text{notional amount} \times \text{period length}$$
$$\times MAX[0, (\text{floor rate} - \text{Kenny Index})]$$
$$\$25.00 = \$5000 \times 0.5 \text{ year}$$
$$\times MAX\ [0, (4.00\% - 3.00\%)]$$

The gross and net payoff profiles for a floor owner and a floor writer are shown in panels A and B of Exhibit 7–10. Again, the payoffs result in a zero-sum game. The floor owner pays a floor premium or some other type of compensation to the floor writer for writing the series of floor put options.

Black's Valuation Model for Caps

From the perspective of a cap or floor owner, a payment (the cap or floor premium) is made for the purchase of interest rate insurance, and a stream of future cash flows will be received that is dependent on unknown future levels of the interest index. The payment of the cap or floor premium can take the form of a single up-front payment, a reduction in the coupon rate of the underlying debt instrument, or the granting of an option under which the cap or floor owner becomes a floor or cap writer. We will present more information about cap and floor premium payment options in the next section.

Now the question is: How do we value these cap and floor options? In the case of cap and floor options for municipal derivative securities, future payments are dependent upon the future level of the Kenny Index versus a prespecified cap or floor rate. Thus, the value of the cap or floor option itself is crucially dependent on expected future Kenny Index levels. This is where *expectational analysis* and *implied forward rates* come into play. Most cap and floor

EXHIBIT 7–10

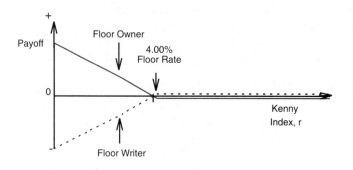

Panel A
Gross Payoffs on Floor Options

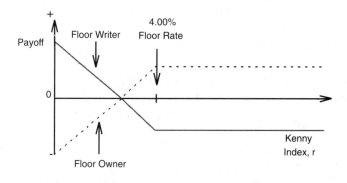

Panel B
Net Payoffs on Floor Options

option pricing models use implied forward rates to calculate the expected interest index levels, which in turn determine the expected cash-flow payments of the cap or floor options.

Like the other valuations discussed in this book, the valuation of cap and floor options involves estimating uncertain future cash flows. Since the cap and floor rates generally are fixed throughout the life of the option, option pricing concentrates on estimating the probabilities that the underlying index (in our example, the Kenny

Index) will exceed the cap rate or be less than the floor rate. Inputs to a typical option pricing model are the volatility of the index, the time to maturity of the option, the specified level of the cap or floor option, and a risk-free rate of interest with which to discount cash flows. Therefore, the valuation of cap and floor options is not unlike the valuation process associated with a stock option.

The volatility of the index is used to estimate how movements in the Kenny Index will affect the value of the option. If the volatility is low over the length of the option, the Kenny Index is not expected to diverge much from the expectations of tax-exempt forward rates implied in the yield curve, and the value of the option decreases. The value of a cap or floor option increases as volatility increases, because it increases the probability that the Kenny Index will move away from the forward rates implied by the yield curve. If the movement of the Kenny Index results in incrementally higher cash flows to the cap or floor owner, this volatility increases the potential yield, and hence the value, of the option. Recent (October 1993) studies and pricing analysis by investment banks and pricing services indicate the use of volatility estimates, as measured by the historical semiannual standard deviation of interest rates, of 6 to 10 percent for the BBI-40[3] and 8.00 to 10.00 percent for the Kenny Index.[4] For the valuation of the interest rate cap and floor options in this chapter and in Chapter 8, we use a volatility estimate of 8 percent for both indexes.

The Black-Scholes option pricing model works very well in valuing stock options where the risk-free interest rate, $\tilde{r}$, used in the model is an exogenous variable and is assumed not to affect stock prices. However, prices of interest rate options are very much more dependent on the risk-free interest rate than are stock prices

---

[3]In recent option-adjusted spread analysis for the BBI-40, Goldman Sachs used a standard deviation volatility estimate of 8 percent and Bloomberg Financial Markets used a volatility estimate of 6 percent. A 1988 study by The First Boston Corporation, entitled "Valuation of Call Provisions on Municipal Bonds" estimated the annualized 30-day yield volatility of the BBI-40 to be between 4 percent and 27 percent. The study results suggested that a range of 6 to 15 percent would be a reasonable assumption for future volatility in the municipal market.

[4]A recent study by the authors which examined the volatility of the Kenny Index since its inception suggests on average a volatility, as measured by the semiannual standard derivation of interest rates, of 8.00 to 15.00 percent.

and stock option values, and adjustments must be made in the model to value interest rate options.

Black's model is often used by market participants to value interest rate caps and floors.[5] As previously stated, an interest rate cap can be valued as a portfolio of European call options, with one option being exercised on each settlement date. For instance, a 5-year, 3.50 percent Kenny-based interest rate cap embedded in a long-term municipal bond that pays semiannual interest can be viewed as 10 European call options on the Kenny Index, each with a strike price of 3.50 percent and each with a different exercise date, t ($t = 0.5$ year, 1 year, . . ., 4.5 years, 5 years).

A limitation of Black's model that has been noted by academicians is that the model assumes one volatility measurement associated with each of the European call option payment dates. There are several different theories regarding the term structure of interest rates and the term structure of volatility, and numerous option pricing models are based on the differing theories. Some models, such as the binomial pricing model used in option-adjusted spread analysis, allow the adoption of a term structure of volatility. We have found that interest rate volatility has decreased over time, and that, with the current low level of estimated volatility (e.g., 8 to 10 percent), the incorporation of a term structure of volatility may be more trouble and cause more confusion than it is worth. Therefore, we have opted for simplicity and have stuck with an interest rate option pricing model that we feel works quite well in today's environment.

The *value of the cap*, V_c, is simply the summation of the values of each of the underlying 10 call options on the Kenny Index minus the cap rate, x_c, with settlement dates of 0.5 year, 1 year, etc., and with expected term periods equal to τ (e.g., $\tau = 0.5$ year). The expected cash flows associated with each period are a function of the implied tax-exempt forward rate for the period, $_{t-1}f_t^*$ minus the strike price, x_c, each adjusted by its respective normal distribution function parameters, $N(d_1)$ and $N(d_2)$. The amount of the cash flow is also dependent upon the notional principal

---

[5]See F. Black, "The Pricing of Commodity Contracts," *Journal of Financial Economics* 3 (1976), pp. 167–79 and Hull, op. cit. pp. 348–352.

amount of the option, F, times the expected payment discounted back to the present by the various zero-coupon risk-free rates of interest that are coincident with the expected payment dates, r_t. Finally, the deferred nature of the payments under the cap over the $T(\tau = 0.5$ year) term periods should reflect the loss of current income, which is discounted at the appropriate forward rate $_{t-1}f_t^*$. This gives us the equations shown below, which represent Black's model for caps.

Let:

V_c = value of the cap

x_c = cap rate

F = notional amount of the cap

$_{t-1}f_t^*$ = implied tax-exempt forward rate of interest

r_t = implied zero-coupon rate at time t

τ = individual cap period

T = number of cap periods of length τ

ln = natural logarithm

σ = standard deviation of the implied tax-exempt forward rate

σ^2 = variance of the implied tax-exempt forward rate

Then:

$$V_c = \sum_{t=1}^{T} \frac{\tau}{1 + \tau \,_{t-1}f_t^*} \, Fe^{-r_t t}[_{t-1}f_t^* \, N(d_1) - x_c N(d_2)]$$

where

$$d_1 = \frac{ln(_{t-1}f_t^*/x) + \sigma^2 t/2}{\sigma \sqrt{t}}$$

$$d_2 = d_1 - \sigma \sqrt{t}$$

The expected future Kenny Index rates $_{t-1}f_t^*$ are derived from the yield curve using expectational analysis, and the implied zero-coupon discount rates r_t are used to discount the expected cash flows. σ^2 is the expected volatility of the implied tax-exempt forward rate.

There, that was easy enough! Now let's value a one-year, semiannually payable 3.00 percent Kenny-based interest rate cap. To properly do this, we need a yield curve to derive the implied tax-exempt forward rates and the implied zero-coupon discount rates. Let's assume that the cap has a $5000 notional amount, F, and that the volatility, σ, of the Kenny Index is 8.00 percent. Let's assume a yield curve like the one shown in Exhibit 4–10, where the annualized implied tax-exempt forward rates $_0f_{0.5}{}^* = 3.124$ percent and $_{0.5}f_1{}^* = 3.268$ percent, and the annual implied zero-coupon rates $r_{0.5} = 4.400$ percent and $r_1 = 4.501$ percent.

The interest rate cap can be viewed as a portfolio of two European call options on the Kenny Index, with strike price $x = 3.00$ percent, and settlement dates $t = 0.5$ year and 1 year. Substituting these variables, we get:

$$V_c = \sum_{t=0}^{1} \frac{\tau}{1 + \tau_{\,t-1}f_t{}^*} \; (\$5000)e^{-r_t t}[_{t-1}f_t{}^* \, N(d_1) - 0.03(d_2)]$$

For period $t = 0.5$ and $\tau = 0.5$, we begin by calculating the values of d_1 and d_2 and refer to Exhibit 7–8 to get the values for $N(d_1)$ and $N(d_2)$, as follows:

$$d_1 = \frac{ln(0.03124/0.03) + [(0.08)^2(0.5/2)]}{0.08\sqrt{0.5}}$$

$$d_1 = \frac{0.040502 + 0.0016}{0.056569} = 0.744259$$

$$N(d_1) = 0.7716$$
$$d_2 = 0.744259 - 0.08\sqrt{0.5}$$
$$d_2 = 0.744259 - 0.056569 = 0.687690$$
$$N(d_2) = \$0.7542$$

Now we can calculate the value of the 0.5-year call option, with $r_{0.5} = 0.044$, on the Kenny Index, as follows:

$$V_{0.5} = \frac{0.5}{1 + (0.5)(0.03124)} \; (\$5000)e^{-(0.044)(0.5)} \, [(0.03124)(0.7716)$$

$$- (0.03)(0.7542)]$$
$$V_{0.5} = (0.492310)(\$5000)(0.978)(0.001479)$$
$$V_{0.5} = \$3.561$$

For the period $t = 1$, $\tau = 0.5$, we first calculate the values of d_1 and d_2 and refer to Exhibit 7–8 to get values for $N(d_1)$ and $N(d_2)$, as follows:

$$d_1 = \frac{ln(0.03268/0.03) + (0.08)^2(1/2)}{(0.08)\sqrt{1}}$$

$$d_1 = \frac{0.085566 + 0.0032}{0.08} = 1.109575$$

$$N(d_1) = 0.8664$$

$$d_2 = 1.109575 - 0.08\sqrt{1}$$

$$d_2 = 1.029575$$

$$N(d_2) = 0.8484$$

Now we calculate the value of a one-year call option, with an 0.5-year term—0.5 year out—and with $r_1 = 0.04501$, on the Kenny Index, as follows:

$$V_1 = \frac{0.5}{1 + (0.5)(0.03268)} (\$5000)e^{(-0.04501)(1)} [(0.03268)(0.8664)$$

$$- (0.03)(0.8484)]$$

$$V_1 = (0.491961)(\$5000)(0.956)(0.002862)$$

$$V_1 = \$6.730$$

The value of the Kenny cap is the sum of the values of the two underlying call options, as follows:

$$V_c = V_{0.5} + V_1$$

$$= \$3.561 + \$6.730$$

$$= \$10.291$$

In other words, this cap is valued at $10.29, which represents approximately two-tenths of one percent (0.2 percent) of the $5000 notional principal amount. It is obvious that doing calculations by hand is a laborious task, even for a short, two-period interest rate cap. Luckily, this type of option valuation procedure is not too difficult to program into a computer spreadsheet. Sample printouts of output pages for such a program are included in Chapter 8.

Now let's consider an interest rate floor with the same parameters as the cap we valued above. The interest rate floor can be valued by using put–call parity, as we did for put options in the previous section; however, we must make a slight adjustment, as follows:

$$V_P = V_c - \frac{\tau}{1 + \tau_{t-1}f_t^*} \$5000e^{-r_t t}(-x_c + {}_{t-1}f_t^*)$$

We calculate the value of the put in two steps and sum the individual parts as we did for the cap. Using the numbers from above, we can calculate the 0.5-year value of the put option with $(-x_c + {}_{t-1}f_t^*)$ equal to $(-3\% + 3.124\%)$ on the Kenny Index, as follows:

$$V_{0.5} = 3.443 - (0.492310)(\$5000)(0.978)(0.00124)$$
$$= 3.443 - (2.985)$$
$$= \$0.458$$

Similarly, we can calculate the 1-year value of the put option with $(-x_c + {}_{t-1}f_t^*)$ equal to $(-3\% + 3.268\%)$, as follows:

$$V_1 = 11.288 - (0.491961)(\$5000)(0.956)(0.00268)$$
$$= 11.288 - (6.302)$$
$$= \$4.986$$

The value of the Kenny floor is the sum of the values of the two underlying put options, as follows:

$$V_p = V_{0.5} + V_1$$
$$= \$0.458 + \$4.986$$
$$= \$5.444$$

PRICE DURATION OF AN INTEREST RATE OPTION

Recall from Chapter 3 that the price duration of a security measures the change in price of the security for a given change in interest rates. Since delta is an estimate of the change in price of an option for a corresponding change in the price of the underlying asset, delta can also be used to estimate the price duration of an interest rate option.

The delta of a one period interest rate cap is measured by:

$$\Delta_c = e^{-r_t t} \, N(d_1)$$

Since the value of an interest rate cap increases as interest rates increase, the delta is always positive and falls between 0 and 1. Using the delta, we can estimate the price duration, D^{cap}, by adjusting for the length of the cap period and the notional amount of the cap, as shown below:

$$D^{cap} = \tau F e^{-r_t t} N(d_1)$$

Since an interest rate cap over many periods is essentially a portfolio of single-period caps, the delta of the portfolio is the sum of the individual deltas on the single-period caps. Thus, for a multi-period cap we would calculate the value of the delta as:

$$\Delta_c = \sum_{t=1}^{T} e^{-r_t t} N(d_1)$$

Similarly, the price duration of a multi-period cap would be calculated as:

$$D^{cap} = \sum_{t=1}^{T} \tau F e^{-r_t t} N(d_1) = \tau F \sum_{t=1}^{T} e^{-r_t t} N(d_1)$$

It is easy to extend this analysis to an interest rate floor option. The delta of an interest rate floor is always negative because the value of a floor decreases as interest rates increase. We can estimate the delta of an interest rate floor as:

$$\Delta_p = \sum_{t=1}^{T} e^{-r_t t} [N(d_1) - 1]$$

Therefore, the price duration for an interest rate floor option can be estimated as:

$$D^{floor} = \tau F \sum_{t=1}^{T} e^{-r_t t} [N(d_1) - 1]$$

Example.   Using the numbers from the previous example,

$$F = \$5,000$$
$$r_5 = 4.400\%$$
$$\tau = .5$$
$$N(d_1) = .7716$$

The delta of the cap is equal to:

$$\Delta_c = e^{(-.044)(.5)}.7716 = .7546$$

The price duration of the cap is equal to:

$$D^{cap} = (.5)(\$5,000)(.7546) = \$1,886.56$$

Applying the price duration, if interest rates change by 10 bps, we would expect the value of the cap to change by $(.001)(1886.56) = \$1.886$.

Use of Option-Like Structures in Municipal Derivative Securities

Many of the municipal derivative securities that have been recently marketed either implicitly or explicitly include an option component with a price performance profile similar to either an interest rate cap or an interest rate floor. An *implicit* interest rate cap or floor exists when an interest rate formula on a variable rate bond is *constrained* from floating past a certain level. Implicit interest rate caps are embedded in the RIBS, the inverse floater, the BULL Floater BPO, and the BEAR Floater BPO. Implicit interest rate floors are embedded in the BULL Floater BPO and the BEAR Floater BPO. An *explicit* interest rate cap is embedded in the cap bond.

Let's now look at the interest rate formulas for the five products that we will value in Chapter 8 and see how the option components should be analyzed.

RIBS

The BEY interest rate formula for the RIBS is:

RIBS rate + SAVRS rate = 2 (6.25%) until maturity on 8/1/2014
RIBS rate = 2 (6.25%) − SAVRS rate
RIBS rate = 12.50% − SAVRS rate

What happens if the SAVRS rate goes above 12.50 percent? The answer is that the terms of the SAVRS specify a maximum interest rate, an interest rate cap, so that the SAVRS rate never exceeds 12.5 percent. This formula means that the RIBS contains an implied interest rate cap on the SAVRS rate. This cap (call) option is *written* by the SAVRS owner, has a strike price of 12.50 percent versus the companion SAVRS, is payable every 35 days to coincide with the 35-day interest payment dates of the RIBS and the SAVRS, and has a final exercise date of August 1, 2014.

Inverse Floater

The interest rate formula for the inverse floater is:

$c = 6.15\% + (4.70\% - \text{Kenny Index})$ prior to 8/15/1999

$c = 6.15\%$ from 8/15/1999 until maturity on 8/15/2012

The variable-rate interest rate formula of the inverse floater can also be written as:

$$c = 10.85\% - \text{Kenny Index}$$

Reasonable questions to ask about this security would include the following: What happens if the Kenny Index goes above 10.85 percent? Does the inverse floater owner then lose a portion of its principal? The answers are that the inverse floater contains an implied 10.85 percent Kenny Index interest rate cap that is written by the issuer of the inverse floater and that the interest rate cap caps the Kenny Index at 10.85 percent.

The interest rate cap that is implicitly written by the issuer of the inverse floater holder has value. It will be analyzed in Chapter 8 as a 10.85 percent semiannually payable Kenny Index cap (call option) with a final exercise date of August 15, 1999.

BULL Forward BPO

The interest rate formula for the BULL Forward BPO is:

$c = 5.20\%$ prior to June 15, 1994

$c = 5.20\% + 3$ (interest rate adjustment) from 6/15/1994 until maturity on 6/15/2005

The option components on the BULL Forward BPO are a bit trickier and less obvious than the options on the previous two securities. Embedded in this instrument are three forward-like hedging components that are explained further in Chapter 8. The interest rate formula for c is constrained from going below 0 percent or above 2 (5.20%) = 10.40% by not allowing the interest rate adjustment to go above 1.733 percent or below −1.733 percent.

Because of these constraints on the interest rate adjustment, there are three implied interest rate caps (call options) that are owned by the BULL Forward BPO holder at 7.077 percent on the yield to maturity of the BBI-40. These caps, in effect, are written by an investor that owns a mirrored security to the BULL Forward

BPO, a BEAR Forward BPO. Likewise, these constraints implicitly require the Bull Forward BPO holder to write three interest rate floor (put) options at 4.676 percent on the yield to maturity of the BBI-40. These cap and floor options are one-time European options that are can be exercised on June 15, 1994. They will be further explained and valued in Chapter 8.

BEAR Floater
The interest rate formula for the BEAR Floater is:

c = 6.10% + 2 (Kenny Index − 5.0%) prior to 8/15/2002

c = 6.10% from 8/15/2002 with maturity on 8/15/2022
Prior to August 15, 2002, there is a minimum interest rate of 4.0 percent and a maximum interest rate of 8.20 percent.

The option components associated with a BEAR Floater are dictated by the minimum interest rate of 4.00 percent and the maximum interest rate of 8.20 percent, prior to August 15, 2002. If we solve for the Kenny Index in the above interest rate equation that gives a BEAR Floater rate of 4.00 percent, we find the Kenny rate to be 3.95 percent. Therefore, because the BEAR Floater cannot receive less than 4.00 percent and because there are two embedded hedging components [2 (Kenny Index − 5.00%)], the BEAR Floater owner implicitly owns two embedded semiannually payable interest rate floor (put) options at 3.95 percent versus the Kenny Index, with a final exercise date of August 15, 2002. Even though the maximum and minimum rates are contractual elements of the BEAR Floater and are not subject to being waived, it is useful in an analytic sense to view them as interest rate cap and floor options.

Likewise, if we solve for the interest rate equation for the Kenny Index that gives a BEAR Floater rate of 8.20 percent, we find the Kenny Index rate to be 6.05 percent. Since the BEAR Floater cannot receive more than 8.20 percent and there are two embedded hedging components, the BEAR Floater owner implicitly has written two embedded semiannual pay interest rate cap (call) options at 6.05 percent versus the Kenny Index with a final exercise date of August 15, 2002.

These options are valued in Chapter 8.

Cap Bond
The interest rate formula on the cap bond is:

$c = 6.60\% + MAX$ (0%, PSA Index $- 3.50\%$) until 10/1/1997

$c = 6.60\%$ from 10/1/1997 until maturity on 10/1/2016

It will not surprise you to find out that the option component associated with a cap bond is an interest rate cap. The cap in the above interest rate formula is *explicitly* stated as MAX (0%, PSA Index $- 3.50\%$). This cap option will be valued as a series of semi-annually payable European call options with a strike price of 3.50 percent versus the PSA Index and a final exercise date of October 1, 1997. The cap value is shown in Chapter 8.

SUMMARY

In this chapter, we focused on understanding and valuing the option components of municipal derivative securities: interest rate cap and floor options.

We began with a general description of call options and put options. A *call option* is the right to buy an asset, and a *put option* is the right to sell an asset, at a predetermined price for a predetermined period of time. We also examined the payoff profiles of option contracts and noted that combinations of option contracts can be linked, to replicate payoff profiles of hedging contracts such as futures, forwards, and swaps. An option is a one-sided obligation, unlike the two-sided obligation associated with hedging contracts.

We looked at the valuation of options and began to describe the variables that influence option price and value: the current price, S, of the underlying asset; the strike price, X_c, of the option; the price volatility, σ^2, of the underlying asset; the time to maturity, t, of the option; and the risk-free rate of interest, $\tilde{r}$.

To familiarize ourselves with option valuation models, we used the Black-Scholes model to value a share of non-dividend-paying common stock. We found that the valuation equations, though not necessarily fun, were manageable. We even learned how to use put–call parity to derive the value of put options.

We then focused on the understanding and valuation of interest rate caps and floors. An *interest rate cap* is a call option, and an *interest rate floor* is a put option; the periodic payments of both are based on a notional principal amount and on the level of interest rates as compared to a predetermined strike price. Under an interest rate cap, payments are received by the owner of the cap and paid by the writer of the cap only during periods in which the interest rate, or an interest rate index, exceeds the strike price of the cap. Conversely, under an interest rate floor, payments are received by the owner of the floor and paid by the writer of the floor only during periods in which the interest rate, or the interest rate index, is below the strike price of the floor.

We discussed valuation of interest rate caps and floors and the use of Black's interest rate cap option pricing model to value a one-year, semiannually payable, Kenny Index-based, 3 percent interest rate cap, using the implied tax-exempt yield curve shown in Exhibit 4.10.

We then showed how interest rate caps and floors are embedded in, and should be valued in, each of the five municipal derivative securities that are examined in this book.

CHAPTER 8

VALUATION: THE DERIVATIVE ASSET PRICING MODEL

THE DAP MODEL

Introduction

You—the reader—must have a very strong desire to understand municipal derivative securities. By now, you have trudged through seven chapters of pithy, concise, and occasionally witty descriptions of bond mathematics, expectational analysis, and building-block components. You have finally acquired enough background and expertise to soil your hands and intelligently value municipal derivative securities. This is when the fun begins!

To value complex municipal derivative securities, we use an approach called the *derivative asset pricing (DAP) model*.[1] This approach has been suggested and applied by academicians and practitioners in corporate finance.[2] Financial engineers have shown that this approach makes it possible to break down complex derivative securities into simple securities which may be valued easily.

---

[1]The DAP model approach for valuing municipal derivative securities is used by G. Gray, and P. Cusatis in "Understanding and Valuing Municipal Derivative Securities," *Municipal Finance Journal*, vol. 14, no. 2, Summer 1993, 2, pp. 1–41; and by G. Gray and K. Engebretson, in "Residual Interest Bonds (RIBS)," *Municipal Finance Journal* vol. 13, no. 1, spring 1992, pp. 1–29.

[2]See C. Smith and C. Smithson, "Financial Engineering: An Overview," Chapter 1 of *The Handbook of Financial Engineering*, Harper Business, New York, 1990; and C. Smith, C. Smithson, and D. Wilford, "Managing Financial Risk," *The Journal of Applied Corporate Finance*, vol. 1, no. 4, 1989, pp. 27–48.

Our agenda in this chapter is to take the concepts developed in the previous seven chapters, to interweave their common threads into a consistent valuation approach, and to value five representative but complex municipal derivative securities. Since the DAP valuation model is developed in accordance with accepted financial theory, it can be used to value just about any complex debt-based derivative security—municipal, corporate, or government. After describing the general procedures that are used in the DAP model and discussing *structure value,* we will get into the valuation of RIBS, an inverse floater, a cap bond, a BEAR Floater Bond Payment Obligation (BPO) and a BULL Forward BPO.

Model Procedure

Each of the municipal derivative securities examined below has a hedging and/or an option component embedded in it. The valuations of these hedging components (as shown in Chapter 6) and option components (as shown in Chapter 7) are primarily dependent on the yield curve and on implied tax-exempt forward rates. As discussed in Chapter 4 in the description of expectational analysis, most market participants estimate implied tax-exempt forward rates, $_{t-1}f_t^*$, by using the taxable Treasury or LIBOR curve to calculate implied taxable forward rates, $_{t-1}f_t$, and multiplying by a ratio (e.g., 69 to 75 percent). *The implied tax-exempt forward rates are the key inputs in the process of valuing embedded interest rate swaps, forward contracts, and interest rate cap and floor options.*

The first requirement in valuing a municipal derivative security is to input the yield curve and to derive the implied tax-exempt forward rates. These rates are used to value the hedging and option components.

We have developed simple spreadsheet-based software that incorporates and integrates into the DAP model approach each of the key concepts that we have discussed. We have replicated input and output computer screens that illustrate the valuation process for each of the five municipal derivative securities. It is important to note that most of the calculations in the computer program can easily be done on a handheld calculator; it may take a bit longer, but you'll be surprised to see that these programs are not *black-box* or *voodoo economics.* Solving the equations requires no more than an

understanding of simple mathematics. If you follow the process
with a handheld calculator to see whether the emperor is wearing
clothes, you'll be surprised to find that his garments are not only
real but are also carefully constructed and quite colorful.

Taxable Yield Curve Screen

Our first general screen (see Exhibit 8–1), the *taxable yield curve input
screen,* includes all the inputs and calculations associated with expectational analysis (see Chapter 4). The key input is a full-coupon par
taxable yield curve (Exhibit 8–2). For this we use the full-coupon
Treasury curve. From the par taxable curve we derive implied zero-
coupon rates, r_t, and implied taxable forward rates, $_{t-1}f_t$. From the implied taxable forward rates we calculate the set of implied tax-exempt
forward rates, $_{t-1}f_t^*$, by multiplying the taxable forward rates by a ratio
of 71.0 percent. We also use this screen to calculate an implied at-
market swap rate, as described in Chapter 6, for a par interest rate
swap that is coincident with the term of the hedging component. The
implied at-market swap rate is the cumulative present value of the
implied tax-exempt forward rates over the term of the swap divided
by the sum of the discount factors (calculated in accordance with
Exhibit 6–14, without regard to dealer Bids–Receives spreads).

EXHIBIT 8–1
Taxable Yield Curve Input Screen (January 3, 1994)

```
Name of Yield Curve: Treasury 1/3/1994 Target Short-Term Ratio(%)  :    71.00
Term of Swap / Bond:     21 years      Avg. Exp. Short-term rate    :     4.70

     Full   Implied Implied  Tax-Ex. |      Full   Implied Implied  Tax-Ex.
Year Coupon  Zero   Forward  Forward | Year Coupon  Zero   Forward  Forward
 1   3.710   3.710   3.71     2.63   |  16  6.300   6.572   7.67     5.44
 2   4.300   4.319   4.93     3.50   |  17  6.350   6.648   7.88     5.59
 3   4.680   4.713   5.51     3.91   |  18  6.400   6.729   8.11     5.76
 4   5.050   5.109   6.30     4.48   |  19  6.450   6.814   8.36     5.94
 5   5.310   5.389   6.52     4.63   |  20  6.500   6.904   8.63     6.13
 6   5.470   5.562   6.43     4.57   |  21  6.510   6.906   6.95     4.93
 7   5.670   5.793   7.19     5.10   |  22  6.520   6.912   7.03     4.99
 8   5.750   5.876   6.46     4.59   |  23  6.530   6.920   7.09     5.03
 9   5.870   6.020   7.18     5.10   |  24  6.540   6.930   7.15     5.08
10   5.960   6.128   7.10     5.04   |  25  6.550   6.941   7.22     5.12
11   6.020   6.197   6.89     4.89   |  26  6.560   6.954   7.29     5.17
12   6.080   6.271   7.09     5.03   |  27  6.570   6.969   7.36     5.23
13   6.140   6.349   7.29     5.17   |  28  6.580   6.986   7.44     5.28
14   6.200   6.431   7.50     5.32   |  29  6.590   7.005   7.53     5.35
15   6.250   6.499   7.46     5.30   |  30  6.600   7.025   7.62     5.41
                    Implied SWAP Rates
          3 year        3.33%           10 year        4.27%
          5 year        3.79%           20 year        4.69%
          7 year        4.05%           30 year        4.77%
```

EXHIBIT 8–2
Yield Curve (January 3, 1994)

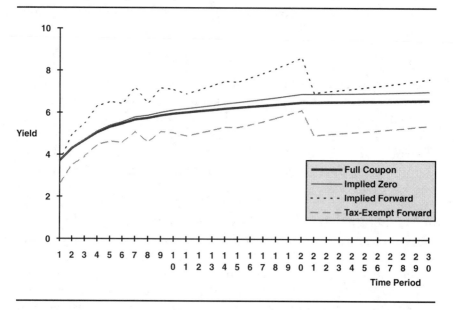

For example, the Treasury full-coupon par taxable yield curve is input in columns 2 and 7 of Exhibit 8–1. The implied zero-coupon rates are calculated by the program and are shown in columns 3 and 8. They may be overridden in our program by directly inputting, in columns 3 and 8, an observed zero-coupon scale. The implied taxable forward rates are also calculated by the program and are shown in columns 4 and 9. The implied tax-exempt forward rates in columns 5 and 10 are simply columns 4 and 9 times our target short-term ratio (71.0 percent, which is an input at the upper righthand corner of Exhibit 8–1). The implied swap rates for 3, 5, 7, 10, 20, and 30 years are also shown. To get any other term of implied swap rate, or average expected short-term rate, we would simply input into the "Term of Swap/Bond" cell the desired year (e.g., 21 years), and the average expected short-term rate (e.g., 4.70 percent) would appear in the upper righthand area of the screen.

Suffering swaptions! That sure seems like a lot of information on one screen! And none of it is dependent upon the credit rating or yield of a municipal derivative security. In fact, this one screen can and will be used in valuing each of the five municipal derivative securities. The key inputs, the full-coupon taxable rates and the implied tax-exempt forward rates, will be the same for each of our municipal derivative securities. The only thing that will change is the term of the hedging component.

Cap–Floor Valuation Screen
In our second general screen (Exhibit 8–3), the *cap–floor valuation screen,* we have listed all the inputs associated with interest rate cap and floor option valuation, as described in Chapter 7.

Explicit inputs on this screen include the cap strike price (e.g., 3.00 percent) and the floor strike price (e.g., 3.00 percent), the volatility (e.g., 8 percent) of the interest rate index (e.g., the Kenny Index), and the term of the option (e.g., five years).

Variables that are implicitly input into this screen are the implied tax-exempt forward rates, $_{t-1}f_t^*$, which are incorporated from columns 5 and 10 of Exhibit 8–1, and the zero-coupon discount rates, r_t, which are incorporated from columns 3 and 8 of Exhibit 8–1.

Given these inputs, Exhibit 8–3 uses Black's model for caps. A cumulative distribution function for the standard normal random variable (Exhibit 7–8), is embedded in the computer program, and is used to calculate theoretical interest rate cap values for periods of 0.5 year to 30 years. The program applies put–call parity to

EXHIBIT 8–3
Cap–Floor Valuation Screen (January 4, 1994)

Name of Bond: AA Bond 1/4/1994   Volatility: 8.00 %
            Type of Index: Kenny   Term of Option: 5 years
        Cap Strike Price: 3.00 %   Cap Value: 3.767%
      Floor Strike Price: 3.00 %   Floor Value: 0.365%

Year	CAP	FLOOR	Year	CAP	FLOOR	Year	CAP	FLOOR
0.5	0.000%	0.181%	7.5	6.857%	0.370%	19.0	17.958%	0.419%
1.0	0.000%	0.358%	8.0	7.359%	0.372%	20.0	18.765%	0.422%
1.5	0.238%	0.359%	8.5	7.992%	0.373%	21.0	19.243%	0.434%
2.0	0.473%	0.363%	9.0	8.606%	0.374%	22.0	19.702%	0.446%
2.5	0.879%	0.364%	9.5	9.181%	0.376%	23.0	20.140%	0.458%
3.0	1.276%	0.364%	10.0	9.738%	0.378%	24.0	20.556%	0.469%
3.5	1.896%	0.364%	11.0	10.724%	0.383%	25.0	20.952%	0.480%
4.0	2.499%	0.365%	12.0	11.707%	0.388%	26.0	21.328%	0.491%
4.5	3.141%	0.365%	13.0	12.686%	0.392%	27.0	21.686%	0.501%
5.0	3.767%	0.365%	14.0	13.656%	0.397%	28.0	22.028%	0.510%
5.5	4.347%	0.366%	15.0	14.549%	0.402%	29.0	22.353%	0.519%
6.0	4.912%	0.367%	16.0	15.427%	0.407%	30.0	22.662%	0.528%
6.5	5.636%	0.368%	17.0	16.288%	0.411%			
7.0	6.340%	0.368%	18.0	17.132%	0.416%			

calculate interest rate floor values for each period. For example, for a five-year option term, 8.00 percent volatility, and 3.00 percent cap and floor strike prices, the model calculates a cap value of 3.767 percent and a floor value of 0.365 percent.

As with the hedging component values, option component values are also independent of the credit rating or yield on a municipal derivative security. The key inputs that won't change from security to security are the implied tax-exempt forward rates and the zero-coupon discount rate. The inputs that *will* change are the cap and/or floor strike price, the term of the option, and the type of index and its associated volatility.

Tax-Exempt Yield Curve Screen

Our third general screen (Exhibit 8–4) is the *tax-exempt yield curve screen*. This screen is important in the valuation of municipal derivative securities that can be *stripped* into its component cash flows, such as BPOs, and sold, through a preset CUSIP mechanism at the investor's option.

To handle the valuation of debt components of *strippable* and annuity, level-debt-style securities, we use the approach described in Chapter 4 in which an implied zero curve is derived. For example, in Exhibit 8–4, we start with a *tax-exempt, issue-specific, full-*

EXHIBIT 8–4

Tax-Exempt Yield Curve Screen (January 3, 1994)

Name of Bond: Sample AA Bond 1/3/94
Term of Bond: 30 years

Year	Full Coupon	Implied Zero	Actual Zero	Full Cou. Duration	Year	Full Coupon	Implied Zero	Actual Zero	Full Duration
1	2.400	2.40	2.400	0.99	16	5.100	5.37	5.374	11.12
2	3.200	3.22	3.220	1.95	17	5.150	5.44	5.441	11.53
3	3.550	3.58	3.577	2.87	18	5.200	5.51	5.512	11.90
4	3.800	3.84	3.837	3.75	19	5.200	5.49	5.495	12.29
5	3.950	3.99	3.993	4.59	20	5.250	5.57	5.575	12.61
6	4.100	4.15	4.154	5.38	21	5.250	5.56	5.558	12.96
7	4.250	4.32	4.320	6.13	22	5.300	5.65	5.646	13.24
8	4.350	4.43	4.430	6.84	23	5.300	5.63	5.630	13.55
9	4.450	4.54	4.544	7.51	24	5.300	5.62	5.616	13.85
10	4.550	4.66	4.661	8.14	25	5.300	5.60	5.603	14.13
11	4.650	4.78	4.782	8.73	26	5.350	5.71	5.709	14.33
12	4.750	4.91	4.907	9.28	27	5.350	5.69	5.694	14.58
13	4.850	5.04	5.036	9.79	28	5.350	5.68	5.682	14.82
14	4.950	5.17	5.171	10.26	29	5.350	5.67	5.671	15.04
15	5.050	5.31	5.310	10.69	30	5.350	5.66	5.660	15.25

coupon municipal yield curve in columns 2 and 7. Exhibit 8–4 shows the tax-exempt yield curve for an AA-rated bond on January 3, 1994 (see Exhibit 2–3). This yield curve is very much dependent on the bond's credit rating, alternative minimum tax (AMT) status, type of issue, etc. From the full-coupon municipal yield curve, an implied zero-coupon, issue-specific yield curve is derived. The appropriate zero-coupon discount rate, r_t, is used to price each expected semiannual cash flow to determine a market value for the debt component. In Exhibit 8–4, we also calculate the duration, in accordance with Chapter 3, of a comparable full-coupon par bond, to provide a comparison of yields and price volatilities.

Security-Specific Screens

To complete the valuation process, we use a series of security-specific computer screens. Each screen incorporates the implied forward rates and hedging component values that are derived in Exhibit 8–1 and the option component values that are derived in Exhibit 8–3. The valuations of strippable bonds and BPOs also incorporate the issue-specific implied tax-exempt, zero-coupon rates that are derived in Exhibit 8–4.

The security-specific screens incorporate the special features that are embedded in each of the five securities that we will examine. In valuing each derivative security, we go through the same basic process: (1) We use expectational analysis to calculate implied forward rates. (2) We define the building-block components and quantify the expected cash flows. (3) We assign a structure value to the security. (4) We use the DAP model to value it. Then, as we describe the valuation process of each derivative security, we outline the procedures in the four steps.

Structure Value

As previously discussed, successful derivative securities package combinations of cash-flow streams in ways that are more highly valued by certain investors than the sum of the underlying cash flows. Successful derivative products have a *positive structure value:* the value of the output is greater than the sum of the values of the inputs. At least for a time, until the activity of arbitrageurs can take it away (if arbitrage is practical), investors may be willing to discount these unique cash flows at a lower rate than they would otherwise pay for fixed-rate bonds, thereby paying a higher price for the derivative security.

In his examination of the process of financial innovation and security design in the corporate finance market, John Finnerty finds that innovation can add value for investors and issuers.[3] The three ways in which he sees innovation as having the potential to add value are:

1. It can introduce structural features into a security that will reduce risk to an investor or reallocate risk to another entity.
2. It can develop financing structures that will lower issuance expenses and underwriting discounts.
3. It can develop financing structures that enhance the tax characteristics of the cash flows, thereby increasing the value of a derivative security.

The concept of structure value is very important in the valuation of municipal derivative securities. The cash-flow characteristics of municipal derivative securities have unique tax-related features that the cash flows of building-block securities do not have. For example, the raw cash flows of municipal inverse floating-rate bonds can be created synthetically by (1) owning a fixed-rate, tax-exempt bond with a fixed coupon, a maturity date, credit characteristics, and redemption features; plus (2) being the floating-rate payer in an interest rate swap with a set reference rate and term. In this example, the raw cash flows for the inverse floater and the two building-block components (fixed-rate bond plus interest rate swap) are identical, but the treatments for federal income tax purposes are quite different. All the interest associated with inverse floaters is treated as *tax-exempt* interest, while the interest associated with an interest rate swap that is not embedded in a tax-exempt bond generally is treated as *taxable* interest.

---

[3]See J. Finnerty, "Financial Engineering in Corporate Finance: An Overview," *Financial Management*, vol. 1, no. 4, 1989, pp. 49–58.

To address the unique structural aspects of a municipal derivative security, a *structure value* is incorporated into the valuation process. The DAP model takes this valuation approach; the building blocks are modeled and valued, and a *subjective* structure value is assigned. A positive structure value (lower discount rate or yield) results if there are beneficial tax aspects, lower intermediary costs, or efficiencies of structure. A negative value (higher discount rate or yield) results if there are negative tax aspects, higher intermediary costs, and lower liquidity of the instrument. Successful municipal derivative products will have positive structure values (generally due to advantageous tax treatment) in excess of negative structure values (usually due to reduced liquidity of the security). *The value of a successful municipal derivative security will be greater than the sum of the simpler underlying cash flows.*

In each of the valuations that follows, we theoretically estimate value, in accordance with the DAP model, on two bases:

1. With *no structure value,* under which the whole is equal to the sum of the parts.
2. With a *subjective structure value,* in which we uniformly assign a 10-BP structure value for each security (although there are good arguments for higher structure values for some and lower for others). This effectively lowers the discounting rate and raises the value of the municipal derivative security.

Now, "Let the wild rumpus start!"[4]

VALUATION OF A RESIDUAL INTEREST BOND[5]

In March 1990, Lehman Brothers introduced Residual Interest Bonds (RIBS), a new type of municipal security which has an interest rate that varies *inversely* with the tax-exempt market's short-term interest rate. RIBS are issued in the primary market in tandem with Select Auction Variable Rate Securities (SAVRS). The sum of

---

[4]M. Sendak, *Where the Wild Things Are,* Harper & Row, New York, 1963, p. 12.

[5]This section is based on Gray and Engebretson, loc. cit.

the interest rates on a set proportion of RIBS and SAVRS is fixed to maturity, providing absolutely fixed-rate financing to the issuer. However, RIBS investors have a valuable option: they can either link proportional amounts of the RIBS and SAVRS to produce a fixed rate of interest through maturity (thus creating a *linked coupon*), or they can unlink the RIBS and SAVRS. If they choose to unlink the RIBS and SAVRS, they can either sell them separately or hold them as floating-rate and inverse floating-rate bonds. Assuming that the historical relationship between municipal yields and Treasury yields continues (see Chapter 4), RIBS will exhibit unique payment and price performance characteristics, including higher current yields and greater call premiums than comparable fixed-rate bonds.

RIBS were introduced as part of a fixed-rate financing program for municipal bond issues offered in the primary market. Many investment banks have introduced inverse floating-rate products similar to RIBS. In some recent (Autumn 1993) transactions, floating-rate/inverse floating-rate structures were marketed in which there were three floating-rate securities for every one inverse floating-rate security. The RIBS–SAVRS program was also adapted to the secondary markets through the use of *custodial receipts* (CRs) or *trust receipts* (TRs) structures that mimic the performance of RIBS and SAVRS.

Inverse floating-rate securities were first introduced into the corporate bond market in the mid-1980s and have frequently been used in the CMO marketplace. The breakthrough in structure, in our opinion, that enabled inverse floaters to be embraced by municipal investors was due to the following:

1. The creation of SAVRS as a *companion security*, to be marketed in concert with RIBS.
2. The creation of the CUSIP *linkage mechanism* and *rate lock option* (see below) that allows a RIBS owner to acquire a SAVRS, to request that the two securities be designated through a separate CUSIP number as linked RIBS–SAVRS, and to lock in the fixed, linked coupon paid by the issuer.

The RIBS–SAVRS linkage mechanism and the CUSIP system, in effect, created *Humpty-Dumpty* securities that, contrary to the nursery rhyme, *can be put back together again* after initially being separated. The ability to recombine complex derivative securities into *plain-vanilla* fixed-rate bonds is a feature that is being broadly adopted in the derivative securities marketplace.

General Description of RIBS–SAVRS

Interest Rate Mechanism

From a bond issuer's perspective, the RIBS–SAVRS program raises long-term funds with an aggregate fixed interest rate. As such, it has the mirrored-security, fixed-rate structure that was described in Chapter 2. It segments the issuer's fixed payment stream into two components, each of which is sold to investors as a separate security. The components, which are issued in proportional principal amounts, are:

- SAVRS, variable-rate securities with interest rates that are reset every 35 days or every six months through a Dutch auction.
- RIBS, which have an interest rate equal to the difference between the issuer's fixed interest payment stream and the interest and expenses paid on the SAVRS.

Due to their unique payment characteristics and anticipated high yields, RIBS are attractive to sophisticated institutional investors such as mutual bond funds. SAVRS are typically purchased by corporations that seek short-term, tax-exempt instruments for cash-management purposes, and by investors that evaluate tax-advantaged products, such as municipal bonds and preferred stock, on an after-tax yield basis relative to taxable money market instruments.

The interest rate on SAVRs, called the *auction rate,* is determined every 35 days or every six months by a Dutch auction. The total interest rate, called the *SAVRS rate,* for each interest period is the auction rate plus the service charge. The service charge generally includes a broker-dealer fee of 25 BPs (0.25 percent) and an auction agent fee of 3 BPs (0.03 percent) per annum, in each case charged only on the outstanding amount of SAVRS eligible to participate in the auction. For example, if the auction rate is 2.72 percent and the service charge is 0.28 percent, the SAVRS rate equals 3.00 percent, as shown below.

$$\text{SAVRS rate} = \text{auction rate} + \text{service charge}$$
$$3.00\% = 2.72\% + 0.28\%$$

Interest on SAVRS is subject to maximum and minimum interest rates, which are functions of a market index at the time of the auction. Interest is payable every 35 days or every six months on the actual number of days in the interest period, based on a 360-day year. In a Dutch auction, if there are more sellers than buyers and if, because of this disequilibrium, an auction fails (in which case it is called a *failed Auction*), then the interest rate for the subsequent interest period goes to the maximum rate. Proportional amounts of RIBS and SAVRS must be redeemed on any redemption date to maintain proportional amounts of outstanding RIBS and SAVRS. If equal amounts of RIBS and SAVRS are issued and the auction takes place every 35 days, the interest rate for the RIBS is equal to the difference between twice the fixed rate (the linked coupon) paid by the issuer and the SAVRS rate. The formula is adjusted to compensate for the actual/360-day bond year applied to the SAVRS versus the actual/365-day interest accrued on RIBS. For example, if the 35-day linked coupon equals 6.173 percent (for a 6.25 percent BEY) and the SAVRS rate equals 3 percent, the RIBS rate equals 9.304 percent, as shown in the following equation:

$$\text{RIBS rate} = (2 \times \text{linked coupon}) - [(\text{SAVRS rate})(365/360)]$$
$$9.304\% = (2 \times 6.173\%) - [(3.00\%)(365/360)]$$

The interest rate on RIBS will:

1. Increase as the SAVRS rate decreases.
2. Decrease as the SAVRS rate increases.

If the SAVRS rate is lower than the linked coupon, the RIBS will bear an interest rate higher than the linked coupon. Conversely, if the SAVRS rate exceeds the linked coupon, RIBS holders will receive an interest rate lower than the linked coupon.

The interest rate on RIBS can never go below 0 percent. This limit effectively places an interest rate ceiling or cap on the SAVRS holder. In the above example, the RIBS owner also owns an embedded interest rate cap at twice the linked coupon, or a BEY of 12.50 percent, and the SAVRS owner has *written* the interest rate cap at the same level. We will value this cap below.

Rate Lock Option
The rate lock option is a feature of the RIBS–SAVRS program that enables a holder of RIBS to purchase an equal amount of SAVRS; to request that the two securities be designated, through a separate CUSIP number, as *linked RIBS–SAVRS;* and to lock in the fixed, linked coupon paid by the issuer. During the period that the RIBS and SAVRS are linked, these particular SAVRS are ineligible for sale in auctions and the owners are *not* charged the 28 BP service charge. Therefore, a linked RIBS-SAVRS holder will receive a higher rate of interest than will a holder of both RIBS and SAVRS that are not linked. The holder may link and unlink the RIBS and SAVRS as frequently as desired. The existence of the rate lock option allows us to value RIBS, that have been issued in concert with an *equal* amount of SAVRS, as a combination of the following:

1. The ownership of the cash flow associated with two fixed-rate bonds with a known maturity and an interest rate equal to the linked coupon.
2. The ability to finance (or lever) the purchase price of one of the bonds at an interest rate equal to the SAVRS rate.

Investment Characteristics of RIBS

The cash flows associated with RIBS are dependent on two variables: the linked coupon, which is set at the date of issuance and does not vary, and the SAVRS rate, which is reset through a Dutch auction every 35 days. The current market value of RIBS, therefore, is crucially dependent upon investors' expectations of future SAVRS rates.

Observed *auction rates* on SAVRS have on average been 22 BPs higher than the rates on tax-exempt floating-rate demand notes and the Kenny Index. Historically, tax-exempt interest rates on short-term notes have been significantly lower than rates on fixed-rate, long-term debt with a similar rating. For example, the average difference between the BEYs of the Kenny Index and the Bond Buyer Revenue Bond Index from September 1981 to September 1993 was 3.07 percent (see Chapter 4). If the municipal yield curve is consistent with its upward-sloping history, and we assume no upward shift in interest rates, a RIBS holder should expect higher returns on both a current and total return basis, relative to holders of either fixed-rate or floating-rate debt.

J. Randall Woolridge prepared a study which simulated the historic interest rate performance of hypothetical RIBS issued on the first day of any calendar month during the period from September 1981 to September 1989.[6] As proxies for the linked coupon and the SAVRS rate, respectively, Woolridge used the Bond Buyer Revenue Bond Index and the Kenny Index. The results of his simulation show that a RIBS holder would have received, on average, a 352-BP-per-annum higher yield than the holder of a comparable fixed-rate bond. He noted that the superior simulated yield performance of RIBS declined over the period of his study, due to a general decline in interest rates and a corresponding reduction in the slope of the yield curve.

RIBS have higher call premiums than comparable full-coupon bonds. Since SAVRS are callable at par, RIBS generally are callable at twice the premium level of a typical fixed-rate bond (e.g., 104 percent in 10 years, as compared to a typical 102 percent full-coupon bond call). This provides issuers with the same total costs of an early redemption as they face with full-coupon fixed-rate bonds.

If we assume that the tax-exempt yield curve continues to be upward-sloping, the inherent structural aspects of RIBS should lead to the following payment and price performance characteristics, relative to full-coupon, fixed-rate bonds of similar maturity and rating:

1. Higher current yields.
2. Higher expected yields to maturity.
3. Greater call premiums.
4. Increased price volatility (see the discussion of duration below).
5. A rate lock option that allows an internal levering–delevering feature to help insulate the yield on RIBS from adverse movements in short-term rates.

---

[6]See J. Woolridge, "An Economic Analysis of Residual Interest Bonds (RIBS)," unpublished manuscript commissioned by Shearson Lehman Hutton, Inc., February 1990.

Expected RIBS performance is similar to that of a leveraged municipal bond, where the cost of leverage is the short-term, tax-exempt borrowing rate (i.e., the SAVRS rate). The unusual features and expected performance of RIBS have made them highly desirable to certain investors.

Valuation of RIBS

The RIBS that we value is an AA-rated revenue bond that matures on August 1, 2014, is callable on August 1, 2003, at a price of 104 percent, and pays interest every 35 days at a linked coupon rate of 6.173 percent (BEY of 6.25 percent) and a RIBS rate of 2(6.173 percent) minus the SAVRS rate. The interest rate profile for the RIBS appears in Exhibit 8–5.

Our first order of business is to divide the RIBS into its building blocks. For ease of analysis, we assume that the 6.173 percent linked 35-day payment is comparable to a 6.25 percent semiannual

EXHIBIT 8–5
RIBS Interest Rate Profile

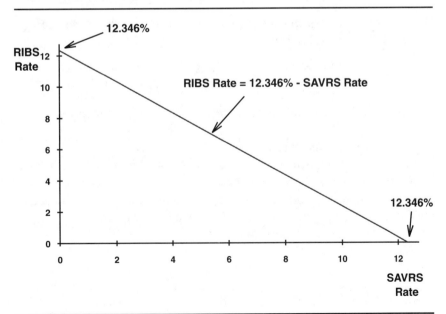

BEY payment. Donald Smith[7] and Woolridge[8] have shown that the interest payment characteristics of taxable inverse floaters, which are analytically similar to RIBS, may be created synthetically by combining several building blocks. Specifically, for the RIBS that we are valuing, the building blocks are:

1. A *debt component* that has a 6.25 percent BEY, a maturity date of August 1, 2014, and a redemption feature of August 1, 2003, at 104 percent, declining to 100 percent on August 1, 2005.

2. A *hedging component* of a fixed-to-floating interest rate swap of the form 6.25 percent minus the SAVRS rate, with maturity on August 1, 2014 (a term of 20.5 years). The RIBS holder is the floating-rate payer, and the issuer is the fixed-rate payer.

3. An *option component* in which the RIBS holder is the owner of a 20.5-year interest rate cap at 12.50 percent, because the interest rate formula does not allow the RIBS rate to be less than zero.

We can write out the RIBS interest rate formula, in accordance with the above discussion. If we do so, it appears as follows:

$$\text{RIBS rate} = 6.25\% + (6.25\% - \text{SAVRS rate})$$

Based on the above, the theoretical DAP value of the RIBS may be expressed as shown below.

DAP price (inverse floater) = price (fixed-rate bond + fixed-to-floating swap + interest rate cap)

Now let's get into the valuation of the various components.

Valuation of the Hedging Component
As a starting point for valuing derivative securities and to determine the value for the hedging and option components, we begin with the Treasury yield curve on the date of valuation. Exhibit 8–6 shows the *taxable yield curve input screen*, using the full-coupon Treasury yield curve of January 3, 1994.

---

[7] See D. Smith, "The Arithmetic of Financial Engineering," *The Journal of Applied Corporate Finance*, winter 1989; pp. 49–58.

[8] See Woolridge, loc. cit.

EXHIBIT 8–6
Taxable Yield Curve Input Screen (January 3, 1994)

```
Name of Yield Curve: Treasury 1/3/1994 Target Short-Term Ratio(%)   :   71.00
Term of Swap / Bond:      20.5 years    Avg. Exp. Short-term rate    :    4.69
      Full   Implied Implied  Tax-Ex. !        Full   Implied Implied  Tax-Ex.
Year Coupon  Zero    Forward  Forward  ! Year Coupon  Zero    Forward  Forward
 1   3.710   3.710   3.71     2.63     !  16  6.300   6.572   7.67     5.44
 2   4.300   4.319   4.93     3.50     !  17  6.350   6.648   7.88     5.59
 3   4.680   4.713   5.51     3.91     !  18  6.400   6.729   8.11     5.76
 4   5.050   5.109   6.30     4.48     !  19  6.450   6.814   8.36     5.94
 5   5.310   5.389   6.52     4.63     !  20  6.500   6.904   8.63     6.13
 6   5.470   5.562   6.43     4.57     !  21  6.510   6.906   6.95     4.93
 7   5.670   5.793   7.19     5.10     !  22  6.520   6.912   7.03     4.99
 8   5.750   5.876   6.46     4.59     !  23  6.530   6.920   7.09     5.03
 9   5.870   6.020   7.18     5.10     !  24  6.540   6.930   7.15     5.08
10   5.960   6.128   7.10     5.04     !  25  6.550   6.941   7.22     5.12
11   6.020   6.197   6.89     4.89     !  26  6.560   6.954   7.29     5.17
12   6.080   6.271   7.09     5.03     !  27  6.570   6.969   7.36     5.23
13   6.140   6.349   7.26     5.17     !  28  6.580   6.986   7.44     5.28
14   6.200   6.431   7.50     5.32     !  29  6.590   7.005   7.53     5.35
15   6.250   6.499   7.46     5.30     !  30  6.600   7.025   7.62     5.41

                          Implied SWAP Rates
          3 year          3.33%          10 year          4.27%
          5 year          3.79%          20 year          4.69%
          7 year          4.05%          30 year          4.77%
```

The present value of the 20.5-year, 6.25 percent fixed-to-floating SAVRS swap component that is embedded in the RIBS is equal to the discounted value of its anticipated future cash flows. In Exhibit 8–6, the full-coupon Treasury curve is used in calculating implied zero-coupon rates, implied taxable forward rates, and implied tax-exempt forward rates as described in Chapter 4. To calculate the theoretical 20.5-year par swap rate, the present value of the implied tax-exempt forward rates is calculated, as described in Exhibit 6–14, which represent expectations of the weighted average, short-term, tax-exempt rate over the 20.5-year period. The program calculates an average expected short-term rate (see the upper righthand corner of Exhibit 8–6) of 4.69 percent for the 20.5-year period ending August 1, 2014.

The 20.5-year implied swap rate of 4.69 percent represents market expectations of the weighted average, short-term, tax-exempt rate. As a proxy, we use the Kenny Index. The RIBS interest rate formula is based on the companion SAVRS rate, not on the Kenny Index. Studies have shown that auction-rate securities have average interest rates about 22 BPs higher than the Kenny Index. This adjustment would increase the expected auction rate to 4.91 percent over the 20.5-year period. There are also, on average, 28 BPs in auction fees which must be added to the auction rate, to calculate the SAVRS rate. In addition, interest is paid on an actual/360-day basis, every 35 days, which increases the BEY on the SAVRS. The effect of these adjustments is to raise the BEY of the companion SAVRS security to 5.215 percent (look ahead to the output screen of Exhibit 8–8 on page 224). Having made all these adjustments, we are now ready to value the 20.5-year swap.

If the current market of an all-in-cost 20.5-year companion SAVRS swap is 5.215 percent, and the RIBS holder also owns an embedded 20.5-year swap with a BEY fixed rate of 6.25 percent, the swap is in the money, on average, 1.035 percent per year. This results in a swap value of 13.447 percent to maturity and 8.379 percent to the first call date on the RIBS.

Valuation of the Option Component

The next step in valuing RIBS is to use the Treasury yield curve and the implied tax-exempt forward rates on the date of valuation to determine the value of the option components. Exhibit 8–7 shows the *cap–floor valuation screen*, using the inputs from the Treasury yield curve of January 3, 1994.

We have put in a cap strike price of 12.50 percent, a term of option of 20.5 years, and a volatility estimate of 8 percent. Implicitly input into this screen are the implied tax-exempt forward rates and the zero-coupon discount rates from Exhibit 8–6. We use Black's

EXHIBIT 8–7
Cap–Floor Valuation Screen

```
Name of Bond: AA RIBS - 1/3/1994                Volatility:  8.00 %
             Type of Index: Kenny            Term of Option:  20.5 years
           Cap Strike Price:  12.50 %           Cap Value: 0.023%
         Floor Strike Price:   0.00 %         Floor Value: 0.000%
```

Year	CAP	FLOOR		Year	CAP	FLOOR		Year	CAP	FLOOR
0.5	0.000%	0.000%		7.5	0.000%	0.000%		19.0	0.017%	0.000%
1.0	0.000%	0.000%		8.0	0.000%	0.000%		20.0	0.023%	0.000%
1.5	0.000%	0.000%		8.5	0.000%	0.000%		21.0	0.024%	0.000%
2.0	0.000%	0.000%		9.0	0.000%	0.000%		22.0	0.025%	0.000%
2.5	0.000%	0.000%		9.5	0.000%	0.000%		23.0	0.027%	0.000%
3.0	0.000%	0.000%		10.0	0.000%	0.000%		24.0	0.029%	0.000%
3.5	0.000%	0.000%		11.0	0.000%	0.000%		25.0	0.031%	0.000%
4.0	0.000%	0.000%		12.0	0.000%	0.000%		26.0	0.034%	0.000%
4.5	0.000%	0.000%		13.0	0.003%	0.000%		27.0	0.037%	0.000%
5.0	0.000%	0.000%		14.0	0.006%	0.000%		28.0	0.041%	0.000%
5.5	0.000%	0.000%		15.0	0.007%	0.000%		29.0	0.044%	0.000%
6.0	0.000%	0.000%		16.0	0.008%	0.000%		30.0	0.049%	0.000%
6.5	0.000%	0.000%		17.0	0.010%	0.000%				
7.0	0.000%	0.000%		18.0	0.012%	0.000%				

model for caps to get a 20.5-year, 12.5 percent cap value of 0.023 percent, or a dollar price of 23 cents per $1000. This is not a very significant number, because the implied forward rates associated with the yield curve of January 3, 1994, are much lower than the cap rate of 12.50 percent.

Valuation of the Debt Component

The valuation of the 6.25 percent debt component is fairly straight-forward. We simply discount at the relevant market discount rate the cash flows of a 6.25 percent bond with a maturity of August 1, 2014, a call date of August 1, 2003, and a call price of 102 percent. If the required full-coupon yield for an AA-rated, 2014 maturity bond is 5.25 percent (see Exhibit 2–3), a premium 6.25 percent bond due on August 1, 2014, priced to maturity, is 112.485 percent. The market value of the same bond, priced to the August 1, 2003, call date with a 104 percent premium, is 109.882 percent (see Exhibit 8–8).

Valuation Summary—No Structure Value

Combining the values of the three components (with no structure value), and using the assumptions described above, gives the following DAP model valuation of the RIBS:

$$\text{DAP price (to maturity)} = 112.485\% + 12.109\% + 0.023\%$$
$$= 124.617\%$$
$$\text{DAP price (first call)} = 109.882\% + 7.545\% + 0.00\%$$
$$= 117.427\%$$

Valuation Summary—10-BP Structure Value

As previously discussed, inverse floaters can be synthetically created by owning a fixed-rate bond and writing a fixed-to-floating interest rate swap that contains an interest rate cap. RIBS, however, have two features that enhance their value relative to that of a synthetically created security, as follows:

1. Whereas payments on an interest rate swap are taxable to investors, all interest payments on RIBS are tax-exempt.
2. The rate lock option gives a RIBS holder the ability to purchase a SAVRS, create a linked RIBS–SAVRS, and eliminate service charges in exchange for a payment of par plus

EXHIBIT 8–8
RIBS Valuation Program

```
                    R I B S   I n p u t   S c r e e n
                        (No Structure Value)
--------------------------------------------------------------------------
Name of Bond:RIBS example
                                      Linked Bond            RIBS
Trade Settlement Date.....................01/03/1994      01/03/1994
Interest Payment Periods...................    35 days       35 days
Purchase Price............................  100.000        100.000
Maturity Date.............................08/01/2014      08/01/2014
First Optional Redemption Date............08/01/2003      08/01/2003
  First Par Opt. Red. Date................08/01/2005      08/01/2005
  Initial Optional Call Price.............     102            104
Unit Bond Equivalent Yield................    6.250          N.A.
  Unit Coupon(35 day coupon)..............    6.173          N.A.
Current SAVRS Rate(35 day coupon).........    2.600          2.600
Auction Service Fees......................    0.280          0.280
Exp.Short-Term Rate.......................    4.690          4.910
Muni Market Term Swap Rate................    4.690          4.910
Investors Required Full Coupon Bond Yield..   5.250          5.250

                    O u t p u t   S c r e e n
--------------------------------------------------------------------------
        Current (SAVRS+Serv.Fee) B.E.Y.............    2.937%
            Current RIBS Coupon(35 days)...........    9.425%
            Current RIBS Bond Equivalent Coupon....    9.606%
            Current RIBS Yield to Maturity.........    9.606%
        Exp.Short-Term - B.E.Y....................    5.318%
            Exp.Avg.RIBS Coupon(35 days)..........    7.083%
            Exp.Avg.RIBS Bond Equivalent Coupon....    7.185%
            Exp.Avg.RIBS Yield to Maturity.........    7.185%
        Implied Break-Even Avg. Short-Term rate....    6.772%
--------------------------------------------------------------------------

                                           Price to...
                                          First      First
    RIBS Prices:
-------------------------------------- Maturity   Call     Par Call
    Value of Bond............................  112.485%  109.882%  108.588%
    Value of Swap(s).........................   12.109%    7.545%    8.633%
    Value of Cap(s)..........................    0.023%    0.000%    0.000%
        Total Value of RIBS(DAP)..............  124.617%  117.427%  117.221%
```

(effectively) the surrender of the RIBS owner's pro rata share of the interest rate swap.

If we assume that the structure value associated with RIBS, because of their efficiency and the advantageous tax treatment of their interest payments, results in a 10-BP lower discount rate (to 5.15 percent), the market values of the RIBS will increase to the values shown in Exhibit 8–9.

With the 10 BPs of structure value, we have the following DAP model valuation of the RIB:

$$\text{DAP price (to maturity)} = 113.852\% + 12.109\% + 0.023\%$$
$$= 125.984\%$$

$$\text{DAP price (to first call)} = 110.687\% + 7.545\% + 0.00\%$$
$$= 118.232\%$$

EXHIBIT 8–9
RIBS Valuation Program

```
                    R I B S   I n p u t   S c r e e n
                       10 BP Structure Value
----------------------------------------------------------------------
Name of Bond: RIBS example
                                         Linked Bond         RIBS
Trade Settlement Date.....................01/03/1994      01/03/1994
Interest Payment Periods...................    35 days        35 days
Purchase Price.............................   100.000       100.000
Maturity Date.............................08/01/2014      08/01/2014
First Optional Redemption Date............08/01/2003      08/01/2003
   First Par Opt. Red. Date................08/01/2005      08/01/2005
   Initial Optional Call Price.............     102          104
Unit Bond Equivalent Yield.................    6.250        N.A.
   Unit Coupon(35 day coupon)..............    6.173        N.A.
Current SAVRS Rate(35 day coupon)..........    2.600        2.600
Auction Service Fees.......................    0.280        0.280
Exp.Short-Term Rate........................    4.690        4.910
Muni Market Term Swap Rate.................    4.690        4.910
Investors Required Full Coupon Bond Yield..    5.250        5.150
            Current (SAVRS+Serv.Fee) B.E.Y............    2.937%
            Current RIBS Coupon(35 days)............    9.425%
            Current RIBS Bond Equivalent Coupon......    9.606%
            Current RIBS Yield to Maturity..........    9.606%
            Exp.Short-Term - B.E.Y...................    5.318%
            Exp.Avg.RIBS Coupon(35 days)............    7.083%
            Exp.Avg.RIBS Bond Equivalent Coupon......    7.185%
            Exp.Avg.RIBS Yield to Maturity..........    7.289%
            Implied Break-Even Avg. Short-Term rate....    6.772%
----------------------------------------------------------------------
                                                   Price to...
                                                First      First
RIBS Prices:
------------------------------------------------ Maturity   Call    Par Call
Value of Bond.............................. 113.852%  110.687% 109.498%
Value of Swap(s)........................... 12.109%    7.545%   8.663%
Value of Cap(s)............................  0.023%    0.000%   0.000%
   Total Value of RIBS(DAP)................ 125.984%  118.232% 118.131%
```

Time Duration of RIBS

As discussed in Chapter 3, applying the implied forward rates to standard duration measures removes the biases inherent in the use of Macaulay's duration for derivative securities.

Let:

D^* = duration measure that incorporates movements in short-term rates

C = annual coupon payment in dollars

F = principal or redemption amount

$_{t-1}f_t^*$ = implied tax-exempt forward interest rate from $t - 1$ to t

t = time

n = number of years

Then:

$$D^* = \sum_{t=1}^{2n} \left\{ \left[\frac{(C/2)/\prod_t(1 + {}_{t-1}f_t^*)}{P^*} \right] \frac{t}{2} \right\} + \left[\frac{F/\prod_t(1 + {}_{t-1}f_t^*)}{P^*} \; n \right]$$

Using this equation, we can estimate the time duration of RIBS. Since the cash flow is unknown, we calculate the expected RIBS coupon based on implied forward rates in each semiannual period. For simplicity, we assume that there are 41 full semiannual interest periods. Therefore, the time duration of the RIBS can be calculated as shown below.

Let:

D_t^* = time duration of RIBS

P^* = price of the RIBS as calculated using DAP = 125.955

C_t = estimated annual RIBS coupon payment at time t measured in dollars, calculated as: $[(2)(6.25) - ({}_{t-1}f_t^* + 0.28)(360/365)]$

F = \$100

${}_{t-1}f_t^*$ = implied tax-exempt forward interest rate from time $t-1$ to t

$t = 1 - 41$

$n = 20.5$

Then:

$$D_t^* = \sum_{t=1}^{41} \left\{ \left[\frac{(C_t/2)/\prod_t(1 + {}_{t-1}f_t^*)}{125.955} \right] \frac{t}{2} \right\} + \left[\left(\frac{F/\prod_t(1 + {}_{t-1}f_t^*)}{125.955} \right) 20.5 \right]$$

$D_t^* = 12.55$ years

Solving the above equation for D_t^* results in a time duration of 12.55 years for the RIBS. The above equation is actually quite easy to set up in a spreadsheet. The layout is very similar to the duration calculations in Exhibit 3.

Price Duration of RIBS

In Chapter 3, we showed how duration can be used to estimate changes in bond prices. The price duration of RIBS gives us an estimate of the price volatility for a given parallel change in interest rates. For small changes in interest rates, price duration is a good estimate of the corresponding change in the bond price. To calculate the price duration of RIBS, we calculate the duration of each of the components described in the previous section and sum the durations to arrive at a price duration for the security. Assuming 41 semiannual periods for simplicity, we calculate the duration of each of four components as follows:

1. Owning a 6.25% fixed-rate bond with 20.5 years to maturity and a market yield of 5.25%. The time and price duration of the fixed-rate bond component is calculated below.

Let:

$C = \$6.25$

$F = \$100$

$P = \$112.464$

$y = 5.25\%$

$t = 1,2,3,\ldots,41$

$n = 20.5$

Then:

$$D = \sum_{t=1}^{41}\left(\frac{\dfrac{3.00}{(1.02625)^t}}{112.464}\left(\frac{t}{2}\right)\right) + \left(\frac{\dfrac{100}{(1.02625)^{41}}}{112.464}\right)(20.5) = 12.34$$

$$D_m = \frac{12.34}{1.02625} = 12.02 \text{ years}$$

2. Being the floating rate payer in an interest rate swap component with 20.5 years to maturity where the investor pays the SAVRS rate and receives 6.25%. We calculate the duration of the swap component using the methodology discussed in Chapter 6. For the investor, the swap component is the economic equivalent of buying a 6.25% bond and selling an equal amount of variable rate bonds. The modified duration of each of these is:

$$D_m^{fixed\ rate} = 12.02 \text{ years}$$
$$D_m^{variable\ rate} = .49 \text{ years}$$

The duration of the swap component equals the duration of the fixed-rate bond minus the duration of the variable-rate bond:

$$D^{swap} = 12.02 - .49 = 11.54 \text{ years}$$

3. Owning an interest rate cap on the SAVRS at a rate of 12.50%. The duration of this cap is equal to the sum of the delta values, as shown in Chapter 7:

$$D^{cap} = .5 \sum_{t=1}^{21} e^{-r_t t}\, N(d_1) = .034 \text{ years}$$

4. Selling an interest rate floor on the SAVRS rate at 0.00%. The duration of this floor is 0 years.

Using these price duration measures, we can measure the price duration of the RIBS as:

$$D_p^* = 12.02 + 11.54 - 0.034 + 0.000 = 23.526 \text{ years}$$

The price duration of 23.526 years is an estimate of the change in price of the RIBS for a 1.00% change in interest rates. Exhibit 8–10 shows changes the actual price, using our DAP model, and estimated price, using the price duration calculation, for 10-BP, 20-BP and 30-BP increases and decreases in interest rates. The actual price change is based upon the RIBS valuation outlined in the previous section assuming a parallel shift in interest rates. For small changes in interest rates, the price duration provides a good estimate of price volatility. For example, for a 10-BP increase in interest rates, the estimated price change is −2.353% and the actual price change is 2.393%, a difference of only 4-BPs. For larger changes in interest rates, the duration estimate is less accurate. This is due to the convexity associated primarily with the bond component. However, as discussed in Chapter 3, we can adjust the bond component for the convexity and thus have a more accurate measure of price fluctuations for larger changes in interest rates.

EXHIBIT 8–10
Actual and Estimated Price Changes for RIBS

	Actual Price	Actual Change in Price	Estimated Price	Estimated Change in Price	Difference
Rates increase 30 BPs	117.454	−7.163	117.559	−7.058	−0.105
Rates increase 20 BPs	119.874	−4.743	119.912	−4.705	−0.038
Rates increase 10 BPs	122.224	−2.393	122.264	−2.353	−0.040
Rates unchanged	124.617	0.000	124.617	0.000	0.000
Rates decrease 10 BPs	127.034	2.417	126.970	2.353	0.064
Rates decrease 20 BPs	129.506	4.889	129.322	4.705	0.184
Rates decrease 30 BPs	132.141	7.524	131.675	7.058	0.466

VALUATION OF AN INVERSE FLOATER

An inverse floater is a bullish municipal derivative security with an interest rate that varies inversely with an interest rate index. Although it typically has payment characteristics that are similar to RIBS, an inverse floater does not entail the simultaneous issue of an auction rate security. In this section we discuss the structure, valuation and price and time durations of an inverse floater.

General Description of Inverse Floaters

Interest Rate Mechanism
In many ways, inverse floating-rate bonds have an interest rate setting mechanism and investment characteristics that are similar to RIBS. The interest rate formula, prior to August 15, 1999, on the inverse floater that we value is:

Inverse floater rate = 6.15% + (4.70% − Kenny Index)

As with RIBS, the interest rate on the inverse floater will:

1. Increase as the Kenny Index decreases.
2. Decrease as the Kenny Index increases.

However, unlike RIBS with an inverse floater there is no companion security or auction structure, with its attendant service charges (e.g., 28 BPs). Also, because the inverse floater bond rate is based upon an index and not upon the SAVRS rate, there is no 22-BP average difference in yield. Actual/360-day and 35-day pay compounding aspects that effectively increase the BEY for auction-rate securities also do not apply. Therefore, the value of the variable-rate component is solely dependent upon the simple weighted average of the Kenny Index during the six-month interest period. Also observe that, in contrast to RIBS–SAVRS, the fixed or base rate (e.g., 6.15 percent) and the reference rate (e.g., 4.70 percent) are not necessarily the same. In fact, in most cases, the reference rate is substantially below the base rate, reflecting the shorter duration of the hedging component. The investment characteristics of these bonds are described in the next section.

In all the inverse floater transactions of which we are aware, the bond issuer has also entered into an offsetting interest rate swap agreement with a commercial or an investment bank that mirrors the floating-rate component of the inverse floating-rate bond. This offsetting interest rate swap creates a synthetic-asset, fixed-rate structure for the issuer, as described in Chapter 2.

To the extent that the Kenny Index is below the reference rate (e.g., 4.70 percent), the inverse floater will bear an interest rate higher than the fixed-rate component (e.g., 6.15 percent). Conversely, if the Kenny Index exceeds the reference rate, inverse floater holders will receive an interest rate that is lower than the fixed-rate component.

The interest rate on the inverse floater can never go below 0 percent. This limit effectively places an interest rate ceiling and cap on the Kenny Index. The inverse floater owner owns an interest rate cap, at 6.15 percent plus 4.70 percent, or 10.85 percent, and the *issuer* has written the interest rate cap which we value in the sections that follow.

Interest Rate Swap Conversion Mechanism

The interest rate swap conversion mechanism (also called the *conversion option*) is incorporated into many inverse floater transactions. This feature is somewhat analogous to the rate lock option in a linked RIBS–SAVRS transaction. Under the conversion option and prior to the conversion date (e.g., August 15, 1999), an inverse floater investor has an option to convert the inverse floating-rate bond to a fixed-rate interest payment. This conversion option involves either a positive or a negative interest rate adjustment to the fixed-rate bond rate (e.g., 6.15 percent), prior to the conversion date. The interest rate adjustment will be dependent on the movements in the yield curve and the valuation of a hypothetical swap agreement (Exhibit 6–14). The calculation of the interest rate adjustment is somewhat complex, but if interest rates, in general, have declined, the interest rate adjustment to the inverse floater investor should be positive, generating a fixed-rate bond payment above 6.15 percent prior to the conversion date. Conversely, if interest rates, in general, have increased, the interest rate adjustment to the inverse floater investor should be negative, generating a fixed-rate bond payment below 6.15 percent prior to the conversion date.

Investment Characteristics of Inverse Floaters

The cash flows associated with inverse floaters are dependent upon three variables: (1) the fixed-rate component (e.g., 6.15 percent); (2) the reference rate (e.g., 4.70 percent), both of which are set at the date of issuance and do not vary; and (3) the weighted average Kenny Index during each six-month interest payment period. As with RIBS, the current market value of inverse floaters is greatly dependent upon investors' expectations regarding the average of the future Kenny Index.

On August 15, 1999, the interest rate formula on the inverse floater converts to a fixed-rate of 6.15 percent until maturity on August 15, 2014. Thus, in 5.5 years the inverse floater converts to a fixed-rate bond. Assuming a continued upward-sloping municipal yield curve environment, the inverse floater owner will benefit from this steep yield curve for only a short period of time (e.g., 5.5 years). In comparison to RIBS, which have an embedded swap of 20 to 30 years, an inverse floater usually has a short-term embedded interest rate swap and, consequently, a shorter duration than a RIBS (see the discussion of duration below). As a result, the reference rate or embedded swap rate is usually much lower for an inverse floater than for a comparable-maturity RIBS.

Assuming that the tax-exempt yield curve continues to be upward-sloping, the inverse floater should have the following payment and price performance characteristics relative to a fixed-rate bond:

1. Higher current yields.
2. Higher expected yields to maturity.
3. Increased price volatility due to increased duration.

Valuation of an Inverse Floater

The inverse floater that we value is an AA-rated hospital revenue bond that matures on August 15, 2012; is callable on August 15, 2002, at a price of 102 percent, and pays interest on August 15 and February 15 at the annual rate of 6.15% + (4.70% − Kenny Index), prior to August 15, 1999. Thereafter, interest is paid at a fixed rate of 6.15 percent until maturity. The interest rate profile for the inverse floater is in Exhibit 8–11.

Like RIBS, the inverse floater may be divided into building-blocks, as follows:

1. A *debt component*, that has a 6.15 percent coupon, a maturity date of August 15, 2012, and a redemption feature of August 15, 2002, at 102 percent, declining to 100 percent on August 15, 2004.

2. A *hedging component* that is a fixed-to-floating interest rate swap of the form 4.70 percent minus the Kenny Index, with a term that expires on August 15, 1999 (in 5.5 years). The inverse floater holder is the floating-rate payer and the issuer is the fixed-rate payer.

EXHIBIT 8–11
Inverse Floater Interest Rate Profile

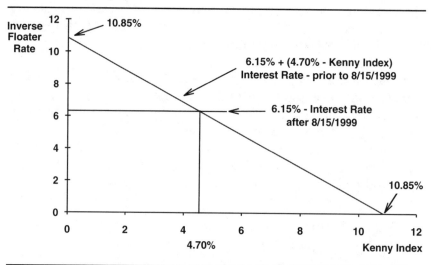

3. An *option component* in which the inverse floater holder is the owner of a 5.5-year interest rate cap at 10.85 percent, because the interest rate formula does not allow the inverse floater rate to be less than zero.

Based on the above, the theoretical DAP value of the inverse floater may be expressed as follows:

DAP price (inverse floater) = price (fixed-rate bond + fixed-to-floating swap + interest rate cap)

Valuation of the Hedging Component

Again we begin with the Treasury yield curve, to determine the value of the hedging and option components. Exhibit 8–12 shows the *taxable yield curve input screen* of January 3, 1994. The theoretical 5.5-year par swap rate is calculated in the upper righthand portion of the screen as 3.86 percent.

The present value of the 5.5-year, 4.70 percent fixed-to-floating Kenny swap component that is embedded in the inverse floater equals the discounted value of its anticipated future cash flows. The average present values of the implied tax-exempt forward rates over the 5.5-year swap period are calculated by the program (as shown in Exhibit 6–16) as 3.86 percent.

EXHIBIT 8–12
Taxable Yield Curve Input Screen (January 3, 1994)

```
Name of Yield Curve: Treasury 1/3/1994  Target Short-Term Ratio(%)   :    71.00
Term of Swap / Bond:      5.5 years      Avg. Exp. Short-term rate    :     3.86
         Full    Implied  Implied  Tax-Ex. !         Full    Implied  Implied  Tax-Ex.
Year  Coupon     Zero    Forward  Forward  ! Year  Coupon     Zero    Forward  Forward
  1    3.710     3.710    3.71     2.63    !  16   6.300     6.572    7.67     5.44
  2    4.300     4.319    4.93     3.50    !  17   6.350     6.648    7.88     5.59
  3    4.680     4.713    5.51     3.91    !  18   6.400     6.729    8.11     5.76
  4    5.050     5.109    6.30     4.48    !  19   6.450     6.814    8.36     5.94
  5    5.310     5.389    6.52     4.63    !  20   6.500     6.904    8.63     6.13
  6    5.470     5.562    6.43     4.57    !  21   6.510     6.906    6.95     4.93
  7    5.670     5.793    7.19     5.10    !  22   6.520     6.912    7.03     4.99
  8    5.750     5.876    6.46     4.59    !  23   6.530     6.920    7.09     5.03
  9    5.870     6.020    7.18     5.10    !  24   6.540     6.930    7.15     5.08
 10    5.960     6.128    7.10     5.04    !  25   6.550     6.941    7.22     5.12
 11    6.020     6.197    6.89     4.89    !  26   6.560     6.954    7.29     5.17
 12    6.080     6.271    7.09     5.03    !  27   6.570     6.969    7.36     5.23
 13    6.140     6.349    7.29     5.17    !  28   6.580     6.986    7.44     5.28
 14    6.200     6.431    7.50     5.32    !  29   6.590     7.005    7.53     5.35
 15    6.250     6.499    7.46     5.30    !  30   6.600     7.025    7.62     5.41

                            Implied SWAP Rates
         3 year          3.33%            10 year          4.27%
         5 year          3.79%            20 year          4.69%
         7 year          4.05%            30 year          4.77%
```

The 5.5-year implied swap rate of 3.86 percent, represents market expectations of the weighted average, short-term, tax-exempt rate. Unlike the RIBS valuation that takes into account the vagaries of SAVRS and the auction-rate security market, no additional adjustments to the 3.86 percent swap rate are necessary.

If the current market for a 5.5-year Kenny-based swap is 3.86 percent, and the inverse floater holder owns an embedded 5.5-year swap which is paying a fixed rate of 4.70 percent, the swap is *in the money* on average 0.91 percent per year. This results in a present value for the 4.70 percent fixed-to-floating rate Kenny swap of 4.491 percent (Exhibit 8–14).

Valuation of the Option Component

The next step in valuing the inverse floater is to determine the value of the option component. Exhibit 8–13 shows the *cap–floor valuation screen,* using the inputs from the Treasury yield curve of January 3, 1994, a cap strike price of 10.85 percent, a term of option of 5.5 years, and a volatility estimate of 8.00 percent.

Implicitly used in Exhibit 8–13 are the implied tax-exempt forward rates and the zero-coupon discount rates from Exhibit 8–12. Black's model for caps values a 5.5-year, 10.85 percent cap value of 0.000 percent—again, not a significant number.

EXHIBIT 8–13
Cap–Floor Valuation Screen (January 3, 1994)

Name of Bond: Inverse Floater 1/3/1994   Volatility: 8.00 %
      Type of Index: Kenny   Term of Option: 5.5 years
      Cap Strike Price: 10.85 %   Cap Value: 0.000%
      Floor Strike Price: 0.00 %   Floor Value: 0.000%

Year	CAP	FLOOR	Year	CAP	FLOOR	Year	CAP	FLOOR
0.5	0.000%	0.000%	7.5	0.000%	0.000%	19.0	0.045%	0.000%
1.0	0.000%	0.000%	8.0	0.000%	0.000%	20.0	0.060%	0.000%
1.5	0.000%	0.000%	8.5	0.000%	0.000%	21.0	0.063%	0.000%
2.0	0.000%	0.000%	9.0	0.000%	0.000%	22.0	0.067%	0.000%
2.5	0.000%	0.000%	9.5	0.002%	0.000%	23.0	0.072%	0.000%
3.0	0.000%	0.000%	10.0	0.003%	0.000%	24.0	0.077%	0.000%
3.5	0.000%	0.000%	11.0	0.007%	0.000%	25.0	0.082%	0.000%
4.0	0.000%	0.000%	12.0	0.008%	0.000%	26.0	0.089%	0.000%
4.5	0.000%	0.000%	13.0	0.009%	0.000%	27.0	0.096%	0.000%
5.0	0.000%	0.000%	14.0	0.011%	0.000%	28.0	0.104%	0.000%
5.5	0.000%	0.000%	15.0	0.014%	0.000%	29.0	0.112%	0.000%
6.0	0.000%	0.000%	16.0	0.018%	0.000%	30.0	0.122%	0.000%
6.5	0.000%	0.000%	17.0	0.024%	0.000%			
7.0	0.000%	0.000%	18.0	0.032%	0.000%			

Valuation of the Debt Component

The valuation of the 6.15 percent debt component is relatively simple. We assume that a required full-coupon yield for an AA-rated, 2012-maturity bond is 5.20 percent (see Exhibit 2–3). A premium, 6.15 percent bond due on August 15, 2012, and priced on January 3, 1994, at 5.20 percent to maturity is 111.237 percent. The market value of the same bond, priced to the August 15, 2002, call date with a 102 percent premium, is 107.809 percent (see Exhibit 8–14).

Valuation Summary—No Structure Value

Combining the values of the three components gives the following DAP model valuation of the inverse floater:

EXHIBIT 8–14
Inverse Floater Valuation Program (No Structure Value)

```
                    BULL/BEAR  I n p u t   S c r e e n
-----------------------------------------------------------------------

    Name of Bond:Sample Inverse Floater
    BULL or BEAR Floater (Press Enter to Change)......BULL
    Trade Settlement Date............................01/03/1994
    Link Coupon......................................   6.150
    Specified (Swap) Rate............................   4.700
    Number of Implied Swaps..........................       1
    Conversion Date..................................08/15/1999
    Maturity Date....................................08/15/2012
    First Optional Redemption Date...................08/15/2002
      First Par Opt. Red. Date.......................08/15/2004
      Initial Optional Call Price....................   102.0
    Purchase Price...................................  100.000
    Current Kenny Rate...............................    2.200
    Muni Market Term Swap Rate.......................    3.856
    Exp. Kenny Short-Term Rate.......................    3.856
    Investors Required Full Coupon Bond Rate.........    5.200
    (Kenny) Cap Rate.................................   10.850
    (Kenny) Floor Rate...............................    0.000
                    O u t p u t   S c r e e n
-------------------------------------------------  BULL     BEAR    ----------
                                                  Floater  Floater
                                                  -------------------
    Current Kenny Rate...................          2.200%   2.200%
    Current Coupon.......................          8.650%   3.650%
    Current Yield to Maturity............          7.177%   5.214%
    Exp.Kenny Short-Term Rate ...........          3.856%   3.856%
      Exp.Avg. Coupon (to Conversion Date)...      6.994%   5.306%
      Exp.Avg. Yield to Maturity............        6.486%   5.824%
-----------------------------------------------------------------------
                                                 Price to...
                                                  First      First
    BULL Floater Bond Prices:                      Call     Par Call
    --------------------------------------- Maturity  Call   Par Call
    Value of Bond............................ 111.237% 107.809% 107.669%
    Value of Swap(s)......................... 4.491%   4.491%   4.491%
    Value of Cap(s).......................... 0.000%   0.000%   0.000%
    Value of Floor(s)........................ 0.000%   0.000%   0.000%
      Total Value of BULL Floater(DAP)......... 115.728% 112.300% 112.160%
```

$$\text{DAP price (to maturity)} = 111.237\% + 4.491\% + 0.0\%$$
$$= 115.728\%$$
$$\text{DAP price (first call)} = 107.809\% + 4.491\% + 0.0\%$$
$$= 112.300\%$$

Valuation Summary—10-BPs Structure Value

Inverse floater owners are accorded the same advantageous tax treatment of interest payments as are RIBS owners. We therefore subjectively assume a 10-BP structure value, which results in a discount rate of 5.10 percent and increases the market values of the inverse floater to the values shown in Exhibit 8–15.

EXHIBIT 8–15

Inverse Floater Valuation Program (10-BP Structure Value)

```
                      BULL/BEAR  I n p u t   S c r e e n
------------------------------------------------------------------------
     Name of Bond: AA INVERSE FLOATER 1/3/94
     BULL or BEAR Floater (Press Enter to Change)......BULL
     Trade Settlement Date.............................01/03/1994
     Link Coupon...................................   6.150
     Specified (Swap) Rate.........................   4.700
     Number of Implied Swaps.......................       1
     Conversion Date...............................08/15/1999
     Maturity Date.................................08/15/2012
     First Optional Redemption Date................08/15/2002
       First Par Opt. Red. Date....................08/15/2004
       Initial Optional Call Price.................   102.0
     Purchase Price................................ 100.000
     Current Kenny Rate............................   2.200
     Muni Market Term Swap Rate....................   3.790
     Exp. Kenny Short-Term Rate....................   3.790
     Investors Required Full Coupon Bond Rate......   5.100
     (Kenny) Cap Rate..............................  10.850
     (Kenny) Floor Rate............................   0.000

                      O u t p u t   S c r e e n
-------------------------------------------------  BULL     BEAR   ----------
                                                 Floater  Floater
                                                 -------------------
     Current Kenny Rate.......................    2.200%   2.200%
     Current Coupon...........................    8.650%   3.650%
     Current Yield to Maturity................    7.177%   5.214%
     Exp.Kenny Short-Term Rate ...............    3.856%   3.856%
       Exp.Avg. Coupon (to Conversion Date)...    6.994%   5.306%
       Exp.Avg. Yield to Maturity.............    6.486%   5.824%
-------------------------------------------------------------------------
                                                     Price to...
     BULL Floater Bond Prices:                      First    First
     ---------------------------------------- Maturity   Call   Par Call -
     Value of Bond............................ 112.519% 108.537% 108.519%
     Value of Swap(s)......................... 4.491%    4.491%   4.491%
     Value of Cap(s).......................... 0.000%    0.000%   0.000%
     Value of Floor(s)........................ 0.000%    0.000%   0.000%
       Total Value of BULL Floater(DAP)....... 117.011% 113.028% 113.011%
```

With the 10 BPs of structure value and the lower discount rate of 5.10 percent, we have the following DAP model valuation of the inverse floater:

$$\text{DAP price (to maturity)} = 112.519\% + 4.491\% + 0.0\%$$
$$= 117.010\%$$
$$\text{DAP price (first call)} = 108.537\% + 4.491\% + 0.0\%$$
$$= 113.028\%$$

Time Duration of Inverse Floaters

To calculate the time duration of an inverse floater, we calculate the duration of the two underlying pieces and combine them into one value, as we did in Chapter 3. Because the cash flows prior to August 15, 1999, are uncertain, we will apply the derivatives time duration measure, as we did in the RIBS example. The cash flows after August 15, 1999, are fixed, and therefore Macaulay's duration is used to calculate the duration on these cash flows.

First, we must calculate the prices of the individual pieces. The prices will be used in the individual duration calculations. For simplicity, we will assume that the bond has 37 full semiannual coupon periods to maturity. Since we know from Exhibit 8–14 that the combined price of the derivative is $115.728, we begin by calculating the price of the fixed-rate piece and subtract it from the total price, as follows:

Piece 1: 1/2 (6.15 + 4.70 − Kenny Index) paid semiannually from 1/3/1994 to 8/15/1999	$115.728 − $81.618 = $34.11
Piece 2: $3.075 semiannual coupon payment from 8/15/1999 to 8/15/2012 plus payment of principal on 8/15/2012	$81.618
Total	$115.728

Duration of Piece 1

To calculate the time duration of piece 1, we will use the derivative duration model and the price we computed above.

Let:

D^* = duration measure that incorporates movements in short-term rates

P^* = price of piece 1 = 34.11

C_t = estimated annual inverse floater coupon at time t measured in dollars, calculated as $(6.15) + (4.70 - {}_{t-1}f_t^*)$

${}_{t-1}f_t^*$ = implied tax-exempt forward interest rate from time $t-1$ to t

$t = 1,2,3, \ldots ,11$

$n = 5.5$

Then:

$$D^* = \sum_{t=1}^{11} \left\{ \left[\frac{(C_t/2)/\prod_t(1 + {}_{t-1}f_t^*)}{34.11} \right] \frac{t}{2} \right\}$$

$D^* = 3.68$ years

Solving this equation for D_t^* results in a duration of 3.68 years for piece 1.

Duration of Piece 2

Let:

D = Macaulay's duration for piece 2

$P = 81.618$

$C = 6.15$

$F = 100$

$y = 5.20\%$

$t = 12,13, \ldots ,37$

$n = 18.5$

Then:

$$D = \sum_{t=12}^{37} \left\{ \left[\frac{3.075/(1.026)^t}{81.618} \right] \frac{t}{2} \right\} + \left[\frac{100/(1.026)^{37}}{81.618} (37) \right]$$

$D = 14.816$ years

After calculating the durations of the individual pieces, we can calculate the time duration of the whole bond by weighting the individual pieces by their prices, as we did in Chapter 3. The result is:

$$D_t^* = 3.68 \left(\frac{34.11}{115.728} \right) + 14.816 \left(\frac{81.681}{115.728} \right) = 11.53 \text{ years}$$

Price Duration of an Inverse Floater

To calculate the price duration of an inverse floater, we calculate the duration of the building block components and sum the durations to arrive at a price duration for the security. Assuming 37 semiannual periods, we calculate the duration of each of four components as we did with the RIBS example.

1. Owning a a 6.15% fixed-rate bond component with 18.5 years to maturity and a market yield of 5.20%. Macaulay's duration and modified duration for this bond are as follow:

$C = \$6.15$

$F = \$100$

$P = \$111.201$

$y = 5.20\%$

$t = 1,2,3, \ldots ,37$

$n = 18.5$

$$D = \sum_{t=1}^{37} \left(\frac{\frac{3.075}{(1.026)^t}}{111.201} \left(\frac{t}{2} \right) \right) + \left(\frac{\frac{100}{(1.026)^{37}}}{111.201} \right)(18.5) = 11.69$$

$D_m = 11.39$ years

2. Being the floating-rate payer in an interest rate swap component with 5.5 years to maturity where the investor pays the Kenny rate and receives 4.70%. For the investor, this swap is the economic equivalent of buying a 4.70% bond and selling an equal amount of Kenny-based variable-rate bonds. The modified duration of each of these is:

$$D_m^{fixed\ rate} = 4.82\ \text{years}$$
$$D_m^{variable\ rate} = .49\ \text{years}$$

The duration of the swap equals the duration of the fixed-rate bond minus the duration of the variable rate bond:

$$D^{swap} = 4.82 - .49 = 4.33\ \text{years}$$

3. Owning an interest rate cap on the Kenny rate at 10.85%. The duration of this cap is equal to the sum of the delta values of the individual caps. In this case, the cap is out of the money and has a delta of 0.00 years:

$$D^{cap} = .5 \sum_{t=1}^{18.5} e^{-r_t t}\ N\ (d_1) = 0.00\ \text{years}$$

4. Selling an interest rate floor on the Kenny rate at 0.00%. The duration of this floor is 0.00 years.

Using these price duration measures, we can measure the price duration of the inverse floater as:

$$D_p^* = 11.39 + 4.33 - 0.00 + 0.00 = 15.72\ \text{years}$$

Thus for a 1.00% change in interest rates, the estimated price change of the inverse floater is 15.72%.

VALUATION OF A CAP BOND

In this section we discuss the valuation and duration of a cap bond. A cap bond is a fixed-rate bond if rates stay below a specified cap rate. However, if rates exceed the cap rate, the cap is in the money and the interest rate is adjusted to reflect this difference. Unlike RIBS and inverse floaters, cap bonds pay a higher rate of interest when interest rates rise.

General Description of Cap Bonds

RIBS and inverse floaters have a *bullish* interest rate characteristic in that their interest rates increase as short-term, tax-exempt rates decrease. A cap bond has a *bearish* interest rate characteristic in that its interest rate increases as short-term, tax-exempt rates increase.

The interest rate formula, prior to October 1, 1997, on the cap bond that we value is:

Cap bond rate = 6.60% + MAX(0%, or PSA Index − 3.5%)

Cap bonds carry a fixed coupon (e.g., 6.60 percent) for the life of the bond, plus additional interest payments, prior to October 1, 1997, equal to the amount, if any, that the PSA Index exceeds 3.50 percent on a weighted daily average basis. Therefore, the cap bond is equivalent to the combination of a fixed-rate bond at 6.60 percent and an interest rate cap option that has a cap rate of 3.50 percent and an expiration date of October 1, 1997.

In most of the cap bond transactions of which we are aware, the bond issuer has also purchased an offsetting interest rate cap from a commercial or investment bank that mirrors the interest rate cap embedded in the cap bond. This offsetting interest rate cap creates a synthetic-asset, fixed-rate structure for the issuer, as described in Chapter 2.

Investment Characteristics of Cap Bonds

The cash flows associated with the cap bond are dependent upon three variables: (1) the fixed-rate component (e.g., 6.60 percent), (2) the weighted average PSA Index during each six-month interest payment period, and (3) the preset cap rate (e.g., 3.50 percent). The market value of a cap bond is dependent upon investors' expectations of the average PSA Index.

Until October 1, 1997, the interest rate on the cap bond will increase with an increase in the PSA Index over 3.50 percent. This increasing interest rate aspect of a derivative security that reacts in tandem with an increase in required yields in the marketplace tends to reduce the price–interest rate volatility of a bond, therefore reducing its price duration (see the discussion of duration, below).

When a cap bond is marketed, the issuer effectively sells a fixed-rate bond at a discount to market yields and writes an embedded interest rate cap. The cap bond investor, in exchange for the interest rate insurance provided by the cap, requires a lower yield on the fixed-rate bond component.

If we compare a cap bond to a similar fixed-rate bond and

assume a continued upward-sloping municipal yield curve, the cap bond should have the following payment and price performance characteristics:

1. Lower current yields.
2. Lower expected yields to maturity.
3. *Decreased* price volatility and decreased duration.

Valuation of a Cap Bond

The cap bond that we value is a Baa-1 general obligation bond that matures on October 1, 2016. It is callable on October 1, 2002, at a price of 101.5 percent. It pays interest on October 1 and April 1, at the annual rate of 6.60 percent plus a *variable rate* equal to the *greater of* 0 percent, or the PSA Index minus 3.5 percent, prior to October 1, 1997. Thereafter, interest is paid at a fixed rate of 6.60 percent until maturity. The interest rate profile for the cap bond appears in Exhibit 8–16.

EXHIBIT 8–16
Cap Bond Interest Rate Profile

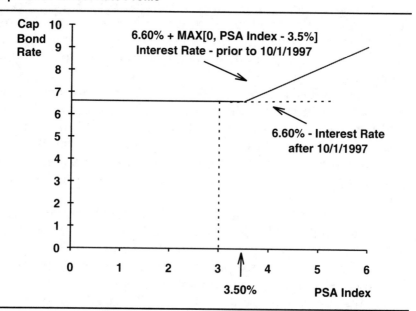

The cap bond may be divided into the following building-block components:

1. A *debt component* that has a 6.60 percent coupon, a maturity date of October 1, 2016, and a redemption feature of October 1, 2002, at 101.5 percent, declining to 100 percent on October 1, 2004.
2. An *option component* in which the cap bond holder is the owner of a 3.5-year interest rate cap at 3.50 percent that expires on October 1, 1997.

There is *no hedging component* embedded in the cap bond. Based on the above, the DAP value of the cap bond may be expressed as follows:

$$\text{DAP price (cap bond)} = \text{price (fixed-rate bond} \\ + \text{interest rate cap)}$$

Valuation of the Option Component
We again start with the Treasury yield curve to determine the value of the option component. Exhibit 8–17 shows the *taxable yield curve input screen* of January 3, 1994.

EXHIBIT 8–17
Taxable Yield Curve Input Screen (January 3, 1994)

```
          T a x a b l e   Y i e l d   C u r v e   I n p u t   S c r e e n
Name of Yield Curve: Treasury 1/3/1994 Target Short-Term Ratio(%)  :   71.00
Term of Swap / Bond:      3.5 years    Avg. Exp. Short-term rate    :    3.47
        Full    Implied Implied  Tax-Ex. |        Full    Implied Implied  Tax-Ex.
Year  Coupon     Zero   Forward  Forward | Year  Coupon     Zero   Forward  Forward
  1    3.710     3.710    3.71     2.63  |  16    6.300     6.572    7.67     5.44
  2    4.300     4.319    4.93     3.50  |  17    6.350     6.648    7.88     5.59
  3    4.680     4.713    5.51     3.91  |  18    6.400     6.729    8.11     5.76
  4    5.050     5.109    6.30     4.48  |  19    6.450     6.814    8.36     5.94
  5    5.310     5.389    6.52     4.63  |  20    6.500     6.904    8.63     6.13
  6    5.470     5.562    6.43     4.57  |  21    6.510     6.906    6.95     4.93
  7    5.670     5.793    7.19     5.10  |  22    6.520     6.912    7.03     4.99
  8    5.750     5.876    6.46     4.59  |  23    6.530     6.920    7.09     5.03
  9    5.870     6.020    7.18     5.10  |  24    6.540     6.930    7.15     5.08
 10    5.960     6.128    7.10     5.04  |  25    6.550     6.941    7.22     5.12
 11    6.020     6.197    6.89     4.89  |  26    6.560     6.954    7.29     5.17
 12    6.080     6.271    7.09     5.03  |  27    6.570     6.969    7.36     5.23
 13    6.140     6.349    7.29     5.17  |  28    6.580     6.986    7.44     5.28
 14    6.200     6.431    7.50     5.32  |  29    6.590     7.005    7.53     5.35
 15    6.250     6.499    7.46     5.30  |  30    6.600     7.025    7.62     5.41

                         Implied SWAP Rates
         3 year              3.33%             10 year              4.27%
         5 year              3.79%             20 year              4.69%
         7 year              4.05%             30 year              4.77%
```

Exhibit 8–18 shows the *cap–floor valuation screen* that implicitly uses the implied tax-exempt forward rates and implied zero-coupon rates calculated in Exhibit 8–17 as inputs into the valuation of the 3.50 percent interest rate cap option.

Explicitly, we put into our pricing model a cap strike price of 3.50 percent, a term of option of 3.5 years, and a volatility estimate of 8 percent. By using Black's model for caps, we arrive at a cap value of 0.929 percent.

Valuation of the Debt Component

The valuation of the 6.60 percent, Baa-1 22-year fixed-rate debt component is the next step. Using Exhibit 2–3, we see that an A-rated security maturing in 2016 has a required full-coupon yield of 5.50 percent. Adding a 10-BP risk premium to compensate for the lower rating, we use 5.60 percent as the required yield for a Baa-1 comparable security. A premium 6.60 percent bond due on October 1, 2016, and priced on January 1, 1994, at 5.60 percent to maturity, is 112.761 percent. The market value of the same bond, priced to the October 1, 2002 call date with a 101.5 percent call premium, is 107.754 percent (see Exhibit 8–19).

Valuation Summary—No Structure Value

Combining the values of the debt and option components gives the following DAP model valuation of the cap bond:

EXHIBIT 8–18
Cap–Floor Valuation Screen (January 3, 1994)

Name of Bond: Baa-1 Cap Bond 1/3/94   Volatility: 8.00 %
                Type of Index: PSA   Term of Option: 3.5 years
              Cap Strike Price: 3.50 %   Cap Value: 0.929%
            Floor Strike Price: 0.00 %   Floor Value: 0.000%

Year	CAP	FLOOR	Year	CAP	FLOOR	Year	CAP	FLOOR
0.5	0.000%	0.000%	7.5	4.474%	0.000%	19.0	13.236%	0.000%
1.0	0.000%	0.000%	8.0	4.832%	0.000%	20.0	13.921%	0.000%
1.5	0.053%	0.000%	8.5	5.319%	0.000%	21.0	14.299%	0.000%
2.0	0.118%	0.000%	9.0	5.792%	0.000%	22.0	14.644%	0.000%
2.5	0.315%	0.000%	9.5	6.233%	0.000%	23.0	15.015%	0.000%
3.0	0.517%	0.000%	10.0	6.660%	0.000%	24.0	15.350%	0.000%
3.5	0.929%	0.000%	11.0	7.403%	0.000%	25.0	15.670%	0.000%
4.0	1.333%	0.000%	12.0	8.164%	0.000%	26.0	15.978%	0.000%
4.5	1.783%	0.000%	13.0	8.933%	0.000%	27.0	16.271%	0.000%
5.0	2.221%	0.000%	14.0	9.708%	0.000%	28.0	16.553%	0.000%
5.5	2.624%	0.000%	15.0	10.422%	0.000%	29.0	16.821%	0.000%
6.0	3.015%	0.000%	16.0	11.134%	0.000%	30.0	17.079%	0.000%
6.5	3.570%	0.000%	17.0	11.841%	0.000%			
7.0	4.109%	0.000%	18.0	12.542%	0.000%			

EXHIBIT 8–19
Cap Bond Valuation Program (No Structure Value)

```
Name of Bond:Baa-1 CAP BOND 1/3/1994
              Trade Settlement Date................01/03/1994
              Maturity Date........................10/01/2016
              First Optional Redemption Date.......10/01/2002
              First Par Optional Redemption Date...10/01/2004
              Coupon (Linked B.E.Y.)...............   6.600
              Purchase Price.......................  100.000 %
              Initial Optional Call Price..........  101.5
              Cap Term.............................    3.5 years
              Cap Rate.............................    3.500 %
              Discount Rate........................    5.600 %
                                            Price to...
                                           First     First
                              Maturity      Call    Par Call
              Value of Bond.............. 112.761% 107.754% 107.981%
              Value of Cap...............   0.929%   0.929%   0.929%
                Total Bond Value(DAP)..... 113.690% 108.683% 108.910%
```

DAP price (to maturity) = 112.761% + 0.929% = 113.690%

DAP price (first call) = 107.754% + 0.929% = 108.683%

Valuation Summary—10-BP Structure Value

The cap bond also has tax-related structure value to an investor. Generally, interest on an interest rate cap is treated by its recipients as taxable income, while all the interest associated with tax-exempt cap bonds is, in the opinion of bond counsel, exempt from taxation. We therefore again subjectively assume a 10-BP structure value, which results in a discount rate of 5.50 percent and increases the market values of the cap bond to the values shown in Exhibit 8–20.

With the 10 BPs of structure value and the lower discount rate of 5.50 percent, we have the following DAP model valuation of the cap bond:

DAP price (to maturity) = 114.167% + 0.929% = 115.096%

DAP price (first call) = 108.478% + 0.929% = 109.407%

Time Duration of Cap Bonds

The calculations for the time duration of a cap bond are similar to the calculations for the duration of an inverse floater in the previous section. We must calculate the duration of the two underlying pieces and combine the durations into one value. For the cap bond,

EXHIBIT 8–20
Cap Bond Valuation Program (10-BP Structure Value)

```
Name of Bond:Baa-1 CAP BOND 1/3/1994
               Trade Settlement Date................01/03/1994
               Maturity Date.......................10/01/2016
               First Optional Redemption Date.......10/01/2002
               First Par Optional Redemption Date...10/01/2004
               Coupon (Linked B.E.Y.)...............   6.600
               Purchase Price......................  100.000 %
               Initial Optional Call Price..........  101.5
               Cap Term............................    3.5 years
               Cap Rate............................    3.500 %
               Discount Rate.......................    5.500 %
                                              Price to...
                                                  First    First
                                       Maturity   Call    Par Call
               Value of Bond.............. 114.167%  108.478% 108.824%
               Value of Cap..............   0.929%   0.929%   0.929%
                  Total Bond Value(DAP).....  115.096%  109.407% 109.753%
```

the cash flows prior to October 1, 1999, are uncertain and therefore we will apply the derivatives duration measure. Since the cash flows after October 1, 1997, are fixed, Macaulay's duration can be used to calculate their duration.

First, we must calculate the prices of the individual pieces. For simplicity, we will assume that the bond has 47 full semiannual coupon periods to maturity. Since we know from Exhibit 8–18 that the combined price of the derivative is $113.691, we can calculate the price of the fixed-rate piece and subtract it from the total to arrive at the variable-rate price.

Piece 1: $1/2$ [6.60 + MAX (0, PSA − 3.50)] paid semiannually from 1/3/1994 to 10/1/1997	$113.691 − $90.754 = $22.937
Piece 2: $3.30 semiannual coupon payment from 10/1/1997 to 10/1/2016 plus principal on 10/1/2016	$90.754
Total	$113.691

Duration of Piece 1
To calculate the duration of piece 1, we will use the derivative duration model and the price we computed above.

Let:

$P^* =$ price of the piece 1 = 22.937

$C_t =$ estimated annual cap bond coupon at time t measured in dollars, calculated as 6.60 + MAX $(0, _{t-1}f_t^* - 3.50)$

$_{t-1}f_t^* =$ implied tax-exempt forward interest rate from time $t - 1$ to t

$t = 1,2,3, \ldots ,7$

$n = 3.5$

Then:

$$D_t^* = \sum_{t=1}^{7} \left\{ \left[\frac{(C_t/2)\prod_t(1 + {}_{t-1}f_t^*)}{22.937} \right] \frac{t}{2} \right\}$$

$D_t^* = 1.97$ years

Solving this equation for D^* results in a duration of 1.97 years for piece 1.

Duration of Piece 2

Let:

$D =$ Macaulay's duration
$P = 90.754$
$C = 6.15$
$F = 100$
$y = 5.60\%$
$t = 8,9, \ldots ,47$
$n = 23.5$

Then:

$$D = \sum_{t=8}^{47} \left[\left(\frac{3.30/(1.028)^t}{90.754} \right) \frac{t}{2} \right] + \left(\frac{100/(1.028)^{47}}{90.754} (23.5) \right)$$

$D = 15.366$ years

After calculating the durations of the individual pieces, we can calculate the time duration of the whole bond by weighting the individual pieces by their prices, as we did in Chapter 3. The result is:

$$D_t^* = 1.97 \left(\frac{22.937}{113.691} \right) + 15.366 \left(\frac{90.754}{113.691} \right) = 12.66 \text{ years}$$

Price Duration of a Cap Bond

Their are two components to a cap bond—a fixed-rate bond and a Kenny-based interest rate cap. By calculating the duration of these two components, we can arrive at a price duration for the cap bond. The two components have the following characteristics and durations:

1. Owning a 6.60% fixed-rate bond component with 23.5 years to maturity and a market yield of 5.60%. Macaulay's duration and modified duration of this bond are as follow:

$C = \$6.60$
$F = \$100$
$P = \$112.98$
$y = 5.60\%$
$t = 1,2,3, \ldots ,47$
$n = 23.5$

$$D = \sum_{t=1}^{47} \left(\frac{\frac{3.30}{(1.028)^t}}{112.98} \left(\frac{t}{2} \right) \right) + \left(\frac{\frac{100}{(1.028)^{47}}}{112.98} \right) (23.5) = 12.91 \text{ years}$$

$$D = \frac{12.91}{1.028} = 12.56 \text{ years}$$

2. Owning an interest rate cap on the Kenny rate at 6.60% with a maturity of 3.5 years. The price duration of this cap is equal to the sum of the delta values:

$$D^{cap} = .5 \sum_{t=1}^{3.5} e^{-r_t t} N(d_1) = 1.67 \text{ years}$$

Since the value of the cap moves in the same direction as interest rates (unlike the price of the bond component that will move opposite of interest rates) we must subtract the value of the price duration of the cap. Therefore, the price duration of the cap bond is equal to:

$$D_p^* = 12.55 - 1.67 = 10.88$$

Based on the price duration, the price of the cap bond is estimated to decrease by 10.88% for a 1.00% increase in interest rates.

VALUATION OF A BEAR FLOATER

In this section we turn the discussion to the valuation and duration of a BEAR floater. As the mirror image of an inverse floater, a BEAR floater has interest rates that move in the same direction as an index. BEAR floaters have less price volatility and, therefore, lower price duration measures than comparable maturity fixed-rate bonds.

General Description of a BEAR Floater

A BEAR Floater, like a cap bond, has a *bearish* interest rate—its interest rate increases as short-term, tax-exempt rates increase. The interest rate formula, prior to August 15, 2002, on the BEAR Floater that we will value is:

BEAR Floater rate = 6.10% + 2 (Kenny Index − 5.0%)

There is a minimum interest rate of 4.0 percent and a maximum interest rate of 8.2 percent. After August 15, 2002, the BEAR Floater rate is 6.10 percent.

Based on the above formula and prior to August 15, 2002, the interest rate on the BEAR Floater will either increase or decrease with changes in the Kenny Index at *twice* the rate of change in the Kenny Index (assuming that the BEAR Floater rate is not at the minimum or maximum rate).

As in the RIBS–SAVRS program, the BEAR Floater has a companion security—a BULL Floater. The interest rate formula on the BULL Floater is equal to 6.10% + 2 (5.0% − Kenny Index). BEARS and BULLS, like RIBS and SAVRS, are *mirrored* securities that result in an absolutely fixed rate of interest for an issuer (see Chapter 2). They may be *linked* through a CUSIP mechanism similar to RIBS and SAVRS. However, there is no auction mechanism, service charges, unusual interest compounding periods, or 35-day payments. Interest is paid every six months, and the formula for interest payment is based on the weighted daily average of the Kenny Index during the 6-month interest period.

If the Kenny Index is *above* the reference rate (e.g., 5.00 percent), the BEAR Floater will bear an interest rate that is higher than the fixed-rate component (e.g., 6.10 percent). Conversely, if the Kenny Index is less than the reference rate, BEAR Floater holders will receive a lower rate than the fixed-rate component.

The interest rate on the BEAR Floater can never go below 4.0 percent or above 8.2 percent. As discussed in Chapter 7, the BEAR Floater holder implicitly owns two embedded interest rate *floor* options at 3.95 percent versus the Kenny Index, with a final exercise date of August 15, 2002. Likewise, the BEAR Floater owner implicitly has written two embedded interest rate *cap* options at 6.05 percent versus the Kenny Index, with a final exercise date of August 15, 2002. These options are valued below.

Investment Characteristics of a BEAR Floater

The cash flows associated with a BEAR Floater are dependent upon three variables: (1) the fixed-rate component (e.g., 6.10 percent); (2) the reference rate (e.g., 5.0 percent), both of which are set at the date of issuance and do not vary; and (3) the weighted average Kenny Index during each six-month interest payment period. The market value of a BEAR Floater, like the market values of RIBS and an inverse floater, is greatly dependent upon investors' expectations regarding the future Kenny Index.

Until August 15, 2002, the interest rate on the BEAR Floater that we value will increase or decrease at twice the rate of change of the Kenny Index, subject to the maximum and minimum interest rates. The two times leverage in interest rates tends to reduce the normal inverse price–interest rate volatility of a bond and greatly reduces its duration (see the discussion of duration, below).

Relative to a fixed-rate bond and assuming a continued up-ward-sloping municipal yield curve, BEAR Floaters should have the following payment and price performance characteristics:

1. Lower current yields.
2. Lower expected yields to maturity.
3. Greatly decreased price volatility and lower price duration.

Valuation of a BEAR Floater

The BEAR Floater that we value is an AAA-rated insured hospital revenue bond that matures on August 15, 2022. It is callable on August 15, 2002, at a price of 102 percent, and it pays interest on August 15 and February 15, at the annual rate of 6.10% + 2 (Kenny Index − 5.00%), subject to a *minimum* interest rate of 4.0 percent, and a maximum interest rate of 8.2 percent prior to August 15, 2002. Thereafter, interest is paid at a fixed rate of 6.10 percent until maturity. The interest rate profile for the BEAR Floater appears in Exhibit 8–21.

EXHIBIT 8–21
BEAR Floater Interest Rate Profile

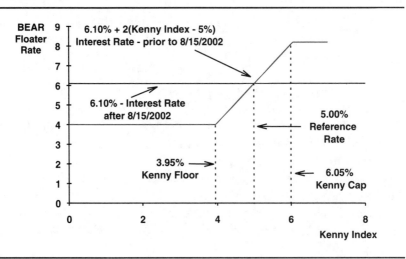

The BEAR Floater may be divided into the following building-block components:

1. A *debt component* that has a 6.10 percent coupon, a maturity date of August 15, 2022, and a redemption date of August 15, 2002, at 102 percent, declining to 100 percent on August 15, 2004.

2. *Hedging components* consisting of *two* floating-to-fixed interest rate swaps of the form (Kenny Index − 5.0%) and a term that expires on August 15, 2002 (after 8.5 years). The BEAR Floater holder is the fixed-rate payer, and the BULL Floater holder is the floating-rate payer.

3. *Option components* in which the BEAR Floater holder, because the interest rate can't go below 4.00 percent, is the owner of two embedded interest rate floor options at 3.95 percent versus the Kenny Index, with a final expiration date of August 15, 2002. Because the interest rate on the BEAR Floater can't go above 8.20 percent, its holder implicitly has *written* two embedded interest rate *cap* options at 6.05 percent versus the Kenny Index, with a final expiration date of August 15, 2002. (See Chapter 7 for a description of the floor and cap structure.)

Based on the above, the theoretical DAP value of the BEAR Floater may be expressed as follows:

DAP price (BEAR Floater) = price [fixed-rate bond
+ 2 (floating-to-fixed swap) + 2 (interest rate floor)
− 2 (interest rate cap)]

Valuation of the Hedging Components
Exhibit 8–22 shows the *taxable yield curve input screen* of January 3, 1994, with the theoretical, 8.5-year par swap rate calculated, in the upper righthand portion of the screen, to be 4.16 percent.

The present value of the two 8.5-year, 5.0 percent floating-to-fixed Kenny swap components that are embedded in the BEAR Floater is equal to the discounted value of its anticipated future cash flows. The 4.16 percent, 8.5-year implied swap rate represents the market's expectation of the weighted average, short-term, tax-exempt rate.

EXHIBIT 8–22
Taxable Yield Curve Input Screen (January 3, 1994)

```
         T a x a b l e   Y i e l d   C u r v e   I n p u t   S c r e e n
Name of Yield Curve: Treasury 1/3/1994 Target Short-Term Ratio(%)  :   71.00
Term of Swap / Bond:      8.5 years      Avg. Exp. Short-term rate   :    4.16
        Full    Implied Implied  Tax-Ex. !           Full    Implied Implied  Tax-Ex.
Year Coupon     Zero    Forward  Forward ! Year Coupon       Zero    Forward  Forward
  1   3.710     3.710    3.71     2.63  !   16  6.300        6.572    7.67     5.44
  2   4.300     4.319    4.93     3.50  !   17  6.350        6.648    7.88     5.59
  3   4.680     4.713    5.51     3.91  !   18  6.400        6.729    8.11     5.76
  4   5.050     5.109    6.30     4.48  !   19  6.450        6.814    8.36     5.94
  5   5.310     5.389    6.52     4.63  !   20  6.500        6.904    8.63     6.13
  6   5.470     5.562    6.43     4.57  !   21  6.510        6.906    6.95     4.93
  7   5.670     5.793    7.19     5.10  !   22  6.520        6.912    7.03     4.99
  8   5.750     5.876    6.46     4.59  !   23  6.530        6.920    7.09     5.03
  9   5.870     6.020    7.18     5.10  !   24  6.540        6.930    7.15     5.08
 10   5.960     6.128    7.10     5.04  !   25  6.550        6.941    7.22     5.12
 11   6.020     6.197    6.89     4.89  !   26  6.560        6.954    7.29     5.17
 12   6.080     6.271    7.09     5.03  !   27  6.570        6.969    7.36     5.23
 13   6.140     6.349    7.29     5.17  !   28  6.580        6.986    7.44     5.28
 14   6.200     6.431    7.50     5.32  !   29  6.590        7.005    7.53     5.35
 15   6.250     6.499    7.46     5.30  !   30  6.600        7.025    7.62     5.41
                               Implied SWAP Rates
         3 year              3.33%              10 year            4.27%
         5 year              3.79%              20 year            4.69%
         7 year              4.05%              30 year            4.77%
```

If the current market for a 8.5-year Kenny-based swap is 4.16 percent, and the BEAR Floater holder owns two embedded 8.5-year swaps and is paying a fixed rate of 5.0 percent, the swap has a *negative value* to the tune of an average 0.84 percent per year. This results in a hedging component value (using the methodology in Exhibit 6–16) of −6.256 percent per swap and for the two receive Kenny Index and pay 5.0 percent fixed swaps of −12.511 percent. (Exhibit 8–24)

Valuation of the Option Components
Exhibit 8–23 shows the *cap–floor valuation screen,* using the inputs from the Treasury yield curve of January 3, 1994, a cap strike price of 6.05 percent, a floor strike price of 3.95 percent, a term of option of 8.5 years, and a volatility estimate of 8.00 percent.

Implicitly used in Exhibit 8–23 are the implied tax-exempt forward rates and the zero-coupon discount rates from Exhibit 8–22. Black's model calculates the 8.5-year, 6.05 percent cap value of 0.201 percent, and the 8.5-year, 3.95 percent floor value of 2.201 percent. Remember that the BEAR Floater investor is the owner of two floor options with a value of 2(2.201%), or 4.402 percent, and is

EXHIBIT 8–23
Cap–Floor Valuation Screen (January 3, 1994)

```
Name of Bond: AAA Insured Bear Floater 1/3/1994        Volatility:  8.00 %
              Type of Index: Kenny              Term of Option:   8.5 years
          Cap Strike Price:   6.05 %               Cap Value: 0.201%
        Floor Strike Price:   3.95 %             Floor Value: 2.201%

Year     CAP      FLOOR  !   Year     CAP     FLOOR  !   Year    CAP      FLOOR
0.5    0.000%    0.649%  !   7.5    0.132%   2.140%  !   19.0   1.691%    2.669%
1.0    0.000%    1.286%  !   8.0    0.150%   2.183%  !   20.0   1.918%    2.691%
1.5    0.000%    1.501%  !   8.5    0.201%   2.201%  !   21.0   2.004%    2.753%
2.0    0.000%    1.717%  !   9.0    0.250%   2.221%  !   22.0   2.091%    2.810%
2.5    0.000%    1.803%  !   9.5    0.297%   2.245%  !   23.0   2.179%    2.864%
3.0    0.000%    1.901%  !  10.0    0.344%   2.269%  !   24.0   2.267%    2.917%
3.5    0.002%    1.926%  !  11.0    0.425%   2.336%  !   25.0   2.355%    2.964%
4.0    0.004%    1.951%  !  12.0    0.530%   2.395%  !   26.0   2.442%    3.011%
4.5    0.011%    1.973%  !  13.0    0.651%   2.445%  !   27.0   2.528%    3.053%
5.0    0.019%    2.000%  !  14.0    0.799%   2.488%  !   28.0   2.615%    3.093%
5.5    0.028%    2.033%  !  15.0    0.944%   2.536%  !   29.0   2.702%    3.130%
6.0    0.039%    2.071%  !  16.0    1.103%   2.577%  !   30.0   2.789%    3.164%
6.5    0.075%    2.085%  !  17.0    1.279%   2.612%  !
7.0    0.116%    2.099%  !  18.0    1.477%   2.642%  !
```

the writer of two cap options with a value of $-2(0.201\%)$, or -0.401 percent.

Valuation of the Debt Component
The 6.10 percent, AAA-rated, 29-year, fixed-rate debt component is the last component that we value. Referring to Exhibit 2–3, we see that an AAA-rated, insured bond maturing in 2022 has a required full-coupon yield of 5.45 percent. The value of a premium 6.10 percent bond due August 15, 2022, and priced on January 3, 1994, at 5.45 percent to maturity is 109.359 percent. The market value of the bond, priced to the August 15, 2002, call date, with a call price of 102 percent, is 105.674 percent. (Exhibit 8–24)

Valuation Summary
Assuming no structure value, combining the values of the debt, hedging, and option components results in the following DAP model valuation of the BEAR Floater:

$$\text{DAP price (to maturity)} = 109.359\% - 12.511\% + 4.402\%$$
$$- 0.401\% = 100.849\%$$
$$\text{DAP price (to first call)} = 105.674\% - 12.511\% + 4.402\%$$
$$- 0.401\% = 97.164\%$$

EXHIBIT 8–24
BEAR Floater Valuation Program (No Structure Value)

```
                 BULL/BEAR  I n p u t   S c r e e n
---------------------------------------------------------------------
    Name of Bond:AAA Insured BEAR Floater 1/3/94
    BULL or BEAR Floater (Press Enter to Change)......BEAR
    Trade Settlement Date............................01/03/1994
    Link Coupon......................................  6.100
    Specified (Swap) Rate............................  5.000
    Number of Implied Swaps..........................      2
    Conversion Date..................................08/15/2002
    Maturity Date....................................08/15/2022
    First Optional Redemption Date...................08/15/2002
      First Par Opt. Red. Date.......................08/15/2004
      Initial Optional Call Price....................  102.0
    Purchase Price...................................  100.000
    Current Kenny Rate...............................    3.950
    Muni Market Term Swap Rate.......................    4.161
    Exp. Kenny Short-Term Rate.......................    4.161
    Investors Required Full Coupon Bond Rate.........    5.450
    (Kenny) Cap Rate.................................    6.050
    (Kenny) Floor Rate...............................    3.950

               O u t p u t   S c r e e n
----------------------------------------------- BULL     BEAR  ---------
                                               Floater  Floater
                                               -------------------
    Current Kenny Rate......................    3.950%   3.950%
      Current Coupon........................    8.000%   4.000%
      Current Yield to Maturity.............    7.142%   5.178%
    Exp.Kenny Short-Term Rate ..............    4.161%   4.161%
      Exp.Avg. Coupon (to Conversion Date)...   7.778%   4.422%
      Exp.Avg. Yield to Maturity............    6.922%   5.355%
-----------------------------------------------------------------------

                                               Price to...
                                               First     First
    BEAR Floater Bond Prices:                  Call      Par Call
------------------------------------------- Maturity  Call   Par Call

    Value of Bond...........................  109.359%  105.674% 105.180%
    Value of Swap(s)........................  -12.511%  -12.511% -12.511%
    Value of Cap(s).........................   -0.401%   -0.401%  -0.401%
    Value of Floor(s).......................    4.402%    4.402%   4.402%
      Total Value of BEAR Floater(DAP)......  100.849%   97.164%  96.670%
```

Valuation Summary—10-BP Structure Value

The BEAR Floater also has tax-related structure value to an investor, because the payment on the embedded swaps and caps results in tax-exempt income to the BEAR Floater holder. If we again assume a subjective 10-BP structure value that results in a discount rate of 5.35 percent, we get the market values for the BEAR Floater that are shown in Exhibit 8–25.

With the 10 BPs of structure value and the lower discount rate of 5.35 percent, we get the following DAP model valuation of the BEAR Floater:

$$\text{DAP price (to maturity)} = 110.917\% - 12.511\% + 4.402\%$$
$$- 0.401\% = 102.407\%$$
$$\text{DAP price (first call)} = 106.386\% - 12.511\% + 4.402\%$$
$$- 0.401\% = 97.876\%$$

Time Duration of BEAR Floaters

The time duration calculation for a BEAR Floater is similar to the calculations for the duration of an inverse floater or a cap bond. Based on the derivatives time duration measure that we developed in Chapter 3, we first calculate the duration of the uncertain cash flows to August 15, 2002. The cash flows after the conversion date are fixed, and therefore we will use Macaulay's duration to calculate their duration. First, we must calculate the prices of the individual pieces to be used in the duration calculations. For simplicity, we will assume that the bond has 57 full semiannual coupon periods to maturity. Since we know from Exhibit 8–23 that the combined price of the BEAR Floater is $100.849, we can calculate the price of the fixed rate piece and subtract it from the total.

Piece 1: 1/2 (6.10 + 2 (Kenny Index − 5.00)) paid semiannually from 1/3/1994 to 8/15/2002	$100.849 − $67.862 = $32.987
Piece 2: $3.05 semiannual coupon payment from 8/15/2002 to 8/15/2022 plus principal on 8/15/2022	$67.862
Total	$100.849

Duration of Piece 1

To calculate the duration of piece 1, we will use the derivative duration model and the price we computed, above.

Let:

D^* = duration measure that incorporates movements in short-term rates

P^* = price of piece 1 = 32.987

EXHIBIT 8–25
BEAR Floater Valuation Program (10-BP Structure Value)

```
                      BULL/BEAR  I n p u t   S c r e e n
-----------------------------------------------------------------------------
    Name of Bond:AAA Insured BEAR Floater 1/3/94
    BULL or BEAR Floater (Press Enter to Change)......BEAR
    Trade Settlement Date.............................01/03/1994
    Link Coupon.......................................    6.100
    Specified (Swap) Rate.............................    5.000
    Number of Implied Swaps...........................        2
    Conversion Date...................................08/15/2002
    Maturity Date.....................................08/15/2022
    First Optional Redemption Date....................08/15/2002
      First Par Opt. Red. Date........................08/15/2004
      Initial Optional Call Price.....................   102.0
    Purchase Price....................................  100.000
    Current Kenny Rate................................    3.950
    Muni Market Term Swap Rate........................    4.161
    Exp. Kenny Short-Term Rate........................    4.161
    Investors Required Full Coupon Bond Rate..........    5.350
    (Kenny) Cap Rate..................................    6.050
    (Kenny) Floor Rate................................    3.950
                      O u t p u t   S c r e e n
-------------------------------------------------  BULL      BEAR  ---------

                                                  Floater   Floater
                                                  --------------------
    Current Kenny Rate......................        3.950%    3.950%
       Current Coupon.......................        8.000%    4.000%
       Current Yield to Maturity............        7.142%    5.178%
    Exp.Kenny Short-Term Rate ..............        4.161%    4.161%
       Exp.Avg. Coupon (to Conversion Date)...      7.778%    4.422%
       Exp.Avg. Yield to Maturity............       6.922%    5.355%
-----------------------------------------------------------------------------

                                                        Price to...
                                                     First      First
    BEAR Floater Bond Prices:                        Call       Par Call
---------------------------------------------- Maturity  Call      Par Call

    Value of Bond............................. 110.917%  106.386%  106.008%
    Value of Swap(s).......................... -12.511%  -12.511%  -12.511%
    Value of Cap(s)...........................  -0.401%   -0.401%   -0.401%
    Value of Floor(s).........................   4.402%    4.402%    4.402%
       Total Value of BEAR Floater(DAP).......  102.407%  97.876%  97.498%
```

C_t = estimated annual BEAR Floater coupon at time t measured in dollars, calculated as $6.10 + 2(_{t-1}f_t^* - 5.00)$

$_{t-1}f_t^*$ = implied tax-exempt forward interest rate from time $t-1$ to t

$t = 1,2,3,\ldots,17$

$n = 8.5$

Then:

$$D = \sum_{t=1}^{18} \left\{ \left[\frac{(C_t/2) \prod_t (1 + {}_{t-1}f_t^*)}{32.987} \right] \frac{t}{2} \right\}$$

$D = 5.28$ years

Solving the above equation for D_1^* results in a duration of 5.28 years for piece 1.

Duration of Piece 2
Let:

$$D = \text{Macaulay's duration}$$
$$P = 67.862$$
$$C = 6.10$$
$$F = 100$$
$$y = 5.45\%$$
$$n = 28.5$$
$$t = 18-57$$

Then:

$$D = \sum_{t=18}^{57} \left[\left(\frac{3.05/1.02725^t}{67.862} \right) \frac{t}{2} \right] + \left(\frac{100/1.02725^{57}}{67.862} \, 28.5 \right)$$

$$D = 20.63 \text{ years}$$

After calculating the durations of the individual pieces, we can calculate the duration of the whole bond by weighting the individual pieces by their respective prices, as we did in Chapter 3. The result is:

$$D_t^* = 5.28 \left(\frac{32.987}{100.849} \right) + 20.63 \left(\frac{67.862}{100.849} \right) = 15.61 \text{ years}$$

Price Duration of BEAR Floaters

The price duration of a BEAR Floater is the sum of the durations of its underlying components. The four components have the following characteristics and durations:

1. Owning a 6.10% fixed-rate bond component with 28.5 years to maturity and a market yield of 5.45%. Macaulay's duration and modified duration for this bond are as follow:

$C = \$6.10$
$F = \$100$
$P = \$109.35$
$y = 5.45\%$
$t = 1,2,3,\ldots,57$
$n = 28.5$

$$D = \sum_{t=1}^{57}\left(\frac{\dfrac{3.05}{(1.02725)^t}}{109.35}\left(\frac{t}{2}\right)\right) + \left(\frac{\dfrac{100}{(1.02725)^{57}}}{109.35}\right)(28.5) = 14.45$$

$$D = \frac{14.454}{1.0275} = 14.07 \text{ years}$$

2. Being the fixed-rate payer in two interest rate swaps with 8.5 years to maturity where the investor receives the Kenny Index and pays 5.00%. For an investor, this swap is the economic equivalent of selling a 5.00% bond and buying an equal amount of Kenny-based variable-rate bonds. The modified duration of each of these is:

$$D_m^{fixed\ rate} = 6.91 \text{ years}$$
$$D_m^{variable\ rate} = .49 \text{ years}$$

The duration of the swap component equals the duration of the fixed-rate bond minus the duration of the variable rate bond:

$$D^{swap} = 0.49 - 6.91 = -6.42$$

3. Selling two 6.05% interest rate caps on the Kenny Index with a maturity of 8.5 years. The cap has a duration of 0.447.

$$D^{cap} = .5 \sum_{t=1}^{17} e^{-r_t t}\, N\,(d_1) = 0.447 \text{ years}$$

4. Owning two 3.95% interest rate floors on the Kenny Index with a maturity of 8.5 years. The floor has a duration of -2.91.

$$D^{floor} = .5 \sum_{t=1}^{17} e^{-r_t t}\, N\,(-d_1) = -2.91 \text{ years}$$

By combining the values of all four components, we can get a price duration for the BEAR Floater as follows:

$$D_p^* = 14.07 - 2(6.42) + 2(0.45) - 2(2.91) = -3.69 \text{ years}$$

Using the price duration, for a 1.00% increase in rates we would estimate an increase in the BEAR Floater price of 3.69%.

VALUATION OF A BULL FORWARD BPO

In April 1993, in transactions for the Pennsylvania Housing Finance Agency and the Puerto Rico Telephone Authority, Lehman Brothers introduced a revolutionary new program for segmenting cash flows from municipal bonds at original issuance into *strips and pieces* that may be more highly valued than *plain-vanilla* bonds by certain investors. The BPO program allows an issuer to create and market separate and distinct portions of interest payments on a municipal bond in a wide range of packages that create value for investors and lower the interest costs for issuers. Under the BPO program, municipal bonds are marketed at initial issuance with embedded structural components. Through the use of separate CUSIP numbers for each BPO, and through pre-set linkage and delinkage provisions, an investor can hold a *linked* bond or separate it into several defined BPOs and either hold or sell the various BPOs. Note that, in the use of CUSIP numbers and linkage provisions, BPOs are similar to RIBS–SAVRS.

An important aspect of the program is that the separation of these BPOs is *at the investor's option*. The program allows an investor to isolate and strip cash-flow streams that can be analyzed and valued as combinations of original issue discount (OID) stripped-coupon bonds, tax-exempt futures contracts, tax-exempt interest rate swaps, and tax-exempt interest rate caps and floors. This *selective stripping option* is valuable to an investor, and interest rates on a bond that has this option should be lower than the rates on a comparable bond that does not have this option.

In this section, we describe BULL and BEAR Forward Bond Payment Obligations (BBF-BPOs) and value a BEAR Forward BPO. BBF-BPOs are municipal bonds with unique payment characteristics that allow investors to hedge against or speculate on changes in municipal bond *market values* due to changes in future long-term, tax-exempt interest rates.

General Description of BULL and BEAR Forward BPOs

BBF-BPOs have the following characteristics:

1. They are semiannually payable, stepped-coupon, mirrored securities that result in a fixed borrowing cost (the *linked coupon*) for the issuer.
2. All cash flows to holders are either tax-exempt interest income or a return of principal.
3. There are two categories of cash flows associated with each BBF-BPO, as follows:
   a. Interest cash flows (interest payments) which are initially fixed (e.g., 5.20 percent) and subsequently are divided (in the interest rate adjustment) between BULL Forward BPO holders and BEAR Forward BPO holders in amounts determined by the level of an index [e.g., the yield to maturity on the Bond Buyer 40 Index (BBI-40)] at some time in the future [the *interest adjustment date* (IAD)].
   b. Principal cash flow (the *principal payment*), which represents a lump-sum payment (e.g., $5000), similar to the cash flow of a zero-coupon bond that matures on a future date.
4. The present value of the payments of the BEAR Forward BPO interest rate adjustment is designed to replicate, on a tax-exempt basis, the cash payoff from shorting the BBI-40 contract (or the Treasury bond futures contract). An owner of a BEAR Forward BPO benefits if the yield to maturity on the BBI-40 is greater on the IAD than on the date of issuance.
5. The present value of the payments of the BULL Forward BPO interest rate adjustment is designed to replicate, on a tax-exempt basis, the cash payoff from buying a BBI-40 contract. An owner benefits if the yield to maturity on the BBI-40 is less on the IAD than on the date of issuance.
6. Pricing the BPOs incorporates Treasury futures (and municipal forwards) *cost of carry* pricing concepts (which take into

account the shape of the yield curve) and the *convergence* of future prices to cash prices over time (see Chapter 6). In an upward-sloping yield curve, and assuming no shift in interest rates, the BULL Forward BPO will have a lower price and greater expected yield than the BEAR Forward BPO. This is analogous to the situation in which buyers of Treasury bond futures benefit from convergence in an upward-sloping yield curve in the Treasury market. Therefore, the initial prices and expected yields of BULL Forward BPOs and BEAR Forward BPOs are different.

Structure and Interest Rate Setting Mechanism of BULL and BEAR Forward BPOs

BULL Forward BPOs and BEAR Forward BPOs are issued in equal amounts in denominations of $5000 each, and pay interest semiannually. A fully linked BBF-BPO pays interest at the linked-coupon rate (e.g., 5.20 percent) and has substantial linkage and stripping provisions, with CUSIPS assigned at issuance to each of the embedded BPOs. For example, a 10-year linked BBF-BPO can be stripped into 20 separate semiannual interest payments and a corpus. There are 21 CUSIPS assigned to these pieces. Alternatively, a linked BBF-BPO can be stripped into a BULL Forward BPO and a BEAR Forward BPO *at the investor's option.*

The interest payment characteristics of BBF-BPOs are similar to those of a stepped-coupon bond. Initially, interest payments to BULL and BEAR holders are equal (e.g., 5.20 percent). On the IAD (e.g., one year from issuance) the market agent determines the BBF adjustment amount and the interest rate adjustment, which may be positive or negative.

The BBF-BPO adjustment amount is designed to replicate the change in market value of a noncallable municipal bond with a 20-year maturity. It has a coupon equal to the yield to maturity on the BBI-40 on the date of issuance, discounted on a semiannual basis, at a rate equal to the yield to maturity on the BBI-40 on the IAD. The BBF adjustment amount is equal to an adjusted bond value minus $5000. The adjusted bond value is the present value, discounted at a rate equal to the yield to maturity of the BBI-40 on the IAD, of a hypothetical noncallable tax-exempt bond. The hypothetical bond has a face value of $5000, a maturity of 20 years, and a coupon equal to the yield to maturity of the BBI-40 on the date of issuance. Examples of these calculations follow.

Assumptions

Date of issuance	August 26, 1993
BBI-40 yield to maturity on 8/26/1993	5.76%
IAD	6/15/1994
Maturity date of bond	6/15/2005

Example 1. Assume that on the IAD the yield to maturity on the BBI-40 is 6.50 percent. Using standard semiannual discounting methods, the adjusted bond value is $4589.14. The BBF-BPO adjustment amount is $4589.14 − $5000 = −$410.86.

Example 2. Assume that on the IAD the yield to maturity on the BBI-40 is 5.10 percent. The adjusted bond value is $5410.73. The BBF-BPO adjustment amount is $5410.73 − $5000.00 = $410.73.

Example 3. Assume that on the IAD the yield to maturity on the BBI-40 is 5.76 percent. The adjusted bond value is $5000.00. The BBF-BPO adjustment amount is $5000.00 − $5000.00 == $0.00.

Using the BBF-BPO adjustment amount, the market agent calculates the annual adjustment amount and the interest rate adjustment. The annual adjustment amount is an annuity with a discounted present value that equals the BBF-BPO adjustment amount. The annual adjustment amount is calculated using a discount rate equal to the yield maturity on the BBI-40 and an annuity period from the IAD to the maturity date of the BULL and BEAR Forward BPOs.

Some examples of these calculations follow. We use the same assumptions as above, with a maturity date on the BPOs of June 15, 2005 − 11 years after the IAD.

Example 1a. The BBF-BPO adjustment amount is −$410.86. The 11-year annuity stream of −$50.94 per year (−$25.47 paid every six months), discounted at a yield of 5.76 percent, will give an annuitized present value of −$410.86. The interest rate adjustment on a percentage basis (−$50.94/$5,000) is −1.019 percent.

Example 2a. The BBF-BPO adjustment amount is $410.73. An 11-year annuity stream of $50.92 per year ($25.46 paid every six months), discounted at 5.76 percent, will give an annuitized present value of $404.51. The interest rate adjustment, on a percentage basis ($50.92/$5000), is 1.018 percent.

Example 3a. The BBF-BPO adjustment amount is $0.00. The interest rate adjustment, on a percentage basis, is 0.00 percent.

After the IAD, the future interest rates on the BULL Forward BPOs and the BEAR Forward BPOs are as follows:

BEAR Forward BPO future rate = 5.20% − 3 (interest rate adjustment)

BULL Forward BPO future rate = 5.20% + 3 (interest rate adjustment)

As seen in the above examples, a BEAR Forward BPO holder benefits when the yield to maturity on the BBI-40 increases above the yield to maturity on the BBI-40 on the date of issuance and the interest rate adjustment is negative. The investment characteristics are similar to those achieved by shorting the Treasury bond or municipal bond futures market. The converse is true for the BULL Forward BPO holder.

In the example above, the leverage factor is 3. The interest rate adjustment is limited to the linked coupon divided by 3. BBF-BPO holders can receive no more interest than twice the linked coupon and no less interest than zero.

Investment Characteristics of BULL Forward BPOs

The cash flows associated with BULL Forward BPOs after the IAD are dependent upon three variables: (1) the fixed-rate component (e.g., 5.20 percent), (2) the initial yield to maturity on the BBI-40 (e.g., 5.76 percent), and (3) the yield to maturity of the BBI-40 on the IAD. Both the fixed-rate component and the initial yield to maturity are set at the date of issuance and do not vary. As can be seen in the above examples, the cash flows on the BULL Forward BPO, and therefore its market value, depend greatly upon investors' expectations of the yield to maturity of the BBI-40 on the IAD.

The interest payment structure of BULL Forward BPOs is designed to perform like a combination of a 12-year fixed-rate bond at 5.20 percent and three embedded tax-exempt interest rate forwards contracts. The forwards contracts have a payment based on the yield to maturity on the BBI-40 of 5.76 percent and a contract expiration date of June 15, 1994. Because of the embedded forward structure, the price volatility and duration for a BULL Forward BPO are significantly greater than those of a comparable fixed-rate bond.

Valuation of a BULL Forward BPO

The BULL Forward BPO that we value is an AAA-rated insured water system revenue bond that matures on June 15, 2005. It is noncallable, and pays interest until June 15, 1994 at the annual rate of 5.20 percent. Thereafter it pays interest on each June 15 and December 15 until maturity at the annual rate of 5.20 percent plus 3 (interest rate adjustment). The interest rate profile for the BULL Forward BPO appears in Exhibit 8–26.

The BULL Forward BPO may be divided into the following building-block components:

1. A *debt component* that has a 5.20 percent coupon and a maturity date of June 15, 2005.

2. *Hedging components* consisting of three embedded forward contracts based on a yield to maturity on the BBI-40 of 5.76 percent which expire on June 15, 1994. The BULL Forward BPO holder is long the contracts and the BEAR Forward BPO holder effectively is short the three forward contracts.

3. *Option components* in which the BULL Forward BPO holder, because the interest rate can not go below 0 percent, is the owner of three embedded European interest rate cap options at 7.077 percent versus the yield to maturity of the BBI-40 with an exercise date of June 15, 1994. Because the interest rate on the BULL Forward BPO cannot go above 10.40 percent, its holder implicitly has written three embedded European interest rate floor options (to the BEAR Forward BPO owner) at 4.676 percent versus the yield to maturity on the BBI-40 with an exercise date of June 15, 1994. (See Chapter 7 for a description of the floor and cap structure.)

EXHIBIT 8–26
BULL Forward BPO Interest Rate Profile

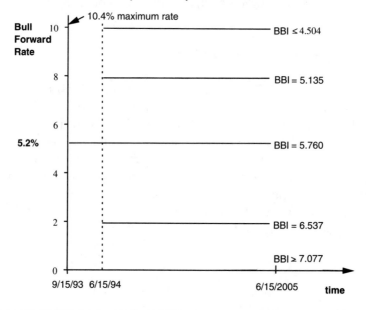

BULL Forward BPO Interest Rate Profile
BULL Forward Rate = 5.20% prior to 6/15/1994
Initial Yield-to-Maturity on Bond Buyer 40 Bond Index = 5.76%
BULL Forward Rate after 6/15/1994 depends on Yield to
Maturity of Bond Buyer 40 Bond Index on 6/15/1994

Based on the above discussion, the DAP value of the BULL Forward BPO may be expressed as follows:

DAP price (BULL Forward BPO) = price[fixed-rate bond
+ 3 (forward contract) + 3 (interest rate cap)
− 3 (interest rate floor)]

Valuation of the Hedging Component
To value the forward contracts embedded in the BULL Forward BPO, we use the *cost of carry* approach discussed in Chapter 6. In this approach, a theoretical forward value is calculated as a function of the yield, y, on the spot commodity (i.e., the current yield to maturity on the BBI-40), the current financing cost, $_{t-1}f_t^*$ (i.e., the

current implied tax-exempt forward rate), the time to contract expiration date, t, and the present value of the asset price, P. The theoretical forward price, B_t, is related to these variables as follows:

$$B_t = P \frac{(1 + c)^t}{(1 + y)^t}$$

In this case, P is the BBF-BPO adjustment amount, which depends on the yield to maturity on the BBI-40 on the date of valuation. The date of valuation is January 3, 1994, and the yield to maturity on the BBI-40 is 5.54 percent. Based on these assumptions and if interest rates remain at this level until the IAD of June 15, 1994, the BBF-BPO adjustment amount would be $5131.99 − $5000 = $131.99, which, when divided by the $5,000 face value, equals 2.639 percent.

The BBF-BPO Adjustment Amount of $131.99, is equivalent to an 11-year annuity stream of $16.36 per year ($8.18 paid semiannually) discounted at 5.76 percent. The interest rate adjustment on a percentage basis ($16.36/$5,000) is 0.327 percent, which equals 0.981 percent for the three forward contracts (Exhibit 8–29).

The current financing rate is the cost of financing the position until settlement and is equal to the tax-exempt implied forward

EXHIBIT 8–27
Taxable Yield Curve Input Screen (January 3, 1994)

```
        T a x a b l e   Y i e l d   C u r v e   I n p u t   S c r e e n
Name of Yield Curve: Treasury 1/3/1994 Target Short-Term Ratio(%)  :   71.00
Term of Swap / Bond:     11 years     Avg. Exp. Short-term rate     :    4.31
      Full     Implied Implied  Tax-Ex. !       Full     Implied Implied  Tax-Ex.
Year Coupon     Zero   Forward  Forward ! Year Coupon     Zero   Forward  Forward
  1   3.710    3.710    3.71     2.63   !  16  6.300     6.572    7.67     5.44
  2   4.300    4.319    4.93     3.50   !  17  6.350     6.648    7.88     5.59
  3   4.680    4.713    5.51     3.91   !  18  6.400     6.729    8.11     5.76
  4   5.050    5.109    6.30     4.48   !  19  6.450     6.814    8.36     5.94
  5   5.310    5.389    6.52     4.63   !  20  6.500     6.904    8.63     6.13
  6   5.470    5.562    6.43     4.57   !  21  6.510     6.906    6.95     4.93
  7   5.670    5.793    7.19     5.10   !  22  6.520     6.912    7.03     4.99
  8   5.750    5.876    6.46     4.59   !  23  6.530     6.920    7.09     5.03
  9   5.870    6.020    7.18     5.10   !  24  6.540     6.930    7.15     5.08
 10   5.960    6.128    7.10     5.04   !  25  6.550     6.941    7.22     5.12
 11   6.020    6.197    6.89     4.89   !  26  6.560     6.954    7.29     5.17
 12   6.080    6.271    7.09     5.03   !  27  6.570     6.969    7.36     5.23
 13   6.140    6.349    7.29     5.17   !  28  6.580     6.986    7.44     5.28
 14   6.200    6.431    7.50     5.32   !  29  6.590     7.005    7.53     5.35
 15   6.250    6.499    7.46     5.30   !  30  6.600     7.025    7.62     5.41
                              Implied SWAP Rates
        3 year              3.33%              10 year              4.27%
        5 year              3.79%              20 year              4.69%
        7 year              4.05%              30 year              4.77%
```

rate that is coincident with the period of time ending on the settlement date, t, of June 15, 1994. In Exhibit 8–27, we see that $_{t-1}f_t^*$, the one-period tax-exempt forward rate, is 2.63 percent.

The time, t, represents the period from valuation, January 3, 1994, to the contract settlement date, June 15, 1994, or 164 days. Adjusted for 182.5-day periods, this equals 0.899 periods.

If we assume that y equals 5.54 percent (paid semiannually), $_{t-1}f_t^*$ equals 2.63 percent (paid semiannually), t equals 0.899 periods, and the current spot commodity price (the BBF-BPO adjustment amount) is 2.639 percent, we can calculate a theoretical forwards value as follows:

$$\text{Forwards value} = 2.639\% \; \frac{(1 + 0.0263/2)^{0.899}}{(1 + 0.0554/2)^{0.899}}$$

$$\text{Forwards value} = 2.639\% \; \frac{1.0118}{1.0249}$$

$$\text{Forwards value} = 2.606\%$$

As we previously discussed, the value of a BULL Forward BPO increases if the yield to maturity of the BBI-40 decreases. In this example, the yield to maturity on the BBI-40 decreased from 5.76 percent on the date of issuance, August 26, 1993, to 5.54 percent on the valuation date, January 3, 1994. This resulted in an increase in the value of the hedging component, the forwards value, (as discussed in Chapter 6) of 2.606 percent, and also in an increase in the value of the three embedded forward contracts, for a total increase of 7.818 percent. (See Exhibit 8–29 on page 270.)

Valuation of the Option Components
Exhibit 8–28 shows the *cap–floor valuation screen*. The value of the option components is dependent on the movement and volatility of the yield to maturity on the BBI-40, which is a long-term interest rate index. Unfortunately, the pure expectations theory of the yield curve addresses only movements in short-term interest rates. Several yield curve models exist for expected future long-term interest rates, but they have little theoretical justification and have not been embraced by many municipal market participants. Furthermore, the market inefficiencies regarding the municipal yield curve that were discussed in Chapter 4 make projecting future long-term mu-

nicipal bond rates from the municipal yield curve very dicey. Therefore, for implied long-term forward rates, we simply assume that *rates stay constant,* which means a flat 5.54 percent yield to maturity on the BBI-40 through June 15, 1994.

Using this assumption and inputting a cap strike price of 7.077 percent, a floor strike price of 4.676 percent, and a volatility of 8 percent, we get a cap value of 0.00 percent and a floor value of 0.00 percent for the interest rate cap and floor options (see Exhibit 8–28).

Valuation of Debt Component
The valuation of the 5.20 percent, AAA-rated, fixed-rate debt component is relatively simple. As shown in Exhibit 2–3, an AAA-rated, insured bond maturing in 2005 has a required full-coupon yield of 4.75 percent. The value of a premium 5.20 percent bond due on June 15, 2005, and priced on January 3, 1994, at 4.75 percent to maturity is 103.936 percent (see Exhibit 8–29). There is no early redemption option on the bond, therefore we only price the debt component to maturity.

Valuation Summary—No Structure Value
Combining the values of the debt, hedging, and option components we get the following DAP model valuation of the BULL Forward BPO:

EXHIBIT 8–28
Cap–Floor Valuation Screen (January 3, 1994)

```
Name of Bond: BULL Forward 1/3/94              Volatility:   8.00 %
            Type of Index: YTM-BBI-40      Term of Option:   0.5 years
          Cap Strike Price:    7.08 %           Cap Value: 0.000%
        Floor Strike Price:    4.68 %         Floor Value: 0.000%
```

Year	CAP	FLOOR		Year	CAP	FLOOR		Year	CAP	FLOOR
0.5	0.000%	0.000%		7.5	0.155%	0.299%		19.0	1.178%	1.616%
1.0	0.000%	0.000%		8.0	0.184%	0.344%		20.0	1.281%	1.737%
1.5	0.003%	0.001%		8.5	0.217%	0.393%		21.0	1.383%	1.859%
2.0	0.004%	0.005%		9.0	0.253%	0.441%		22.0	1.484%	1.975%
2.5	0.006%	0.015%		9.5	0.288%	0.492%		23.0	1.586%	2.092%
3.0	0.009%	0.024%		10.0	0.327%	0.546%		24.0	1.688%	2.206%
3.5	0.014%	0.040%		11.0	0.401%	0.655%		25.0	1.789%	2.318%
4.0	0.023%	0.060%		12.0	0.488%	0.771%		26.0	1.887%	2.428%
4.5	0.033%	0.084%		13.0	0.574%	0.888%		27.0	1.985%	2.534%
5.0	0.047%	0.112%		14.0	0.663%	1.008%		28.0	2.081%	2.637%
5.5	0.063%	0.143%		15.0	0.763%	1.131%		29.0	2.175%	2.738%
6.0	0.083%	0.179%		16.0	0.865%	1.252%		30.0	2.266%	2.837%
6.5	0.106%	0.213%		17.0	0.969%	1.374%				
7.0	0.129%	0.252%		18.0	1.071%	1.495%				

EXHIBIT 8–29
BULL Forward Valuation Program

```
              B U L L Forward  I n p u t   S c r e e n
                    (No Structure Value)
-----------------------------------------------------------------
  -
  Name of Bond:BULL Forward
  BULL or BEAR Forward (Press Enter to Change).BULL
  Trade Settlement Date........................01/03/1994
  Link Coupon..................................    5.200
  Number of Implied Futures Contract...........        3
  Interest Rate Adjustment Date................06/15/1994
  Maturity Date................................06/15/2005
  First Optional Redemption Date...............06/15/2005
    First Par Opt. Red. Date...................06/15/2005
    Initial Optional Call Price................    100.0
  End of Interest Rate Adjustment Period.......06/15/2005
  Reference BBI-40 Yield-to-Maturity...........    5.760
  Current BBI-40 Yield-to-Maturity.............    5.540
  Expected Short-term (164-day)tax-exempt rate.    2.630
  Investors Required Full Coupon Bond Rate.....    4.750
  (BBI-40) Cap Rate............................    7.077
  (BBI-40) Floor Rate..........................    4.676

              O u t p u t   S c r e e n
-----------------------------------------------------------------
  -
  Expected BBF Adjustment Amount...............   131.99
  Expected BBF Annual Annuity Value............    16.37
  Expected Interest Rate Adjustment............    0.981%
  Expected Adjusted Coupon.....................    6.181%
-----------------------------------------------------------------
  -

                                        Price to...
  BULL Forward Prices:                    First       Par
  -------------------------------- Maturity  Call      Call
  Value of Bond....................103.936% 103.936%  103.936%
  Value of Forward(s)..............  7.818%   7.818%    7.818%
  Value of Cap(s)..................  0.000%   0.000%    0.000%
  Value of Floor(s)................  0.000%   0.000%    0.000%
    Total Value DAP...............111.754% 111.754%  111.754%
```

$$\text{DAP price (to maturity)} = 103.936\% + 7.818\% + 0.00\%$$
$$- 0.00\% = 111.754\%$$

Valuation Summary—10-BP Structure Value. The BULL Forward BPO also has a tax-related structure value to an investor, because the payments on the embedded forward contracts result in tax-exempt income to the BULL Forward BPO holder. If we again assume a subjective 10-BP structure value, which results in a

EXHIBIT 8–30
BULL Forward Valuation Program

```
              B U L L  Forward  I n p u t   S c r e e n
                   (10 b.p. Structure Value)
---------------------------------------------------------------
  -
  Name of Bond:BULL Forward
  BULL or BEAR Forward (Press Enter to Change).BULL
  Date of Issuance.............................08/26/1993
  Trade Settlement Date........................01/03/1994
  Link Coupon..................................   5.200
  Number of Implied Futures Contract...........      3
  Interest Rate Adjustment Date................06/15/1994
  Maturity Date................................06/15/2005
  First Optional Redemption Date...............06/15/2005
    First Par Opt. Red. Date...................06/15/2005
    Initial Optional Call Price................   100.0
  End of Interest Rate Adjustment Period.......  06/15/2005
  Reference BBI-40 Yield-to-Maturity...........   5.760
  Current BBI-40 Yield-to-Maturity.............   5.540
  Expected Short-term (164-day)tax-exempt rate.   2.630
  Investors Required Full Coupon Bond Rate.....   4.650
  (BBI-40) Cap Rate............................   7.077
  (BBI-40) Floor Rate..........................   4.676

                 O u t p u t   S c r e e n
---------------------------------------------------------------
  -
  Expected BBF Adjustment Amount...............  131.99
  Expected BBF Annual Annuity Value............   16.37
  Expected Interest Rate Adjustment............   0.981%
  Expected Adjusted Coupoun....................   6.181%
---------------------------------------------------------------
  -

                                        Price to...
  BULL Forward Prices:                  First      Par
  ------------------------- Maturity     Call      Call
  Value of Bond....................104.837%  104.837%  104.837%
  Value of Forward(s)..............  7.818%    7.818%    7.818%
  Value of Cap(s)..................  0.000%    0.000%    0.000%
  Value of Floor(s)................  0.000%    0.000%    0.000%
    Total Value of DAP............112.655%  112.655%  112.655%
```

discount rate of 4.65 percent, the market values for the BULL Forward BPO are as shown in Exhibit 8–30.

With the 10 BPs of structure value and the lower discount rate to 4.65 percent, the DAP model valuation of the BULL Forward BPO is as follows:

$$\text{DAP price (to maturity)} = 104.837\% + 7.818\% + 000\%$$
$$- 0.00\% = 112.655\%$$

Time Duration of BULL Forward BPOs

Since we do not have an acceptable model for estimating long-term tax-exempt rates for BULL Forward BPOs, we continue to assume that rates stay the same until the IAD. If we do this, we can easily calculate the time duration of a fixed-rate bond that pays a 5.20 percent coupon until June 15, 1994 (one period), and converts to a 6.181 percent coupon from June 15, 1994, to June 15, 2005 (22 periods). We will assume that we have 23 full semiannual periods, for simplicity. We substitute into the duration equation as shown below.

Let:

C = $5.20 to 6/15/1994, $6.181 thereafter
F = $100
P = $112.088, based on the coupon payments, C, above
t = 1, 2, 3, . . ., 23
n = 11.5

Then:

$$D_t^* = \frac{2.60}{1.02375} \, 0.5 + \sum_{t=2}^{23} \left[\left(\frac{3.0905/1.02375^t}{112.088} \right) \frac{t}{2} \right]$$

$$+ \left(\frac{100/1.02375^{23}}{112.088} \right) 11.5 = 8.635 \text{ years}$$

Price Duration of BULL Forward BPOs

To calculate the price duration of BULL Forward BPOs prior to the interest rate adjustment date, we decompose the bond into a fixed-rate bond and three 20-year municipal bond contracts. Assuming 23 semiannual periods for simplicity, we calculate the duration of each of the components as follows:

(1) Owning a 5.20% fixed-rate bond with a 11.5 years to maturity and a market yield of 4.75%. The time and price duration of the fixed-rate bond component is:

C = $5.20
F = $100
P = $103.952

$y = 4.75\%$

$t = 1, 2, 3, \ldots, 23$

$n = 11.5$

$$D = \sum_{t=1}^{23} \left(\frac{\frac{2.60}{(1.02375)^t}}{103.952} \left(\frac{t}{2} \right) \right) + \left(\frac{\frac{100}{(1.02375)^{23}}}{103.952} \right) (11.5) = 8.86$$

$$D = \frac{8.86}{1.02375} = 8.65 \text{ years}$$

(2) Owning three 20-year municipal bonds with a coupon equal to the reference BBI-40 yield-to-maturity of 5.76 and a market yield equal to the current BBI-40 yield-to-maturity of 5.54% which implies a market price, P, of $102.639. The price duration of the one of these components is:

$C = \$5.76$

$F = \$100$

$P = \$102.639$

$y = 5.54\%$

$t = 1, 2, 3, \ldots, 40$

$n = 20$

$$D = \sum_{t=1}^{40} \left(\frac{\frac{2.88}{(1.0272)^t}}{102.639} \left(\frac{t}{2} \right) \right) + \left(\frac{\frac{100}{(1.0272)^{23}}}{102.639} \right) (20) = 12.23$$

$$D = \frac{12.23}{1.0272} = 11.91 \text{ years}$$

(3) Owning three interest rate caps on the adjusted bond rate at 7.077% until the interest rate adjustment date. The duration of this cap is equal to the delta value of the one-period option. The price duration of this cap is 0.00 years.

(4) Selling three interest rate floors on the adjusted bond rate at 4.676% until the interest rate adjustment date. The price duration of this floor is 0.00 years.

Using these price duration measures, we can measure the price duration of the BULL forward BPO as:

$$D_p^* = 8.65 + 3(11.91) - 0.00 + 0.00 = 44.38 \text{ years}$$

The price duration of 44.38 is an estimate of the change in price of the BULL forward BPOs for a 1.00% change in interest rates. This is a long price duration for a bond that matures in 11 years.

SUMMARY

If there is one word that effectively summarizes Chapter 8, it is *long*.

In this chapter we have tried to integrate all of the theories, concepts and models that we described in the first seven chapters. In short, this chapter is a description and summary of municipal derivative finance in action!

We began the chapter by describing the DAP Model and its procedures—how the taxable yield curve screen, the cap and floor valuation program, the tax-exempt yield curve screen, and the security specific screens are used in the valuation process. We described the concept of structure valve and how and why the value of a successful municipal derivative security will be greater than the sum of the underlying cash flows.

We then led the reader through the valuation process (some might argue in excruciating detail) for RIBS, an inverse floater, a cap bond, a BEAR Floater, and a Bull Forward BPO. We described the interest rate mechanism, any special features, and the investment characteristics of each security. In the valuation process for each municipal derivative we divided the bond into its underlying debt, hedging and option components and valued each component. We then used the DAP Model to value the municipal derivative security based on no structure value and with 10 BPs structure value.

The DAP valuation process uses expectational analysis and the concepts developed for analyzing fixed-rate bonds, forwards, fixtures, swaps, and cap and floor options. We attempted in this process to use generally accepted financial theories and be consistent in our valuation approach.

We focused extensively on two duration measures for derivative securities—time duration and price duration. Bullish derivative securities like RIBS, inverse floaters and BULL Forward BPOs have price durations that are longer than the durations of comparable maturity fixed-rate bonds. Bearish derivative securities, like cap bonds and BEAR Floaters, have price durations that are shorter than the durations of comparable maturity fixed-rate bonds.

With increased duration and increased price and interest rate volatility, there is an expectation of higher returns to compensate an investor for the increased risk associated with a greater dispersion of returns. As we have stated before, price volatility is not necessarily bad. If a derivative security is properly priced and the investor understands its risks, it may give an investor the best risk/reward trade-off available. Certainly, most investors, to date, have seen outstanding investment performance on a cash flow basis from RIBS and inverse floater type municipal investments.

What lies ahead for municipal derivative products in uncharted and unknown. But even if our crystal ball is a bit cloudy, we see some interesting possibilities—particularly in the area of options—but that is a topic for another book (or, at least a revised edition of this book).

We hope you have found this manuscript helpful and that it is a useful source to you in the future.

INDEX